THE PRACTICAL BOOK
of AMERICAN SILVER

THE
PRACTICAL BOOK
OF
AMERICAN SILVER

BY EDWARD WENHAM

WITH LINE ILLUSTRATIONS BY EDGAR HOLLOWAY
AND REPRODUCTIONS FROM PHOTOGRAPHS

J. B. LIPPINCOTT COMPANY
PHILADELPHIA & NEW YORK

ACKNOWLEDGMENTS

IT IS ONE OF MY REGRETS THAT THE ENGLISH language precludes those dulcet phrases of gratitude possible in the Latin tongues. A writer in English is restricted to a more or less stereotyped form in acknowledging favors; nevertheless, it is my hope that this Preface will convey that sincere sense of indebtedness of which I am and have been conscious for so many years to so many people in America.

During the years since I first became interested in Colonial silver, numerous note books have been filled with rough sketches and hieroglyphics as a result of visits to different museums and of discussing and studying examples with both private and professional collectors, some of whom are no longer with us.

In the preparation of this book, I plead guilty to taking full advantage of that spontaneous kindness which, from my early days, I have met with in America. My vocal inquiries and those made through the mails have been legion, yet have invariably brought a helpful response. In this connection, I would extend my thanks to Edward P. Alexander of Colonial Williamsburg; Mark Bortman, Boston; E. Milby Burton, The Charleston Museum, Charleston, South Carolina; Mrs. Stanley Cunningham, Milton, Massachusetts; Edward M. Davis, III, Norfolk Museum of Arts and Sciences, Norfolk, Virginia; H. F. du Pont, Winterthur, Delaware; Stephen G. C. Ensko, New York; Miss Helen S. Foote, The Cleveland Museum of Art, Cleveland, Ohio; Mrs. Lloyd K. Garrison, New York; John M. Graham, 2d, The Brooklyn Museum, Brooklyn, New York; Mrs. Alexander Duer Harvey, New York; Pierre Jay, New York; Richard J. Koke, The New York Historical Society, New York; Mrs. A. E. MacSwiggan, The Essex Institute, Salem, Massachusetts; and Charles Messer Stow, New York.

My gratitude is due to Mrs. Yves Henry Buhler of the Museum of Fine Arts, Boston, for her valued help when I last had the pleasure of discussing American silver with her, in 1947, and for her helpful answers to later questions. Similarly, am I indebted to Dr. John Marshall Phillips, Director of Yale University Art Gallery both for his many courtesies and for allowing me to have photographs at various times.

To Major Hiram H. Parke of Parke-Bernet Galleries, Inc., New York, I am under obligation for his supplying me with details relating to early American silver which has been sold at those Galleries during the past twenty years; and that obligation must be extended to cover Major Parke's unsparing helpfulness in permitting me, at all times, to have photographs of examples that have passed under his hammer.

Through the generosity of collectors and others in America, it had been possible to assemble a large number of illustrations, some of which have been reproduced as drawings in the following pages; but well-equipped as my files seemed to be, like Oliver Twist, I was compelled to ask for more.

All those additional requests were met with characteristic liberality and I would express my appreciation of the gracious assistance accorded me by Edwin J. Hipkiss and W. Germain Dooley of the Museum of Fine Arts, Boston; H. F. Jayne, Miss C. Louise Avery, Miss Faith Dennis and others of the Metropolitan Museum of Art, New York; and Charles Whitenack of the Philadelphia Museum of Art, Philadelphia, each of whom generously allowed me to select a number of photographs.

Other photographs from which drawings have been made have come from various sources at different times over the years; and among those to whom I am thus indebted are: The Cleveland Museum of Art, Cleveland, Ohio; Robert Ensko, Inc., New York; The Essex Institute, Salem, Massachusetts; Worcester Art Museum, Worcester, Massachusetts. And I would also express my thanks to Christie, Manson & Woods, Ltd; Sotheby & Company; and Victor A. Watson of London, England.

E. W.

INTRODUCTION

The Rediscovery of American Silver

TO SOME EXTENT, THE REDISCOVERY OF AMERICAN
Colonial silver resembled that of the various hoards of ancient Roman
treasures in Europe—a thought which came to the writer when he was
examining the great find of Roman silver at Mildenhall, Suffolk in
1946. Both Roman and Colonial silverwork represent the acme of
craftsmanship, both graced the houses of their time and both disappeared and were forgotten to be again brought to light and admired in
later centuries.

Admittedly fewer centuries passed before Colonial silver was restored
to its proper place, but even so, more than two hundred years elapsed
between the time the first silversmiths were established in the Colonies
and the period when their work received its full recognition; in fact,
less than fifty years ago, the suggestion that America possessed so great
a heritage of craftsmanship in silver was received with incredulous
shrugs.

From what source the interest in American silver stemmed must
remain in doubt. But it is noticeable that it was almost coincidental
with the increased collector interest in English silver, which showed
itself at the Dunn Gardner sale in 1902. Previous to that sale, though
English silver was in fairly good demand, the competition among collectors was what might be termed normal; but at Christie's, when the
Dunn Gardner silver was offered, competition increased to a very
marked degree and the prices realized not only set a new standard of
values for early examples, but may be said to have started that upward
trend which has since been maintained—except during brief periods of
world depression.

This might seem to have no relation to the stimulation of interest in
Colonial silver. The suggestion is not entirely illogical, however, for
this reason: at the Dunn Gardner sale, prices were undoubtedly influ-

enced by 'American interests'; an appreciable number of the pieces found their way to America, where they were seen and admired. This, as it were, spread the gospel of collecting with the result that more and more English, Scottish and Irish silverwork began to find its way to America.

Among the many articles that were brought across the Atlantic, it was natural for some to show a close resemblance to pieces which had belonged to different American families for generations. And we can assume that this resemblance led to comparison and the discovery that while one might be almost a duplicate of another, the imported piece was punched with several marks, whereas the 'family' piece bore only one or possibly two marks and of a different character. At this point the influence of that great discoverer Curiosity came into play; the history of the pieces with only one punch was traced and, as always, the search brought to light other facts and the great tradition of Colonial silversmithing was gradually rediscovered and recognized.

It should not be overlooked, however, that J. H. Buck had made an effort some twenty-five years before to bring the work of the early American silversmiths to public notice. In 1888, he published a work, titled *Old Plate,* which, in addition to dealing with European silver, included a chapter on that made by Colonial silversmiths. Obviously the available data concerning the latter was at that time limited and the book attracted very little interest. But when public notice was at last directed to the fact that silver equal to that imported from Britain had been made in America, Mr. Buck considerably increased the scope of the American section of his book and this revised edition was published in 1903.

It was at about that time that a small group of enthusiasts began seriously to collect American silver. The names of these men are today well known in the world of collecting, for they include William Loring Andrews, Francis Hill Bigelow, Judge A. T. Clearwater, Hollis French, R. T. H. Halsey, Dr. Theodore S. Woolsey and others nearly as familiar.

In his Preface to *American Silver of the XVII and XVIII Centuries,* A Study Based on the Clearwater Collection, by Miss C. Louise Avery which was issued by the Metropolitan Museum of Art in 1920, R. T. H. Halsey relates a story of a Paul Revere teapot. This teapot had been acquired by William Loring Andrews less than twenty years before and had inspired Mr. Andrews to write the now almost forgotten monograph, *Paul Revere and His Engraving,* which, as Mr. Halsey pointed out, "made New York collectors aware of the fact that silver plate was made in the Colonies, previous writings by Dr. Theodore S. Woolsey and John H. Buck having failed to reach their attention."

This monograph gave some impetus to the interest in Colonial silver, but apparently it was for several years restricted largely to finding other pieces by Paul Revere. Then, as Mr. Halsey has recorded, it occurred to a few enthusiasts that other silversmiths were working in Colonial times and many heirlooms which previously had been regarded as of English origin were found to bear no English hall-marks.

It was at this time too that the search began for information concerning silversmithing and the men who worked at it in the Colonies; early newspapers, family records and other possible sources were carefully examined and within a relatively short time these revealed that "literally hundreds of silversmiths lived in the Colonies."

Public notice was first attracted to Colonial silver in 1906 when, at the suggestion of R. T. H. Halsey, Francis Hill Bigelow assembled a large number of examples which had been believed to be the work of English silversmiths but, when examined in the light of the facts that had been gathered, were proved to have been made by men working in America. The outcome of Mr. Bigelow's enthusiastic energy was the first exhibition of Colonial silver. This was held at the Museum of Fine Arts, Boston, in 1906 and the museum issued a descriptive catalogue by J. H. Buck with an Introduction by R. T. H. Halsey.

In the following year, an exhibition of American silver was organized by the Colonial Dames of the State of New York at the Metropolitan Museum of Art, and two years later a number of examples were shown at the same Museum at the time of the Hudson-Fulton celebrations. In the meantime, more Colonial silver had come to light, more data concerning the early American silversmiths had been assembled and, in 1911, a second exhibition was held at the Boston Museum of Fine Arts. This consisted of nearly twelve hundred examples, but, though the handsome illustrated catalogue was titled *American Church Silver,* a very considerable proportion of the pieces were of an essentially domestic character which, together with the fact that the catalogue contained the most complete list of Colonial silversmiths issued up to that time, added greatly to the value of the exhibition.

In that and subsequent years exhibitions were held at New York; Philadelphia; Hartford, Connecticut; Worcester, Massachusetts; and elsewhere, each of which stimulated the examination of family silver and resulted in further discoveries of previously unrecognized pieces of early American silver.

Today, there are a large number of important private collections in addition to those in different museums. Many pieces of this early silverwork have come to the museums by gift, others are lent by their owners, for the true collector is always willing to share his knowledge and his treasures.

Among the earlier collectors whose names are perpetuated by their generous gifts to our public museums are: Judge A. T. Clearwater, Hollis French, Francis P. Garvan and Philip L. Spalding. Others, of whom Francis Hill Bigelow, R. T. Halsey and Dr. Theodore S. Woolsey are prominent, are remembered both for their gifts and for their literary contributions to the history of American silver.

Judge Clearwater's keen interest began at the time when attention was first attracted to Colonial silver and he lent examples to the Metropolitan Museum as early as 1910. From the beginning he had in mind a collection in which all periods would be represented and which would include examples by each of the several groups of men who worked in different parts of America.

It is only necessary to know the Clearwater Collection, now in the Metropolitan Museum of Art, New York, to realize the comprehensive ambition of the man who assembled it. Larger pieces, such as tankards, teapots, coffee-pots and the like may be more impressive, but Judge Clearwater set out to show equally the American silversmith's skill in producing buckles for shoes and knee breeches, tobacco boxes, and other small objects which were in use in the long ago. Like his fellow enthusiasts, he was a great admirer of the work of Paul Revere, of which he acquired a number of important examples, as well as a few by Revere's father, Apollos Rivoire.

Apollos Rivoire who was born at Riancaud, France, in 1702, came to Boston when a young lad and was there apprenticed to John Coney. When he was twenty-one, he started in business as a silversmith and at that time changed his name to the anglicized form, Paul Revere, his celebrated son of the same name being born in 1735.

As time went on and the number of collectors increased, need arose for a work of reference relating to the silversmiths. The pioneer book on this subject was issued in 1915 by Robert Ensko, who for many years had contributed largely to the identification of American silver and the men who made it.

x

Two years later, Hollis French compiled the first list of American silversmiths with facsimiles of their individual marks which was published by the Walpole Society; but no similar record appeared until 1927, when Stephen G. C. Ensko issued his *American Silversmiths and Their Marks* which has been brought up to date in later editions and is the standard work on the subject. Another important contribution to the history of Colonial silver was made in 1917 by Francis Hill Bigelow who published his book, *Historic Silver of the Colonies and Its Makers,* which deals very largely with the silverwork of New England.

Hollis French, as well as devoting himself to research, was a particularly eclectic connoisseur and the two hundred and twelve pieces which he gave to the Cleveland Museum of Art in 1940 are of an outstanding character. As Miss Helen S. Foote has said, the possession of this fine collection places the Cleveland Museum among the great repositories of American silver.

Another keen enthusiast, Francis P. Garvan, began to assemble the well-known collection now in the Yale University Art Gallery some few years after Judge Clearwater and his fellow pioneers. Dr. John Marshall Phillips, the Director of the Gallery, told the writer that Mr. Garvan first began to show an interest in American silver before the first World War. When peace was restored, he became increasingly active and within a relatively short time had acquired a large number of unusually fine early specimens.

In 1931, some four hundred lots of Americana selected from the Garvan collections were offered at auction, having, as Mr. Garvan explained "been found unnecessary to the comprehensiveness of the Mabel Brady Garvan collections at Yale." The catalogue included about fifty lots of American silver and the prices paid were convincing proof of rising values, particularly of the work by the earlier Boston and New York silversmiths.

In view of the length of time that has elapsed since that sale, it is of interest to recall some of the final bids: Of the pieces by Boston men, a bulbous cann or mug by Joseph Loring brought $1,125; a trifid spoon by Edward Winslow, $475; a tablespoon by Paul Revere, $325; a straight-sided tapering mug with reeded strap handle by Edward Winslow, $700; a porringer by John Dixwell, $1,300; a dome-top tankard by Edward Winslow, $2,500; a brazier by Jacob Hurd, $2,800; a bulbous cann, $1,200; a dome-top tankard, $2,100; and an inverted pyriform coffee-pot, $1,700, by Benjamin Burt; a dome-top tankard by Jacob Hurd, $2,200; a similar one by John Burt, $2,400;

a porringer by Paul Revere, $2,300; and a caudle cup by Jeremiah Dummer, $4,500.

These bids were exceeded, however, by those made for some of the New York pieces among which a flat-top tankard by Peter Van Dyck brought $9,000; one by Henricus Boelen, $8,500; a pear-shaped teapot by Adrian Bancker, $3,500; a similar teapot by Thauvet Besley, $2,600; a pear-shaped cream pitcher on three legs by Jacob Ten Eyck, $650; and a porringer by Elias Pelletreau, $675.

As might be expected, the Museum of Fine Arts, Boston, which may be regarded as the alma mater of American silver, has a splendid collection as a result of early acquisitions and gifts and loans. These include the gift of fifty fine specimens collected by Philip L. Spalding who devoted his attention to the work of the earliest Boston silversmiths. As Mr. Edwin J. Hipkiss remarks in the informative catalogue, the importance of the Spalding Collection lies in the fact that thirty-two of the pieces were made by local silversmiths who were born before the year 1700.

There are a number of examples of early American silver in the Essex Institute, Salem, including a collection of spoons representing the various styles fashionable from the late 17th century onward. The Worcester Art Museum, too, is the fortunate owner of many fine examples by early New England men including a fluted, straight-sided teapot, a large coffee-pot, and other pieces by Paul Revere.

Much research has been undertaken by the Philadelphia Museum of Art with a view to accumulating data concerning silversmiths who worked in Pennsylvania. That this group was both more numerous and more important than was at one time supposed has been shown by the splendid examples inherited by the present generation of prominent families in Pennsylvania and the South.

Many of these handsome pieces have been shown at the various exhibitions held in Philadelphia and a considerable number have been lent to the Museum where, in addition to other silverwork made by the Philadelphia silversmiths, some splendid New England and New York pieces are also on view.

By about 1920, it was possible to judge the interest in American silver by that reliable barometer, the auction room, for at that time we began to see serious competition for examples; and how keen that competition has become in later years is apparent from the bidding at more recent sales.

Though during the 1920's other collections were sold at auction and prices maintained a steady upward trend, it was not until the examples in the Garvan sale of 1931, previously referred to, that the general public were given unmistakable proof of the valuations placed upon really fine examples of American silverwork. The following prices realized at auction after the disposal of the pieces from the Garvan Collection seem to indicate that many people regard silverwork as an excellent investment.

Values of silver bearing the mark of Paul Revere have risen consistently. In 1931, a boat-shaped sugar bowl bearing the mark of this famous patriot brought $950; in 1934, two salt spoons and a pair of engraved sugar tongs, $450; (1936) a plain tablespoon, $160, a bulbous-shaped cann, $1,100; (1937) a pair of plain tablespoons, $340 and a pear-shaped cream jug on three legs $600; (the Adams-Quincy heirlooms, 1946) a straight-sided fluted teapot and stand, $14,000; (1948) a pair of canns, $7,000.

Other prices in the higher levels paid for early and rare New England examples include: in 1935, a coffee-pot by Daniel Henchman, $1,900; a flat-top tankard by John Noyes, $1,700; (1936) a pair of casters by Benjamin Burt, $900, a porringer by John Coney, $1,500; (1937) a sauce-boat, $1,500 and a globular teapot by Jacob Hurd, $4,400; a small tankard with stepped flat top by Andrew Tyler, $1,500, a shaped water pitcher by Robert Evans, $600; (Adams-Quincy heirlooms, 1946) the Tutor Flynt two-handled cup and cover by John Coney, $15,000.

Collectors have always shown a keen desire for New York flat-top tankards and this is reflected in prices paid at and since the Garvan sale. In 1936, one by Christopher Robert realized $5,900, one by George Fielding, $3,800 and one by Peter Van Dyck, $4,850; (1937) one by Adrian Bancker, $3,100; (1938) one by Bartholomew Schaats, $4,300. In addition to these a sauceboat by George Ridout in the Lawton Collection brought $850, and a small bowl, 6 inches in diameter, by John Vernon, $600 at the Bigelow sale.

While the figures quoted are of interest and important in that field of collecting to which they belong, it strongly is to be emphasized that they should not be regarded as a criterion of the general levels of values. Such prices are exceptional and for every one which attracts bids in the four-figure range, a far greater number of pieces made by early American silversmiths, come on offer which are within the reach of collectors whose acquisitions have to be regulated by their bank balance.

CONTENTS

CHAPTER   PAGE

1   THE SEVENTEENTH CENTURY   3

Drinking Vessels   4

     Standing-cups   7

     Beakers   10

     Tumblers and Drinking Bowls   13

     Tankards   14

     Mugs   20

     Caudle Cups   21

     Spout Cups   27

Other Domestic Silver   29

     Salts   29

     Boxes for Sugar or Sweetmeats   33

     Candlesticks   35

     Dishes and Salvers   37

     Casters   38

2   HIGH STANDARD PERIOD, 1697 TO 1720   40

Drinking Vessels   42

     Tankards   43

     Mugs and Canns   46

     Caudle and Two-handled Cups   47

     Punch Bowls and Monteiths   48

Other Domestic Silver   50

     Saltcellars   50

     Salvers or Tazze   52

     Casters   53

     Candlesticks   56

     Teapots   58

     Coffee-pots and Chocolate-pots   62

CHAPTER   PAGE

Tea-kettles 64
Braziers or Chafing Dishes 64
Porringers 66

3   THE ROCOCO PERIOD, ABOUT 1725 TO 1770 . . . 70
Drinking Vessels 71
Beakers 71
Tankards 72
Mugs and Canns 74
Two-handled Cups with Covers 75
Punch Bowls 77
Other Domestic Silver 80
Saltcellars 80
Sauceboats 81
Casters 83
Candlesticks 84
Teapots 85
Coffee-pots and Chocolate-pots 88
Tea-kettles 90
Cream Jugs 91
Sugar Bowls 93
Salvers and Trays 94
Historical Society of Pennsylvania 97

4   THE CLASSIC PERIOD, ABOUT 1765 TO 1825 . . . 99
Drinking Vessels 100
Beakers 101
Tumblers 103
Tankards 103
Mugs and Canns 106
Punch Bowls 107
Pitchers 108
Other Domestic Silver 111
Saltcellars 111
Sauceboats 112

CHAPTER   PAGE

Casters 113
Candlesticks 114
Teapots and Tea Services 115
Coffee-pots and Chocolate-pots 125
Small Jugs for Milk and Cream 128
Sugar Bowls 131
Salvers and Trays 134

5   SPOONS AND FORKS 137
Seventeenth-century Spoons 137
Eighteenth-century Spoons 139
Sugar Tongs 143
Forks 144

6   BYGONES 148
Argyles 148
Buckles 148
Coasters 151
Dish Crosses 152
Freedom Boxes 152
Papboats 153
Saucepans and Nutmeg Boxes 154
Standishes and Inkstands 155
Tobacco Boxes and Snuffboxes 156
Patch Boxes 158
Punch Strainers and Ladles 159
Tea Caddies 160
Dish Rings 162

7   MARKS ON AMERICAN SILVER 165

8   SCARCITY AND COLLECTIONS 173

BOOKS OF REFERENCE 265

INDEX 269

ILLUSTRATIONS

The illustrations from photographs, referred to by PLATE number throughout the text, are placed in sequence following page 60.

The illustrations from line drawings, referred to by FIGURE number throughout the text, are placed in sequence beginning with page 179.

THE PRACTICAL BOOK
of AMERICAN SILVER

CHAPTER ONE

The Seventeenth Century

EARLY AMERICAN SILVER IS A PARTICULARLY INTER-
esting study of the persistence of tradition and of the modifications
directed by later local conditions and subtle changes in the outlook of
a people affected by their surroundings. There are instances where
the first influence is submerged by those of a different race who later
came to dominate the first settlers; this is the case with the early New
York silver, which, at first wholly Dutch in form and character, in
time merged with the English styles after the English took over the
Colony.

With the exception of that made by the early New York craftsmen
of Dutch origin or descent, Colonial silver is basically English. In
accepting this, however, we should not overlook those minor details
stemming from the less pronounced, but yet present, influences introduced from France by the Huguenots or by the men who came from
Germany, Scandinavia, and other parts of Europe. Nor must we lose
sight of the appreciable amount of silverwork made in various European countries and brought to the New World by the settlers from
those several countries; for even if the Colonial silversmith was not
always attracted sufficiently to accept entirely a piece of European work
as a model, it may be assumed that some detail might appeal to and be
adopted by him.

This last point is well worth considering. The larger proportion of
Colonial silver designs are characteristically English; but the early
American silversmith, while accepting the actual forms, almost invariably refrained from repeating the elaborate ornamentation found
with some of the late 17th- and 18th-century English silverwork. A
few examples of Colonial work which admit of some exceptions to this
have come to light with the steadily increasing interest in native American silverwork. But with rare exceptions even the decoration of these
shows a characteristic moderation; the few unusually ornate pieces
probably were made to order and copied from English originals.

3

All the basic shapes of the many articles of domestic silver through the centuries spring from a common parentage alike in the Old and the New Worlds. Certain variations occur in the interpretations by the silversmiths of different European countries and, in the later more ornamented pieces, the original form is at times almost unrecognizable. In Colonial silver, however, the form is clearly discernible; being free from unnecessary elaboration, the outline is undisguised. It may therefore be claimed that the American styles, like those of the English early 18th century, known as the High Standard period, represent the skill of the silversmith at the height of his achievement.

DRINKING VESSELS

Sir Mathew Hale, the famous English judge during the time of Charles I and Cromwell, insisted "If you pledge one health you oblige yourself to pledge another and a third and so onwards; and if you pledge as many as will drink, you must be debauched and drunk." The custom of health-drinking is so deeply rooted in the distant past, however, that despite condemnation and many well intentioned efforts to combat it, it has survived to the present day.

One of the earliest instances of health-drinking is mentioned by Richard Verstegan, the 17th-century antiquarian. Writing of a banquet given by Hengist, King of Kent (A.D. 454) to Vortigern, King of the Britons, he describes how Rowena, the daughter of Hengist, came with a gold cup of wine into the hall where the kings and their guests were seated. Kneeling before Vortigern, she said, *"Waes hael hlaford cyning"* (*Your health Lord king*); then having drunk from the cup, she presented it to the King who, after being told the meaning of the custom and of what Rowena had said, took the cup and said "Drinc hael" (*Here's to you*), and he too drank from the cup.

It was the custom at Anglo-Saxon feasts for a large cup to be passed round the company, each person in turn drinking to one or more of his fellow guests. Standing while he drank, he held the cup with both hands, in this way leaving himself open to an attack by an enemy; consequently, it was customary for the man next to him to stand and pledge him. In other words, the second man undertook to be responsible for his safety and emphasized this by holding his sword ready to defend his friend while the latter was drinking.

One writer in *Curiosities of London* refers to the survival of this ancient tradition at what he calls "Hall-feasts," i.e. banquets held at

4

the halls of the different Livery Companies. After the banquet, grace is said and the Master and Wardens of the Company drink to their guests. The standing-cup is passed round the table, each guest rising and drinking from it and, wiping the rim with his napkin, passing the cup to his neighbor.

The modern form of the custom lacks the romance associated with the formal observance where the man who pledges another stands holding the cup and bows to his neighbor; the latter, also standing, takes the cover from the cup with his right hand and remains holding it while the other drinks. This is generally regarded as repeating the old-time precaution to keep the right or dagger hand occupied, thus ensuring against treachery.

In some of the customs associated with the ceremony of drinking in bygone times, it was usual for two men to stand beside the one who was drinking from the cup. An early issue of *Notes and Queries* contains a description of the custom observed at Corporation dinners formerly held in the old city of Lichfield. The Corporation cup, which is a massive affair holding upward of a gallon was presented to the Corporation in 1666 by Elias Ashmole, founder of the Ashmolean Museum at Oxford.

According to the description of these dinners, "The Mayor drinks first and, on his rising, the man on his right and the one on his left also rise. The Mayor then hands the cup to the one on his right, when the one next to him rises, the man on the left of the Mayor still standing. Then the cup is passed across the table to him, when *his* left-hand neighbor rises; so that there are always three standing at the same time—one next to the man who drinks and one opposite him."

In Germany, it was at one time the custom when a man of importance drank the health of an inferior, for the latter to place his thumbs on the table and thus be prevented from making any attack on the man who was drinking. And this same custom was observed at one time at Queen's College, Oxford, where those who waited on their fellow scholars placed their thumbs on the table.

When or where the tradition of pledging originated is doubtful; but it was unquestionably more popular among the races of Northern Europe than among those of the South. According to William of Malmesbury, the 12th-century historian, "it first took its rise from the death of young King Edward (called the Martyr), son of Edgar who was, by contrivance of Elfrida his stepmother, traitorously stabbed in the back as he was drinking." And Edward the Martyr was murdered in 978.

While drinking is still a popular indoor sport, history is crowded with curious modes and customs in the observance of which drinking was carried to an extravagance fortunately unknown in our time. For several centuries it had its own language, most of which came from Germany, Denmark and Holland. We will not here attempt to quote at any length from the wide vocabulary of drinking terms, but a few many be of interest.

Tom Nashe, the Elizabethan wit, said, "Now, he is nobody that cannot drink supernagulum: carouse the hunter's hoope; quaff upse freeze crosse; with the healths, gloves, mumpes. . . ." Drinking supernaculum, or "on the nail," seems to have originated in Denmark or Germany. When a man had emptied a cup he turned it bottom upward with the rim on his thumbnail; if the amount of liquid was more than would remain on his nail, he had to refill the cup and drink again.

One suggestion for the origin of drinking to the health of another before offering him the cup was to prove the cup held no poison and the ceremony of the loving cup, as it is called, was similar in all northerly European countries.

Even as late as the middle of the 17th century, the earliest date for Colonial silver, standing-cups, beakers, tankards and other vessels associated with the ceremony of drinking far outnumbered other articles of domestic silver in Europe and Britain; other silver then in use was restricted almost entirely to spoons, ceremonial standing-salts and rose-water dishes with their accompanying ewers.

Obviously, the articles made by the early Colonial silversmiths would be those known to them in the countries from which they came; and the dominant influence in style would be that of the preponderating race of settlers. Thus in New England which was settled by people from England, the silverwork is essentially English in character from the beginning. In New Amsterdam the earliest silver follows the styles introduced from Holland by the first Dutch settlers. In Pennsylvania the English influence is again dominant as it was later in the South, though the Southern silver was affected directly by the Philadelphia designs.

6

Standing-cups

At banquets and feasts of olden times, only two articles of plate were regarded as important—the standing-cup and the standing-salt. But elaborate as some of the salts were, far more attention was given to the massive drinking cups or hanaps, as they were formerly known. The now forgotten word "hanap" has a curious origin: In medieval times, the large drinking cups when not in use were kept in a case known as a hanaper. This case was often merely a strong wicker basket covered with leather, similar to those used in fairly modern times to hold clothes or samples when travelling; and so from "hanaper" we obtained the more familiar word "hamper."

By far the greater variety and the most elaborate of standing-cups were made in Germany during the 16th century and later. And the German styles directly influenced the English cups of the Elizabethan period—an influence noticeable in the shapes and the heavy and profuse ornamentation. It was not long, however, before this ornate type was superseded by simpler forms which, had England not been disturbed by political and religious strife, would have possibly resulted in the emergence of a style deserving acceptance as essentially English.

While a number of the shapes of Elizabethan days were borrowed by the English early 17th-century silversmiths, they none the less produced many that give evidence of originality and versatility. This development toward original designs is illustrated in the so-called "steeple cup" which appeared in the reign of James I, and which typifies English standing-cups of and is peculiar to the early part of the 17th century. It had a conical bowl with a slightly domed cover surmounted by a pierced or solid spire derived from the architectural steeple of the period. The bowl is supported on a short baluster stem, usually with three scroll brackets on a spreading foot not unlike the lower section of the bell-shaped salts described later.

In the First Church of Boston, there is a cup of this type which was given to the church by John Winthrop, founder of Boston, and governor of the Massachusetts Colony. It is 11½ inches high and bears the London hall-marks for 1610-11 and, though now without a cover, there is no doubt it had formerly a cover with the tall steeple-like ornament typical of the time at which it was made.

These steeple cups were often made in sets of three, one slightly taller than the others. A set hall-marked 1611-12 of which the taller cup is 19¼ inches high and the other two 18 inches, appeared at Christie's in 1924 and brought $23,000. They are variously decorated; both the Winthrop cup and the set mentioned being embossed and chased with floral and foliated motifs, fruit and strapwork in a manner indicating a carry-over from the Elizabethan style of ornamentation, introduced by German and Flemish silversmiths.

By the time of Charles I the Puritan influence had become active in all phases of English life, an influence reflected in the plainer domestic silver which began to replace the ornamented styles. These plain robust forms of the early Stuart and Cromwellian silver were familiar to the venturesome founders of New England, many of whom brought with them cups, beakers and other pieces bearing English hall-marks of the time of Charles I and Cromwell.

NEW ENGLAND. Unlike those in New Netherland, where trade with other countries was frowned upon by the Dutch West India Company, the New England Colonists developed considerable trade with Great Britain and the Indies. While perhaps at first sight it might appear that foreign trade had little influence upon the prosperity of the silversmith's craft, actually its earlier expansion in New England was directly attributable to the steadily increasing exports. There are two reasons for this: Foreign trade brought an inflow of coinage and wealth to the people of New England; and as the coinage was mostly silver this, when melted down and refined, supplied metal for the silversmiths.

Prosperous merchants receiving silver coinage in payment for exports would at times be holding a fairly large quantity. Obviously, this could be an embarrassing responsibility in those early days when there were neither such convenient storing places as safety deposits nor banks which would accept coinage for safekeeping. Consequently, the natural desire for silver appointments resulted in the practice of melting and refining the coins and having the metal made into standing-cups, beakers, tankards and other drinking vessels or articles for which the owner had use—the Puritans believed firmly in articles for everyday use and not for ornament.

During the later 17th century, the Colonial silversmiths not only increased in number but began to produce work in every way equal to that of their English contemporaries. And while doubtless silverwork of the late Stuart styles was imported to the Colonies, the more ornamental forms had little or no appeal to the Colonists.

New England remained faithful to the plain silver which the tenets

8

of the Puritans dictated. Standing-cups followed closely the severely plain cups, characteristic of the reign of Charles I, which had been brought or imported from England. Perhaps it would be more correct to say that some of the New England cups referred to as standing-cups were probably copied from individual wine goblets which were among the family possessions brought over by the early settlers. While the goblets resemble the standing-cups in form, they are noticeably smaller and this applies to many of the Colonial pieces designated as standing-cups.

For example, the cup shown in Figure 1 has the tapering cylindrical bowl with the slightly flaring lip common to English standing-cups a few years before and during the Commonwealth period. The bold baluster stem and spreading foot are also copied from a Commonwealth model. English standing-cups of this type are some 12 inches high but goblets are only about 7 inches. It may therefore be assumed that as the cup in FIG. 1 is only 8 inches high it was copied from a goblet.

Colonial standing-cups or goblets are very rare today outside of the not inconsiderable number belonging to different churches. Nor would it seem that many were made except in New England and most of those for religious use. Some fifty-odd examples, each described as a chalice, were included in the exhibition of American Church Silver at the Museum of Fine Arts, Boston, in 1911. By far the larger number then exhibited have the quite plain bowl, the sturdy baluster stem and molded foot and were made by New England silversmiths working during the late 17th and early 18th centuries. In a few instances, however, the lower part of the bowl is spirally fluted (FIG. 2), a form of ornamentation which appeared in England during the last quarter of the 17th century (see also PLATE IV).

These cups which were in the Boston exhibition range in size from one of 5½ inches high made by Hull and Sanderson (John Hull, 1624-83, and Robert Sanderson, c. 1610-1693), lent by the First Church, Boston, to two slightly over 10 inches, by John Edwards (c. 1670-1746), lent by the Church in Brattle Square, Boston.

Some few of the American tall cups used as chalices in churches are engraved with what might be termed family initials, i.e. the initial of the surname and those of the first given name of the man and wife which would suggest that such cups were at one time in domestic use. Examples are seemingly scarce, however, for of the many in the Boston exhibition relatively few bore initials of former owners; among them, four with initials and two with the Hancock arms were lent

9

by the First Church, Boston, one by the Essex Congregational Church, and one by the First Congregational Church, Quincy.

Beakers

One drinking cup which was still in common use when the first settlers sailed for the New World has survived in the present-day table glasses we call tumblers. The shape of these glasses has come down from the beaker, which it is fairly safe to assume was originally a section of an oxhorn with the smaller end closed by a piece of horn or metal.

English silver beakers began to be copied from the Dutch beakers with the slightly flaring lip in the latter part of the 16th century and it is this style which was generally adopted by Colonial silversmiths. At first, the English retained the rather elaborate spreading foot, but in the early Stuart period they were taller and simpler, any decoration being the engraved interlaced bands round the lip and scroll and floral ornaments pendent below, again following the Dutch style (see FIG. 4). Most of the English beakers of the early 17th century have the simple molded base and, though the wide spreading foot was used, it was invariably plain.

NEW ENGLAND. Some few early New England and all New York beakers of the second half of the 17th century show a distinct Dutch influence. But whereas this influence had come direct to New York, it arrived in New England via the English silver beakers brought over by the early settlers; for several well-known silversmiths of Dutch origin, among them Peter Petersen and Timothy Skittowe, were then working in England and beakers bearing their marks are preserved to the present time.

Probably the first style of beaker made in New England was the straight-sided rather squat type less than 4 inches high, sometimes with a slightly flaring lip. As a rule, they are quite plain, but examples do occur with a wide band of frosting or matting round the body (FIG. 3). This form of ornamentation was used to some extent during the Commonwealth in England, to which country it was probably introduced from Germany though it was also popular in the Scandinavian countries. Another feature of these early New England beakers is the absence of a molded band round the base, as in the one illustrated (FIG. 3).

New England beakers showing Dutch influence (FIG. 4) are few

10

and far between and are distinguished by their height (about 6½ inches), their shape and the fact that they are decorated. Most of those known bear the mark of Hull and Sanderson; they repeat the taper of the original horn shape with a decided flare at the lip and have a deep base molding. As a rule the decoration which is engraved follows the usual foliated design enclosed by plain intersecting bands, with an elaborate pointed ornament of scrolls and floral blossoms pendent from the intersecting bands.

This style of beaker, similarly decorated, is found in Norwich and other parts of East Anglia and also in the Northeast of Scotland. There is this interesting difference, however: the English beakers sometimes have a slightly spreading foot below the base molding, whereas the Scottish have only the deep base molding similar to those made in Boston, and furthermore some of them are without the engraved decoration, as in the New England example (FIG. 5).

Early New England beakers generally retained the short and proportionately wide form but, while the first examples have the quite plain bottom, the simple base molding was adopted before the end of the 17th century. Contemporary English beakers are noticeably taller than those made by the Colonial silversmiths; it might be supposed that the size of the latter was reduced owing to shortage of metal but this is contradicted by the fact that most of them are fairly heavy.

NEW YORK. Thanks to the indefatigable work of Mr. Stephen G. C. Ensko, we now have a comprehensive record of a very large number of American silversmiths and their marks. From this, it is possible to arrive at the approximate number of established craftsmen working in New England and New York at various periods. And an analysis of the long list brings out the somewhat surprising information that before 1700 not more than twenty men in New England were of an age to have been working and less than half that number in New York; it would seem that all the latter were of Dutch descent with the exception of Bartholomew Le Roux, a Huguenot who came to New York in the 17th century.

This would explain in part why there is considerably less New York than New England silverwork ascribable to the 17th century. Moreover, in view of the restrictions made by the Dutch government upon foreign trading by New Netherland, compared with the freedom enjoyed by the New England Colonists, there was a shortage of silver coin—in other words, the silversmiths lacked material. Nor was it until the end of the 17th century that various enterprising spirits saw a means to wealth by indulging in such pastimes as privateering, which brought considerable profit to themselves, and increased "raw material" to the silversmiths.

For these reasons, silver articles by New York silversmiths before 1700 are few and limited in variety, and, as might be expected, the silverwork with the exception of the tankard of that period is essentially Dutch in character. All early New York silver has certain distinctive features: The craftsmen seem to have bestowed upon their work that sense of solid respectability typical of the fairly wealthy Hollander; nor were they sparing of silver, for the articles they made are of unusually heavy metal.

Despite the control of the Colony passing to the English and the influx of English settlers, the Dutch influence persisted for many years, gradually being merged with the English forms as more of the latter were imported and copied by native silversmiths. But though New Netherland changed governments in 1664, at a time when the variety of domestic silver in England increased, several articles which were in comparatively common use in New England do not seem to have been made in New York.

Standing-cups held no appeal for the Dutch settlers; their drinking vessels were confined largely to beakers, tankards and two-handled bowls. And in none of the early designs is the Dutch influence more patent than in the beakers. There is one in the First Reformed Church, Albany, New York, made by Ahasuerus Hendricks in 1678, which is a replica of a beaker bearing the mark of Haarlem, Holland, for 1660.

All early New York beakers repeat the shape of the Dutch prototypes, the average height being from 6 to 7 inches. They have a marked downward taper and a flaring or slightly trumpet-shaped rim; and the sides are engraved with the intersecting bands and pendent ornaments previously described (see FIG. 4). The pendent design varies with different beakers and where the silversmith closely followed the Dutch style, it would perhaps include a panel below each intersection with a figure, usually Faith, Hope and Charity, each in a separate panel (FIG. 6).

New York beakers of this period showed little if any variation in shape or size and the engraved ornamentation retained the same general form. The design, however, was freer and the more sophisticated Dutch scrollwork and other forms were replaced by four-petalled flowers and scrolled tendrils with tiny leaves. Another New

12

York feature is the stout lower member of the molded base which served as a slightly projecting foot; and occasionally the New York silversmith would add a shallow band of leaf-like ornamentation above the base molding, an ornament also copied from the Dutch beakers (PLATE II).

Tumblers and Drinking Bowls

While silver goblets and individual wine cups continued to be used in England during the time of Charles II, they do not seem to have been adopted in America. The only cups of that type made by Colonial smiths were those already referred to under Standing-cups.

Toward the end of the 17th century in England there was a revival of the small wine cup called a tumbler (FIG. 7). These rather amusing cups were known in the Middle Ages and are mentioned in records of that time as "bolles" or "boles" of silver. They are about 2 inches high and about the same in diameter, made of thick silver hammered to form a rounded bottom in such a way that the weight of metal in the base is proportionately greater than in the sides. This allows them to roll or tumble but prevents their overturning, even when filled with wine, in the same way as a weighted doll will roll from side to side yet remain on its feet.

NEW ENGLAND. Small plain bowls, known as dram cups, were popular in New England during the late 17th century, if we may judge from the frequent references to them in old wills. These bowls have some similarity to the New York dram cups, but whereas the latter were derived directly from Holland, those of New England had a closer relationship to the English 17th-century shallow vessels about 4 inches diameter called wine-tasters (FIGS. 8 and 9).

These shallow bowls were in use in England as far back as medieval times when they were used as essay cups to test the wine for poison and also for sampling and tasting wine, ale and other liquors.

NEW YORK. American tumbler cups (FIG. 7) are extremely rare. It is possible that a fair number were made by New York silversmiths —they were at no time popular in New England—but being more or less insignificant yet representing an appreciable amount of metal, it is probable many of them went to the melting pot to furnish metal for more fashionable silverwork.

Wine bowls such as were made by the early New York silversmiths

13

do not occur among any other Colonial silver. They vary in size from about 6 to 9 inches diameter, the larger ones being also deeper. They are decidedly Dutch in character and were doubtless inspired by the *brandewijnkom,* a two-handled bowl used at weddings, birthdays and like family celebrations in Holland. The earlier bowls made in Holland had handles with terminal head ornaments, but the later handles are flat triangular-shaped like those of American porringers, though not pierced. There is also a close resemblance between the Dutch-American bowls and those used in Scandinavian countries for national drinks, such as the Danish *orekovsken.*

Larger bowls by New York silversmiths were generally elaborately embossed in the style illustrated by the two (FIGS. 10 and 11) which were made by Cornelius Kierstede (1675-1757). Both show the Dutch inspiration in the arrangement of the panels and the treatment of the embossed floral and leaf forms. The one in Figure 10, which is slightly larger, is more imposing owing to the cast scroll handles with the terminal female head which are similar to the handles found in English two-handled cups of the second half of the 17th century; moreover, it gains some distinction from the ornamental band on the high foot.

Less impressive plain bowls such as that in Figure 12 were also made in New York. The one illustrated was made by Benjamin Wynkoop (1675-1751) and has stout twisted-wire handles and a flat bottom hammered to suggest a low foot; like others of this type, it bears a noticeable relationship to the New England dram cups, although the latter are smaller.

The three New York bowls mentioned above are in the Metropolitan Museum of Art and the New York Historical Society owns a splendid example of the large size by Benjamin Wynkoop. The last mentioned is paneled and embossed with floral forms, fitted with cast handles and is of the same general character as the Kierstede bowl shown in Figure 10.

Tankards

No etymologist has yet established definitely the origin of the word "tankard." Today we associate it with the massive vessels of silver or pewter favored by the lusty beer drinkers of bygone days. But there is little doubt that the name was at one time used for a wooden vessel in which water was carried from the public conduits and pumps.

14

One of a series of quaint pictures of the "Cries of London" drawn in the early 17th century, is titled "A Tankard Bearer." This shows a bearded man wearing the flat cap and dress of the 16th century. A long coarse apron hangs from his neck to protect his clothes and he carries on his shoulder a large tapering jug-shaped vessel made of wood staves bound with iron bands.

This tapered shape was obviously suggested by the ancient drinking horn, and it was adopted for the first silver tankards in Germany and England during the 16th century. In fact, one of the earliest known English tankards is a section of oxhorn with a silver-gilt cover, handle and foot, hall-marked 1561-2. This rare piece appeared at Christie's in 1924 and brought $2,300.

Silver tankards of the pronounced horn shape continued to be made in England for the first few years of the 17th century. But there was a marked change in the shape during the early Stuart and Commonwealth days. The first development was the tall straight-sided cylindrical body (some are 15 inches) usually ornamented with elaborate embossed and chased work; but as the Puritan influence became stronger, the more attractive plain tankard was introduced.

The simpler type made its appearance in the reign of Charles I. The plain body was much shorter and wider and it had a deep concave spreading foot or skirt; the lid, which was flat, had a low stepped member and a projecting rim hinged to the top of a stout reversed S-shaped handle with a simple thumb-piece of the type usually described as a double-cusp. This style was the forerunner of the tankard with a short wide body popular during the Commonwealth which, in turn, inspired the shape that developed into the English late Stuart and the early Colonial tankards (see FIGS. 13 and 14).

Some few English tankards of this time are known as peg tankards. These have a cylindrical body with a slightly rounded base sometimes ornamented with engraved designs. Inside there is a vertical row of studs or pegs set at equal distances, the origin of which is presumed to be the pegs or pins fastened to the side of the ancient drinking horns to mark the amount each man might drink at the passing of the cup. The lids of peg tankards are usually flat with slightly curved edges. One hall-marked York, 1657, which became part of the Pierpont Morgan collection, has a thumb-piece of two pomegranates and three pomegranate feet. Their general character indicates an influence derived from Scandinavia where tankards were made with a slightly rounded bottom and it was a common practice to use rather massive thumb-pieces and feet.

15

During the second half of the 17th century more tankards were produced by English silversmiths than at any other time. The most popular type was the plain slightly tapered cylindrical body with a small base molding and a similar molding round the lip. The lid had a flat top on a deep convex member and a projecting edge waved at the front. The handle was S-shaped, flat on the outside and semi-circular inside, and the thumb-piece a double scroll. They average about 7 inches in height.

NEW ENGLAND. As in England during the 17th century, no drinking vessel was as popular or in more general use in New England than the massive tankards of which many made by Colonial silversmiths have survived to the present time. As with other domestic silver, the New England tankards are essentially English in character but embody various individual ideas and adaptations.

Two features of English Charles I and Commonwealth tankards were not adopted; namely, the wide concave skirt and the lid with the low step rising from a wide projecting edge. On the other hand, New England tankards did follow closely the style popular in England after the Restoration in 1660, though the Colonial silversmiths used ornamental details not found in the English tankards.

Early New England tankards have the plain cylindrical body with the slight upward taper and a small base molding projecting slightly, in every way similar to the English prototypes; the base molding tends to give additional width to the base and thus accentuate the taper of the body. The lid also follows that of the English tankards of the second half of the 17th century, described above.

As a general rule, New England tankards of this shape are about 6 inches high, though several larger ones are in different private and public collections. The various features of Colonial tankards which are rarely if ever found in the English models include a bold V-shaped tongue, rather like the rat-tail on early spoons, as a continuation of the upper part of the handle down the back of the body immediately below the upper joint of the handle (FIG. 14); also the outer side of the handle will be fluted slightly more than halfway down from the top and a small piece of silver turned in a rough scroll applied to the end of the flutes (FIG. 14).

In addition to the twisted volute, known as the ram's horns (FIG. 13) and the spiral or horizontal twist thumb-pieces which the American silversmiths copied from English tankards, there are several which are largely distinctive of New England.

16

One of the most typical thumb-pieces found in New England tankards is a human mask between two inverted dolphins (FIG. 14). It is possible that this was an adaptation by the Colonial silversmiths, for though this exact ornament has not been found in European silver, a thumb-piece of similar form was used with Danish tankards.

While thumb-pieces of this type produced by different Colonial silversmiths are basically similar, there is a noticeable difference in the modeling; from which it may be inferred the thumb-pieces were cast from different molds and the chasing of various examples clearly indicates that some were tooled and finished by more experienced hands than others.

One unusually large tankard (FIG. 15) by John Coney (1655-1722) was shown at the exhibition of New England silver at the Gallery of Fine Arts, Yale University in 1939. It is 8½ inches high with the plain tapering body and flat lid typical of the late 17th-century tankards; the handle, which has the rat-tail continuing down the body below the upper joint, is plain except for a cherub's head on the tip. Its particular interest, however, lies in the cast thumb-piece in the form of an eagle with wings expanded.

It is engraved R⚹A (Richard and Abigail Lord); Richard Lord and Abigail Warren were married in 1692 which fairly definitely dates the tankard which was loaned to the exhibition by Miss Webster Stillman, a descendant of the original owners.

Ornaments applied to the handles are mostly restricted to the lower terminal or tip. This is often a simple shield cut from stout silver and soldered to the end of the handle (FIG. 14), an ornament commonly found with English tankards, which was borrowed from the Scandinavian countries, probably through Germany. But there are a number of tankards with a cast cherub's head or other mask applied to the tip (FIGS. 13 and 15) and these ornaments are both finely modeled and tooled.

Unlike the New York tankard handles which were often elaborately ornamented, those of New England are plain, apart from occasional fluting, though there are a few instances of the New York style of ornamentation being applied to New England tankards.

Perhaps because of the importance with which tankards were regarded, ornamentation was applied more often to them than to any other domestic silver. It is not unusual to find a lid engraved with an often intricate floral design; and in some few, the base is embossed with vertical acanthus and palm leaves, a style of decoration applied to English tankards and drinking-cups in the later 17th century.

17

Another method of ornamenting New England tankards was that known as cut-card work—a form borrowed from England though oddly enough it is found rarely on English tankards. It seems to have been specially favored by Jeremiah Dummer of Boston (1645-1718) and several of his tankards have delicate shapes, some resembling a tulip cut from thin silver, applied on the lid and where the lower part of the handle joins the body (FIG. 16). This style of decoration, which was introduced to England from France, is particularly effective despite its simple character, and for that reason doubtless appealed to the early settlers.

About 1695, Colonial tankards became slightly taller and, while retaining the straight-sided body, took on a more decided taper. This was the beginning of the change leading to the tankards with the domed lids introduced in the 18th century which will be described in a later chapter.

NEW YORK. When remarking previously that early New York silverwork was Dutch in character, we excluded tankards; it is a mistake to suggest that New York tankards were inspired by Dutch prototypes. Actually few silver tankards seem to have been made in Holland and when those made by the early New York silversmiths are studied it is clear that they, like those of New England, were copied from the English late Stuart models, though some of the ornamental details may be regarded as peculiar to New York.

This straight-sided shape with the slight upward taper seems to be one of the few to which English silversmiths may lay claim as their own. The plain drum tankard was used in the Baltic states and the Scandinavian countries and the hexagonal tapering body in Germany, but none had the robust simplicity of the English and American tankards with flat lids.

While similar to those of New England, the New York tankards are a trifle more capacious and have a sturdier appearance. Again, whereas those of New England are usually quite plain, apart from engraved monograms and arms, the early New York silversmiths added various forms of ornamentation. Narrow silver bands punched with a more or less leaf-like form cut to follow the outline were added above the base molding, often accompanied by a wavy wire; the wire was sometimes applied round the rim (FIG. 17), which was suggested by the similar but more refined ornamentation applied round the bases of beakers imported from Holland. This feature is characteristic of New York tankards and is found with many bearing the marks of men who were working in the last half of the 17th and early 18th centuries.

Instances of the use of the wavy wire are extremely rare with English silver. The only example that has come to the writer's notice is a Charles II plain cylindrical mug with a slightly flaring rim. This mug, which is 3 inches high and hall-marked 1681-2, has a band of wavy wire both round the base and down the back of the scroll handle; it came up at Christie's in June, 1935, at which time it brought $585.

Lids were decorated with engraved designs (FIG. 18), some of which were original conceptions of the several engravers and often quite intricate; also following the custom in Scandinavia and Germany, a coin or medal was sometimes inserted in the center of the lid. Even more ambitious ornamentation was applied to the flat backs of the massive handles (FIG. 19), and here some of the designs may have been inspired by the engraved decoration on the Dutch beakers, especially in view of the pendent character of these elaborate handle ornaments.

It has been suggested that this method of decorating the handles of tankards was originated by the early New York silversmiths, but it must not be overlooked that handles of early German and Scandinavian tankards were similarly decorated. It would be natural to suppose that the first New York silversmiths having learned their trade in Holland would be familiar with the styles of German tankards. Again it is not impossible that some influence was derived from England where tankard handles were ornamented occasionally during the late Stuart period.

Some New York tankards have a row of gradated beads applied to the handle (FIG. 17), the purpose of these, like the more elaborate ornaments, being to afford a better grip of these weighty vessels; this same "help to a shaky hand" is found on the handles of the even more massive and more ornate tankards popular in Denmark in the late 17th century.

In view of the decoration applied to many New York tankards, one might expect that the thumb-pieces would be at least as ornamental as those found in New England; such, however, is not so, for most of the early New York thumb-pieces are of the simple double-spiral or corkscrew type sometimes called a chrysalis which it resembles slightly (see FIGS. 17, 18 and 19).

19

Mugs

Many of the shapes of the 17th-century and later tankards were used for the small mugs or canns which became widely popular during the following century—probably among those whose capacity for beer was less than the amount held by one of the great tankards.

The real origin of the word "mug" remains a mystery. It seems to have been first used in the 16th century and to have been imported from the Scandinavian countries where the Swedish and Norwegian *mugge* denoted an earthenware cup. The colloquial word "mug," meaning "face," can also be tentatively traced to the early pottery drinking pots, probably the 16th-century bellied jugs with the molded face of a bearded man, supposedly that of Cardinal Bellarmine much hated in the Low Countries for his persistent persecution of the Protestants. And until fairly modern times it was not uncommon for an unpopular character to be caricatured as a beer mug.

Another use of the word occurs in the term "mug-house" which during the 18th century was the common name for an ale-house. These mug-houses were regular meeting places for drinking and singing where each of the patrons had his own mug, and the place where his mug was to stand was chalked on the table. A chairman was appointed to keep the gathering in order and it was from these mug-house musical evenings that the old-time Free and Easy came into being which in time developed into the modern music-hall.

NEW ENGLAND. One of the first types of mugs and also one of the few with applied decoration made by Colonial silversmiths had the cylindrical neck and globular body.

This shape even if it were copied from the similar English mug might well have been evolved from the German pottery vessels imported into England and mounted in silver, as for example the Winthrop jug belonging to the American Antiquarian Society, Worcester. Some New England mugs of this shape were decorated with a fluted band around the neck and another round the shoulder and the lower part of the body chased with a series of vertical alternating concave and convex flutes rising from a low molded foot, as illustrated in Figure 20. In the arrangement of the flutes it is possible to see some distant relationship with the Scottish late 17th-century bell-shaped mugs, though the likelihood of such an influence is remote.

Forms of other New England late 17th-century mugs were quite obviously borrowed from caudle cups, of both the plain ogee or gourd shape and the slightly tapering straight-sided bowl; and those, too, were sometimes decorated with the cabled band and fluted base (FIG. 21). Beaker shapes were adapted as mugs (FIG. 22) and it is not improbable that when the beaker went out of fashion more than one was transformed into a mug by the addition of a handle; though the latter may generally be recognized, as they are taller than the small beaker-shaped mug.

Most early Colonial mugs were offsprings of the contemporary tankard with the cylindrical tapering body. Some were plain with a molded rim and base, as in Figure 23; others have a molded rib round the body about halfway up and sometimes nearer the rim (FIGS. 24 and 25). The handles of these cylindrical mugs were in every way similar to the stout reversed S-shape of the tankards and some of them were similarly decorated on the back and tip, as illustrated by the beaded ornament in Figure 24 and the mask at the tip in Figure 25.

NEW YORK. As in New England, many of the first New York mugs were copied from the straight-sided tankards, without the cover. The handles ranged from the simple plain sheet silver scroll (FIG. 26) to the sturdy type similar to those of the large tankards. The latter were at times decorated with cast and chased ornamentation on the back which, again, was copied from the tankard handles. Another form of handle adopted by some of the New York silversmiths was a plain tubular scroll as in Figure 27.

The wide molded rib or band was used often with a narrower band round the lip and base (FIG. 26); others were decorated with a narrow foliated band above the base molding as shown in Figure 27.

Caudle Cups

NEW ENGLAND. As the 17th century advanced and the people of New England prospered, there was a gradual submergence of the austerity so strictly observed by the first arrivals. Still maintaining their desire for simplicity in their homes and those things which added to their comfort and convenience, they none the less began to accept tentative decoration. And there was an increase in both the amount and variety of silver articles in use in Colonial homes and of certain English forms of decoration during the later years of the century. But even though the intensity of the Puritan principles was

21

by that time somewhat moderated, such ornamental forms as were acceptable to the people of New England were of the simplest character.

Decoration seems to have been favored in the two-handled cups known as caudle cups. Most of those which have survived were obviously copied from the English two-handled cups without covers generally spoken of in England as porringers. Two of the earliest known New England caudle cups are preserved in churches.

One, by Hull and Sanderson which belongs to the Second Church, Dorchester, was exhibited at the Museum of Fine Arts, Boston, in 1911, and is illustrated in the catalogue. The lower section of the body of this cup is chased with various flowers each in a shaped panel and it is fitted with two short, rather cramped scroll handles. It is pricked with the initials A C E (Augustin and Elizabeth Clement) and was given to the First Church in Dorchester in 1678.

The other was made by John Coney (1655-1722) and was also in the exhibition of 1911, to which it was loaned by the First Parish of Concord. This cup is plain with two scroll handles and the fact that it is engraved with the date, 1676, in which year it was given by Mrs. Margaret Bridges of Finglas, Ireland, would allow the assumption it was made in that year; it also indicates that John Coney was only about twenty-one when he made the cup.

New England caudle cups have the same bulbous form with a short incurved neck (technically ogee shape) as the English porringers; and while plain examples were made by the Colonial silversmiths, they were often decorated with flat-chased and embossed work which again followed that of the English cups. Like all silverwork with curved outlines, caudle cups were hammered up or raised, as it is called, from a circular sheet of metal, the bottom being hammered almost flat and supported on a low foot.

With some exceptions, they are approximately the same size as the similar English cups, namely, about 3½ inches high and slightly more in diameter at the rim. And while all of them demonstrate the skill of the Colonial craftsmen in raising a fine shape, this is particularly noticeable in undecorated examples. One such plain cup (FIG. 28) made by Jeremiah Dummer of Boston at the end of the 17th century is now in the Boston Museum of Fine Arts and to many its graceful and symmetrical curves hold a greater appeal than those in which the outline is broken by ornamentation.

This plain cup weighs 8¼ ounces, whereas those which are embossed and chased around the bulbous part of the body are mostly about half that weight. The inference is that the latter being of thinner silver were stiffened by the decoration as was the case with many of the English models.

Then, too, the caudle cups which were chased and embossed show a considerable difference in the execution of the ornamental work, for with some there is an immaturity both in the drawing and tooling. The Dutch influence which came to New England through England is present in the tulip and leaf forms frequently used as decoration on the lower part of the cups. These forms and the lines intended to divide the design into panels often suggest a lack of experience in chasing, with the result that they are somewhat crudely outlined.

But if a lack of confidence is sometimes suggested by the ornamental details of New England caudle cups, the shaping of the cups themselves is perfect, the small cast handles are noticeably well modeled, and any immaturity evident in earlier examples is certainly absent from the later decorated cups which show both an advanced technic and an originality in the designs. Though many of the individual motifs were similar to those found on English cups, the arrangement of the general design was usually varied; furthermore, the Colonial silversmiths often introduced quite un-English forms of decoration. For example, a large tulip blossom on a rather long stalk with leaves was, with other flowers, used as a band of embossed decoration round the bulbous part of the caudle cup. Other slightly more ambitious designs were a chubby demi-Cupid figure amid sprays of different flowers as in Figure 29.

Like those of the English models, the early handles were S-shaped in outline resembling to some extent the small brackets fixed to the baluster stem of English steeple-cups of the early 17th century; the brackets were a carry-over from the standing-cups of the Tudor days when they were introduced to England from Germany. The handles of Colonial caudle cups were unquestionably copied from English models, many of them having the tapering row of beads on the back, and terminating below in a scroll rather like a bird's head (FIG. 30).

Toward the end of the 17th century, the bulbous shape of the Colonial caudle cups was replaced by the straight-sided type with rounded bottom and slightly flaring lip which had appeared in England. Some of the English examples were decorated with embossed vertical acanthus and palm leaves round the base, and an embossed band round the upper part of the body. The ornamentation of the Colonial straight-sided cups, however, was generally the

23

simpler flutings round the base, a style which appeared in England during the last quarter of the 17th century and remained popular during the early part of the 18th century (FIG. 30).

Large two-handled cups both of the ogee or bulbous and the straight-sided type with a cover, often accompanied by a salver for ceremonial use, came into fashion in England in the second half of the 17th century; the salver being described by one contemporary writer as "a new fashioned peece of wrought plate, broad and flat with a foot underneath and is used in giving Beer or other liquid thing to save the Carpit or Cloathes from drops."

While no American cup with salver to match is known, there are a few two-handled cups with covers appreciably larger than the small caudle cups. One by John Coney, illustrated in Figure 31, was in the Boston exhibition of 1911 and is now in the Mabel Brady Garvan Collection at Yale University; it is nearly 7 inches high and weighs over 31 ounces. The body is quite plain except for an engraved coat of arms and has the more pear-shaped outline copied by the Western silversmiths from Chinese porcelain.

Although quite plain, it is similar in shape to the ornate cups of the English Restoration period and like them has a tight-fitting domical cover. The cover has a spool-shaped knop handle with a wide projecting flat top the purpose of which is to allow the cover to be inverted to serve as a salver for the cup when necessary or to be used as a separate dish. Like those of all the larger and more important cups, the handles have the terminal female busts probably introduced to England by the followers of Charles II from France where handles were often modeled in the form of a female figure (PLATE VII).

NEW YORK. So rare are caudle cups bearing the marks of New York silversmiths that we may assume caudle was not as popular a drink among the Dutch settlers as it was in New England. This was evident in the quite early days of the interest in American silver. Upward of thirty small caudle cups by New England makers were included in the exhibition at Boston in 1911, whereas only two by a New York maker which might be regarded as caudle cups were shown in the exhibition at the Metropolitan Museum in the same year. The latter were two plain bell-shaped cups with a row of beads on the scroll handles, 4½ inches high by Peter Van Dyck (1684-1750), lent by the Presbyterian Church, Setauket, Long Island.

In 1937, however, the Museum of the City of New York held an exhibition of nearly four hundred examples of silver by New York makers among which there were three important caudle cups, one attributed to Jacob Boelen the elder (1654-1729) and two by Gerrit Onkelbag (1670-1732).

Two of the cups demonstrate the advanced technic of the Dutch-American silversmiths in their handling of ornamentation. The one with the cover shown in Figure 32 is believed to be the work of Jacob Boelen who came to New York when an infant in 1660. The shape is similar to that which, about 1675 in England, began to replace the former ogee outline found with New England caudle cups. And like some contemporary English cups it is embossed at the base with vertical acanthus and palm leaves which are repeated as an ornamental circle enclosing a bold floral motif on the domed cover, to which three volute-shaped brackets are fitted. The brackets are intended to serve as handles for lifting the cover or as feet when the cover is used as a stand for the cup or as a separate dish; the fact that the cover is distinctly domed would suggest the latter.

It is possible to say definitely that this cup was made late in the 17th century, because it is engraved with the arms of Phillipse and the initials I$\overset{C}{\underset{*}{}}$E for Jacobus Van Cortlandt and Eve Phillipse, to whom the cup belonged and who were married in 1691.

One of the two caudle cups by Gerrit Onkelbag is the plain ogee shape without a cover and the other, which has a cover with the three brackets, is the same shape and embossed in a manner similar to the Boelen cup. Regarding the Onkelbag plain cup (FIG. 33) we might speculate whether it once had a cover. This speculation is suggested by the fact that it is 5¼ inches high which is virtually the same height as the two cups with covers (5½ and 5¾ inches respectively); moreover, even without the cover, its weight (approx: 23 ounces) is only about an ounce less than the covered cups.

Both Boelen and Onkelbag would be familiar with the embossed acanthus leaf ornament which was used freely in Holland. It was introduced to England about the middle of the 17th century and became very popular during the reign of Charles II. The Dutch had adopted the use of boldly embossed designs of flowers, of which the tulip was particularly common, fruit and acanthus leaves to strengthen the various articles made of thin silver, and the English silversmiths adopted the Dutch style of ornamentation (PLATE VIII).

Later in the century when large amounts of silver were brought from South America to Europe, the embossed designs were applied to larger cups of heavier metal, and there still exist a fair number of English late Stuart large two-handled cups which resemble quite closely the style of those by the two early New York silversmiths. So, while admitting that these men obtained the inspiration for the ornamentation directly from Holland, the shapes and general character of all three cups are so closely related to the contemporary English cups as to indicate that the English styles were adopted by the Dutch silversmiths of New York at an earlier date than might be generally supposed.

As time goes on and more and more early American silver comes to light, we need to modify and readjust our views as to the various sources from which the Colonial silversmiths drew their designs. Perhaps the more elaborate cups such as those by Jacob Boelen and Gerrit Onkelbag are exceptional and were copied direct from English models or from drawings.

Even if we assume that England was the direct source of some models and ornamental designs employed by the late 17th-century New York silversmiths, we must not lose sight of the fact that the decoration used in European countries bordering on Holland was known to men who had learned their trade in Holland. Many of these European forms in English silver showed a strong German feeling during the 16th and equally strong Dutch and French influences in the following century. Therefore it is possible to trace the interweaving of several influences in the New York Dutch interpretations of the various ornamental forms, some of which were undoubtedly affected by local impulses.

In the embossed flowers, acanthus leaves and other forms found with the New York bowls, for instance, there is the characteristically bold and free Dutch treatment unaffected by any other influence. And if this type is compared with similar decoration of English two-handled cups of the second half of the 17th century, it is plain that the New York embossed work gives evidence of having been handled with a confidence inspired by experience and skill and a familiarity with that style of ornamentation.

Then, too, there is the difference in metal used in England and that used in New York. Owing to the need for economy, more particularly during the third quarter of the 17th century, the English metal was comparatively thin, but even for small articles the New York silversmiths used fairly heavy silver which requires more skill to emboss and chase.

Spout Cups

Doubt exists as to the use in America of the so-called "spout cup" which was largely confined to New England. When the shape and arrangement of the spout are compared with the English 17th-century silver posset pots (FIG. 34) and those made at the Bristol (England) pottery, examples of which are in the Philadelphia Museum of Art, the resemblance is unmistakable. Though few have survived, silver cups of this type were known in England at least as early as the time of Charles I and there is an example dated 1642-3 in the Victoria and Albert Museum.

English silver cups of this type occasionally come on the market, but their rarity commands a fairly high figure. One of *circa* 1670 came up at Sotheby's rooms in August 1948, and brought over $1,000, although it was only 2½ inches high and weighed less than 6 ounces. This example has a plain cylindrical body rounding in at the bottom with a spout rising close to the body; it has two scroll handles with the leaf form on the shoulder and each handle placed at right angles with the spout.

In the previous month a glass spout cup, similar to the silver one mentioned, had made its appearance at the same auction rooms. This was 3¼ inches high and was made probably at Salisbury Court Glasshouse during the last quarter of the 17th century. Such a cup is an even greater rarity than its silver counterpart as was evident from the fact that it realized $1,290. Glass vessels of this type with the spout were known as sillabub cups. Sillabub was a drink made of cream or milk curdled by the addition of wine or cider and sweetened.

It is fairly safe to decide that silver spout cups were made in New England during the later 17th century, the earliest known example being one by Jeremiah Dummer (1645-1718), now in the Museum of Fine Arts, Boston (FIG. 35). And the fact that this cup has two handles and is similar in other respects to the English delft posset pots allows the assumption that some of the early New Englanders had a liking for posset.

It is suggested that spout cups were intended for feeding invalids and children; but while they may have been so used, posset was traditionally regarded both as a luxury and a cure for certain ills—more particularly colds. As some of us today enjoy a glass of hot whisky

27

and regard it as a cure-all, so our forefathers enjoyed their hot milk curdled by some potent alcoholic addition, known as The Posset, which was sucked through the "sucking-spout," as the spout of the posset pot (or spout cup) is called.

Most of the New England late 17th-century specimens had the rather squat bulbous body and cylindrical neck similar to the one by Jeremiah Dummer illustrated in Figure 35. But whereas the latter has two handles, other makers used only one, though, like those of the Dummer cup, this was placed at right angles with the spout; and with all the spout cups of this time there is a noticeably persistent use of the reversed S-shaped handle of stout sheet silver stiffened by fluting or reeding.

There is an obvious resemblance between the shape of these first New England spout cups and that of the German and Flemish stoneware jugs imported into England during the later 16th century, which were known as tiger-ware jugs; but like most of the shapes adopted by European potters, that of the stoneware jugs was derived from China where it had been used for many centuries.

Oriental influence is evident, too, in the shapes of other spout cups such as the one illustrated in Figure 36 which is now in the Worcester Art Museum. This unusual shape was developed from the familiar Chinese pear-shaped vase in which the broad part of the pear forms the shoulders with a short cylindrical neck. The New England silversmith in adapting this outline gave the lower part a slight incurve not noticeable in the Chinese vase. The cover is decorated with cut-card work and is of the flatter shape similar to that of the Dummer spout cup (FIG. 35) instead of the more prevalent dome (FIG. 37).

This adaptation of the Oriental pear shape was used in England at the end of the 17th century and Jackson (*Illustrated History of English Plate*) shows a chocolate pot of the same outline bearing the London hall-marks for 1697-8. This is some two inches taller than the spout cup (FIG. 36) as it has above the cover an additional small cylinder over the hole for the stick or brush with which the chocolate was stirred. Except for this addition and its fluted and punch-work decoration, the English pot is virtually identical with the New England spout cup, even to the shape of the handle.

Some spout cups have the pear-shaped body and plain high domical cover and finial in every way like the the early teapots. Others repeat the elongated pear shape developed in coffee-pots and these have a molded domical cover and baluster finial (FIG. 38). There are also the quite simple cups with no covers which are plain straight-sided mugs with a molded base and fitted with a spout (FIG. 39).

A somewhat similar article known as an "argyle," but used for a different purpose, came into use in England later in the 18th century and this will be mentioned more fully later.

OTHER DOMESTIC SILVER

In England after the Restoration of the monarchy in 1660, the royalist followers of Charles II sought to erase every sign of Puritan austerity by indulging in various forms of extravagance in which silverwork was used with unprecedented lavishness. King Charles, during his long exile, had become accustomed to the ostentatious and sumptuous appointments of the French Court and these he and his followers introduced to England.

Every article that could be made of silver and so add to the display was ordered. Furniture was overlaid with embossed plates of thin silver, massive wine fountains and cisterns and punch bowls became fashionable and a variety of pieces new to the English table were introduced from France. Covered dishes of the type which were the forerunners of the later entree dish, bowls with covers for holding broth, plates, salvers, sweetmeat boxes, casters, a new style of ceremonial salt, different types of candlesticks, all made their appearance and, toward the end of the 17th century, teapots and coffee-pots.

Salts

By the second half of the 17th century the significance of the large standing-salt (FIG. 40) was on the decline though there are clear indications that it was observed to some extent in America during that period. And it is of interest to touch upon the ancient tradition associated with this article of silver formerly so important in Europe and in Britain.

When, in 1508, Wynkyn de Worde printed in his *Boke of Keruynge,* "Set your salt on the ryght side where your soverayne shall sitte" he referred to an age-old custom that has remained to the present time. Few of us moderns recognize any connection with a saltcellar in the arrangement of the tables and the seating of the guests at a public banquet; nor is the average hostess conscious of repeating an ancient tradition in her careful placing of her guests at a semi-formal dinner.

Actually, however, these and other modern social usages associated with the dinner table carry on those founded upon the importance of the large standing-salt cellar generally distinguished as The Salt, in the long ago.

Salt itself was formerly regarded almost with reverence and awe; even today people know a fear of spilling salt and those of us who are influenced by this ancient superstition still practice one of the ceremonies observed centuries ago to exorcize the evil which is supposed to result from spilling salt.

In early times, it was not necessarily the one who spilled the salt who was in danger of the evil, but the one toward whom the salt fell. And that person would take a pinch between the thumb and the finger of the right hand and throw it over his left shoulder; the left or sinister shoulder because this was supposed to be more likely to appease Satan.

Various speculative explanations have been given at different times concerning the purpose and signficance of the standing-salt. One widely believed is that The Salt divided the lord or master of the house and his more important guests from the humbler persons and the retainers. Another suggests it was a "barrier between the guest and the menial," thus implying that The Salt served to mark the line between the high and the humble and that all sat at one table.

In medieval times, the master, his guests and the servants did dine together in the great hall, but not at the same table or "borde" which was an early name for table. The master and the more prominent guests were seated at the high table, which was so called because it was raised on a dais slightly above the level of the floor. This high table was placed across the end of the hall, others being at floor level along the side walls; and the same arrangement is repeated to a large extent at public dinners and banquets to the present day.

Moreover, we still unconsciously repeat the almost forgotten tradition of The Salt in seating the various guests at such functions. As Wynkyn de Worde directed, The Salt was placed in front, but slightly to the right of the master or host; and the principal guest was seated on his right and thus as near The Salt as the host. Other guests were seated at the high table on the left or right of the host according to the social rank of each, while those of less importance were placed at the tables at floor level and were thus, as the old phrase has it, "below the salt." A certain number of these great salts have survived to the present time and their very magnificence is proof of their former importance; today they are equally important but more from the viewpoint of their monetary value. Specimens are by no means plentiful and when one does appear it is met with very keen competition, as was demonstrated by two which came up for auction in 1945 and 1946: one bearing the London hall-marks for 1549-50 bringing $23,000, and the other of 1606-7, $19,345.

Always of imposing size, some of the great salts are of curious shapes, as for example, the one known as the "Giant" or "Huntsman's" salt, still preserved at All Souls College, Oxford. This is 17 inches high and is the figure of a primitive bearded man holding a rock crystal salt bowl and cover on his head.

From about 1590 to 1620 the elaborate salts, one of which is illustrated in Figure 40, were largely replaced by the less imposing bell-shaped type. These were in two sections one above the other, the upper one having a domed top with a pierced spherical knob finial. Each of the two sections had a well for salt, so that they might be used separately and the top serve as a pepper caster, or the three parts joined together could be used as a standing-salt.

In the second half of the 17th century, the custom of the master dining with his guests and retainers in the great hall was discontinued and the standing-salt gradually lost its former importance. The separate dining room was introduced and here the master and his principal guests were seated in the usual order of precedence in relation to The Salt. Presumably, less important guests dined with the servants and retainers in the great hall, though at different tables.

During this period few large ceremonial salts were made, the most common form being a salt holder, without a cover, shaped rather like a spool with a narrow waist and a wide spreading foot and rim. Three or four scroll brackets were fixed to the rim, the purpose of which was to support a napkin or, as Samuel Pepys suggested, a dish to protect the salt from the dust. In addition to the standing-salt, smaller salts known as trencher salts, were set at different parts of the table. From these, each guest took salt with his knife and put it on the edge of his trencher (a wood plate), and picking up the slice of meat with his fingers dipped it in the salt and ate it much as we manipulate asparagus.

NEW ENGLAND. That the ceremony of the standing-salt was observed in Colonial homes during the latter part of the 17th century, and possibly for some years later, is evident from the several standing-salts which have come down from that time.

All the known American specimens are of the spool-shaped type with four brackets (FIG. 41) and each of them bears the mark of a Boston silversmith working during the later 17th and early 18th centuries. Each follows the octagonal plan with a cylindrical waist encircled by a molded band, and a bold gadrooned member round the base and also usually below the molded rim. The general style of all these New England standing-salts is very similar, the only noticeable variations being in the gadroon ornament which in some instances is large bold flutes arranged spirally and in others, smaller parallel flutes.

This style of spool-shaped salt follows the shape into which it was developed in England in the last quarter of the 17th century. While most of the existing English spool-shaped salts date from the second half of the 17th century, a few plain circular examples made during the time of Charles I have been preserved. The Mercers' Company has one of 1638-9 and Mr. Bigelow illustrates another which is at Harvard College, believed to date about 1630; it formerly belonged to the Reverend Jose Glover who left London in 1638 for Cambridge, Massachusetts, in connection with the setting up of the first printing press in America, but he died during the voyage.

It is rare indeed for a spool-shaped salt to be offered for sale and the keenness with which they are sought was demonstrated when one from the Swaything Collection was sold at Christie's in 1924, and brought $6,750. And it is safe to prophesy that should an example by an early American silversmith make its appearance on the public market, its value would prove very greatly in excess of the price paid for the English example.

Various Colonial trencher salts have come to light, but the number of examples is, to say the least, limited. The several types made in New England during the late 17th and first part of the 18th centuries appeared more or less concurrently with and were similar to the English trencher salts. The first was circular about 2½ inches high with an incurved body and chased with spiral flutings round the rim (FIG. 42); the contemporary English salts of this shape were the same size as the Colonial but usually chased with flutings round the base as well as the rim.

In considering these now rare salts, it is well to remember they are small and very liable to damage from rough usage; also that as the later styles came into fashion, many of them were regarded as of little value other than for the metal and were therefore consigned to the all-devouring melting pot. This may be said equally of English trencher salts, which like the American belong in that list of rarities which only the fortunate collector is able to possess.

NEW YORK. No salt of a height suggestive of a standing-salt by a New York maker is known, the earliest examples being of the circular trencher type about 2½ inches high, similar to the New England salts illustrated in Figure 42. Examples of these circular salts were shown in the exhibition of silver by New York makers at the Museum of the City of New York in 1937, including a pair by Jacobus Vanderspiegel (1668-1708) (PLATE III-B).

New York trencher salts of this type have a more decided upward taper than their New England counterparts; also they have the band of fluting round both the rim and the foot. Some have, above the base fluting, a small scalloped band, showing a relationship to the ornamental bands largely peculiar to New York beakers, tankards and mugs.

Probably the earliest known New York salt is one by Cornelius Vanderburgh (1653-99) which was in the same exhibition. It is octagonal, and the eight-sided body tapers upward from a molded base to a wide projecting rim; slightly less than 1¼ inches high and 3¼ inches across the base, it has a more squat appearance than the cylindrical style which is 2½ inches high and about 3¾ inches across the base. This Vanderburgh salt is engraved with the initials I $\overset{C}{*}$ E and belonged to Jacobus Van Courtland and Eve Phillipse who were married in 1691, which we may assume was the year in which the salt was made.

Boxes for Sugar or Sweetmeats

Some pieces of the ornate silver which became fashionable during the time of Charles II seem to have overcome the New England preference for simplicity. Admittedly these are very few, but any by Colonial silversmiths are as elaborate and finely wrought as the English models. The outstanding examples of such Colonial silverwork are those beautiful if rare boxes for sugar or sweetmeats which, in the time of Charles II, were regarded as essential to every fashionable establishment. But however many members of the English Court were at that time fortunate enough to own one, any dating from the Restoration period are today few and far between, and the same applies to any made by Colonial silversmiths. We recall one English box hall-marked 1677-8 which in 1929 brought $3,770, at

Christie's, but even so, a similar box by one of the New England silversmiths would be worth many times that amount—they do not seem to have been made in New York.

NEW ENGLAND. These boxes are oval, about 8½ inches long and 7 inches wide, and though in England usually described as sweetmeat boxes, they are referred to in early New England wills as sugar boxes. Judging from those surviving, most of the Colonial examples were made by John Coney (1655-1722) and Edward Winslow (1669-1753) probably at the end of the 17th or the early years of the 18th centuries. They were fashionable in London about 1675, but it would be natural for some years to elapse before one found its way to America and for the Colonists to accept what to them would seem unduly elaborate silverwork (FIGS. 43 and 44).

They were doubtless one of the various extravagances introduced into England by the French followers of Charles II, and that the Colonial boxes were inspired by the English prototypes is obvious from one made by John Coney (FIG. 43) now in the Museum of Fine Arts, Boston. This particular box is for all purposes a replica of the one sold at Christie's mentioned above and illustrated in this writer's *Domestic Silver of Great Britain and Ireland*. It has a similarly lobed body on four cast scroll feet while the lobes and chased work of the hinged cover and the ring handle entwined with a serpent are identical with the English box.

Other Colonial sweetmeat boxes are embossed and chased with gadroon bands, swirling concave and convex flutes and other motifs as illustrated in Figure 44, derived from English models and suggesting a date slightly later than that of the Coney box (FIG. 43). It is perhaps of interest to mention that more than one of these Colonial boxes found their way to Britain. One by Edward Winslow, similar to that in Figure 43, was at one time owned by the late Sir Charles Jackson, who illustrated it in his work on English plate.

For its later history we are indebted to Mr. Willoughby Farr. Jackson placed the box, correctly labeled, on exhibition in London. While on exhibition, it was seen by a man connected with an important American art museum who insisted that no such piece of silver was ever made in America. Although he knew this to be incorrect, Jackson withdrew the box from the exhibition and it was later disposed of to Crichton Bros. of London.

There Mr. Farr's story ends, but it was completed by Charles Messer Stow who adds that Crichton Bros. sold the box to the late

34

George Palmer from whose collection it went to Tiffany & Co. The late Edsel Ford bought it from Tiffany & Co. and it was exhibited in the Detroit Institute of Arts on loan.

Another Winslow box inscribed W P and the date 1702, which this writer discovered in England in 1937, has an even more romantic story. Again to quote Mr. Stow who delved into the history of this box and published the result of his researches in the New York *Sun* (Sept. 18, 1937): The initials W P (possibly William Parkman or William Paine) are those of the man who ordered it as a gift for Daniel and Elizabeth Oliver. Daniel Oliver, the son of Peter and Sarah Oliver of Newdigate, England, was born in 1664. His wife was the sister of Governor Belcher of Massachusetts.

Daniel Oliver died in 1732, leaving his property including his silver to his wife, at whose death, in 1735, it passed to their son Peter. Shortly before 1776, Peter Oliver left the Colony for Scotland and settled in Edinburgh, taking with him a large part of his movable property including the Winslow box. At some later date, it was apparently given to a local church and, in 1937, found its way to a London dealer, from whom it was acquired by Stephen G. C. Ensko and taken back to its native land.

Candlesticks

NEW ENGLAND. It is improbable that silver candlesticks were used to any extent in New England during the 17th century although some few found their way to the Colony from England. The only known examples which can be definitely ascribed to New England, are a pair by Jeremiah Dummer (FIG. 45), one of which is inscribed: *Made to commemorate the marriage of David Jeffries and Elizabeth Usher 1686. Given by Dr. John Jeffries to his son Dr. B. Joy Jeffries 1876.*

One of these candlesticks is still in the possession of a descendant of the Jeffries family; its companion is in the Garvan Collection at Yale University. And there are three by John Coney in the Museum of Fine Arts, Boston, which probably date from the end of the 17th century.

English candlesticks of the late Stuart period are relatively plentiful and from among those that are known it is not difficult to find the prototypes of those made by Dummer and Coney. The pair by Dummer are about 11 inches high and have a pillar of eight engaged columns forming a rectangle with a molded band halfway down the

35

shaft. This style was inspired by early Gothic architecture, an influence which appeared for a short time in English church and some domestic silver early in the reign of Charles II.

The square base as well as the cylindrical section below the shaft, the wide projecting lobed plate—a hang-over of the earlier drip-pan —and the clustered column are almost identical with a candlestick, embossed with the crown and cypher of Charles II, illustrated by Jackson. The principal differences between the candlesticks are: the English is about 4 inches shorter than the Colonial, and Dummer repeated the square plate above the capital of the shaft.

If we are on less safe ground in attributing the Coney candlesticks (FIGS. 46-A and 46-B) to the late 17th century, at least we may be permitted to rationalize by the fact that they relate to those which appeared in England before the High Standard period (1697-1720).

One is decorated with bands of gadrooning round the socket, the projecting collar and the base; and an analysis of this candlestick shows several adaptations. The molded stem and plain cylindrical socket are reminiscent of some of the English 17th-century cups; the projecting collar takes the place of the boss used with English late 17th-century columnar candlesticks, the circular foot and the base are clearly related to the early 17th-century English socket candlestick with an inverted wide cup-shaped base.

With some of the first English baluster candlesticks (FIG. 47) the stems resemble closely the outline of earlier standing-cups and this is apparent in the stem of the Coney candlestick illustrated in Figure 46-B. With this the shape of the cup is clear in the larger knop of the stem (compare FIGS. 46-B and 47). The cup shape was developed later into a variety of forms which will be dealt with in the following chapters.

NEW YORK. Only one candlestick made by a New York silversmith working during the 17th century has come to notice. Like the earliest New England specimens, this is the square columnar type ornamented in the style of the English late 17th-century candlesticks. It was made in all probability by Cornelius Kierstede who became a freeman of the City of New York in 1698 and worked there until 1722, when he moved to New Haven, Connecticut.

This candlestick is illustrated in *Old Plate* (1903) by J. H. Buck who mentions that it was exhibited at the Washington Centennial held in New York in 1889.

And we might speculate whether the snuffer stand by Cornelius

Kierstede (FIG. 48) which is now in the Metropolitan Museum of Art once accompanied the columnar candlestick. Unfortunately the snuffers are missing, but the interesting stand at least has been preserved. It has a square snuffer holder on a knopped stem with a square concave foot and wide molded base. The form and ornamental treatment are suggestive of several sources: The double-headed eagle on the snuffer holder may well be a European coat of arms; the large decorated knop recalls the huge bulbous legs of Elizabethan tables and like them has a Flemish origin; and the projecting collar, foot and base which are also decorated indicate a relation to those of some late 17th-century candlesticks.

Dishes and Salvers

Even if table manners have become more delicate through the centuries, something reminiscent of ancient times still survives in both the modern dishes and plates and in the way a dinner is served.

In the Middle Ages, the joint was carried to table on a large circular dish called a "charger" by a servant who was also known as a "charger." Each guest was served on a trencher, which was of wood, pewter or silver and similar to the plates familiar in our time—though sometimes the trencher was nothing better than a large thick slice of bread. At the end of the meal, the remains from the trenchers were collected on another large dish known as a "voider," a name which was at one time used to denote a servant who cleared a table after a meal. Incidentally, the voider and its companion the voiding knife survived in the crumb tray and scoop beloved in Victorian times.

NEW ENGLAND. Today we more often think of a dish as an oval shape, but the ancient name "charger" has remained with large circular pewter and pottery dishes. Something of the charger survives also in the large plates or dishes made in New England in the late 17th century. The forms and style of these are associated with those of the first half of the 17th century and would suggest that English early Stuart pieces were brought over by the first settlers and served as models for the Boston silversmiths.

This is illustrated by the large plate or dish shown in Figure 49 which is slightly more than 11 inches in diameter and, though larger, resembles the early Stuart dinner plates which, in turn, resemble those of Elizabethan times. It has a similarly deep well and broad molded rim and, also like many of the early English plates, is engraved; the design engraved on the New England plate is composed of three rather adult-looking cherubs' heads, each with what might be a "permanent wave," between sprigs of carnations and tulips; a style of decoration popular during the reign of Charles II. Another plate of the same size with a reeded edge by the same maker (John Coney) is in the Minneapolis Institute of Arts.

Large plates of this same type and about the same size, fitted with a low trumpet foot, were used as salvers for serving glasses of wine, the servant holding the salver by the foot and so leaving the other hand free. A New England example by Timothy Dwight (1645-91) is in the Pickman Collection at the Museum of Fine Arts, Boston. This has the wide border engraved with a unicorn and other animals and floral sprays and while not as elaborate as the English 17th-century salvers which were often accompanied by a large cup, the shape and general design of the decoration were obviously inspired by the English examples which were boldly embossed with similar subjects.

NEW YORK. Examples in any way resembling the 17th-century salvers are so rare among New York silverwork that we must assume that very few were made. In fact the only example we can recall which may date from that time is one by Jacobus Vanderspiegel (1668-1708), which was exhibited at the Museum of the City of New York in 1937-8. This is 8¼ inches in diameter on a low foot with a band of heavy spiral fluting round the rim and the foot; the center of the salver is engraved with the Van Courtland arms.

Salvers of this style, now more often called "tazze," appeared in England at the end of the 17th century when they replaced the larger and more ornate cup salvers mentioned above. Like the one by Vanderspiegel, most of the English examples are quite plain except for a gadrooned or molded edge. They were not popular for long, however, and though they were made during the High Standard period, the first quarter of the 18th century saw them superseded by the small circular and square salvers which were the ancestors of the later tea trays.

Casters

Anyone with a leaning toward purism might insist that this section should be headed, "Dredgers, Casters and Muffineers," for while each of these articles has a similar use the origins of the several names differ.

Dredger is derived from "drudger," the name for the box with holes in the top which was used in old-time kitchens for sprinkling flour. Later these were made of brass or other metal with a plain cylindrical body and a pierced domed tightly fitting cover and smaller ones of the same shape were used for sprinkling pepper. Caster, according to our invaluable friend, Noah Webster, is a small vessel "to contain condiments at the table"; and muffineer, "a vessel with a perforated top for sprinkling muffins with sugar, spice, salt, etc."

NEW ENGLAND. Casters were in fairly general use in England by the late 17th century, and they seem to have quickly found their way to New England, for there are several known examples which were unquestionably copied from the similar type introduced from France during the reign of Charles II.

For instance, the caster by John Coney (1655-1722), shown in Figure 50 repeats the cylindrical body, the high pierced top and baluster finial, the forms and arrangement of the piercing, the molded band, domical foot and bayonet fastener of the English late 17th-century models. This New England caster, however, has two bands round the body which is unusual with the English casters which have only one band; and other differences occur with the moldings. It will be noticed that the piercings are larger than those of later casters and this again shows an English influence and indicates that the caster was intended for salt or possibly for sugar, though the latter was then scarce and hardly likely to have been wasted as so often happens when it is shaken from a caster.

NEW YORK. Cylindrical casters of the same general form as that by John Coney were also made in New York, at the end of the 17th century. But when for instance the caster by Gerrit Onkelbag (FIG. 51) is compared with the contemporary English and New England casters, features showing a marked Dutch influence are observable. These features are the flattish fluted top to the cover, the wide spreading foot which is also fluted and that characteristic New York ornament, the foliated band above the base molding.

Casters of similar shape and decorated in a similar style—with the exception of the foliated band round the base—were made in England during the last ten years of the 17th century. The few examples that survive, however, are slightly larger than the one by Onkelbag.

39

CHAPTER TWO

High Standard Period
1697 to 1720

THIS BRIEF PERIOD OF TWENTY-THREE YEARS SAW A complete change in English silver, a wide increase in the number of articles made for domestic use and a discontinuance of many of the former large pieces intended for ceremonial observances. James II, during the three years he was king, had so out-Stuarted the Stuart extravagance that the people were aroused to such a pitch that this useless monarch was compelled to take a one-way ticket to France and William of Orange reigned in his stead.

All that is history, but its effect upon English and, indirectly, upon American silverwork was significant. The always increasingly lavish use of silver which began after Charles II returned from France in 1660 had resulted in the melting down of so much of the national coinage that it was impossible to find sufficient metal for the Mint. This shortage became so acute that in 1696 Parliament passed an act prohibiting taverns from using any silver articles excepting spoons —any innkeeper displaying other silver usually lost it under seizure.

In the following year, another act was passed fixing a selling price of 5s. 4d. (approximately $1.33) an ounce for articles bearing the London hall-mark. And, to stop the melting of coinage, the standard of metal for silver articles was raised from 11 ounces 2 pennyweights to 11 ounces 10 pennyweights of pure silver to the pound (12 ounces) troy; but the standard of metal for silver coinage remained as it was. This meant that when an article was taken to the Assay Office for marking it had to be of the higher standard, otherwise it was confiscated and the maker punished—and in those days the penalties were fairly severe.

Another change resulting from this was in the hall-marks: the former leopard's head and lion passant were replaced by a lion's head erased (cut off at the neck with a jagged edge) and the figure

40

of Britannia. The lion's head erased and Britannia marks were used during the last five years of William III, the whole of the reign of Queen Anne and the first five years of George I—the practice of regarding all silver bearing these marks as "Queen Anne" is therefore a mistake.

It is also well to remember that while the old standard and the old marks (leopard's head and lion passant) came back in 1720, the higher standard continued to be and is still used. And the Assay Office (it is to be regretted) today mark articles of the high standard with the lion's head erased and Britannia—as more than one collector has probably discovered to his chagrin. A good motto in silver collecting is to look and look well before you buy; it is even better to borrow experienced eyes.

Perhaps to the layman the decrease in the amount of alloy may not seem important. So here, a brief explanation: Alloy is added to silver to harden it—not to save silver; consequently the less the alloy, the softer the metal and the softer the metal the more restricted the type of ornamentation. For that reason the raising of the standard of the metal brought a complete change in English silver. No more of the large and imposing pieces made of thin silver which had graced the dining halls and no more of the extravagant embossed work which had helped to stiffen the thin silver of the late Stuart days.

Much English silver of the High Standard period is similar to that made by American silversmiths—a fact which possibly explains why it has always been keenly sought by those in the United States who are interested in silver for their tables, rather than for "museum-izing" behind the locked glazed doors of cabinets.

Not all English silver of this time is quite plain; but the men who made it realized that in view of the softer metal any decoration of a delicate character would tend quickly to show signs of wear under the lusty rubbing of some energetic servant.

Such ornamentation as was applied to English High Standard silverwork was restricted to designs in cut-card work, deep flutings both concave and convex, sometimes arranged vertically and some-times spirally, gadrooning, various cast masks and foliage which were usually finely tooled. Some pieces were engraved, but this type of decoration does not seem to have been employed to any great extent.

During this period, the merchants began to accumulate wealth and lay the foundations of what we now call the middle classes. These families built finer houses and furnished them in a manner which their rise on the ladder of prosperity and social status warranted. Furniture for the first time developed real design, forecasting the splendid work that later came from the shops of Chippendale, Hepplewhite and their contemporaries.

Fine porcelain was imported in always growing quantities from the Far East and ships brought various exotic foods and drinks. The last two, calling for suitable articles in which to serve them, prompted a wide increase in the number and variety of domestic silver articles, the shapes of many of which were evolved from the imported porcelain vases, bowls and other pieces.

Tea, coffee and chocolate which had been introduced to Europe in the previous century became fashionable drinks during the early part of the 18th century; and their popularity stimulated both the European and American silversmiths to adapt and design a large number of previously unknown articles. In the shapes and treatment of some silverwork of the English High Standard period it is possible to see the French influence which was introduced by the Huguenots and which was later to be dominant in English silver. This influence, too, is reflected in American silverwork; but, as we shall see, the Colonial silversmiths very rarely adopted the more exuberant ornaments of the rococo style.

DRINKING VESSELS

By the end of the 17th century, standing-cups and wine goblets were almost forgotten, though the former were, and still are, used upon ceremonial occasions; a few beakers were made, most of them of large proportions intended as mantel ornaments. Similarly, while the two-handled cups of the type known in America as caudle cups remained popular for the first few years of the High Standard period, they, too, gradually went out of fashion.

Capacious tankards with the flat lid such as were in general use during the late Stuart times continued to be made for the first few years of the 18th century. Then, though the same tapering shaped body was used, they lost much of their character when the former flat lid was replaced by the domed shape and, somewhat later, the line of the body was broken by a small molded band about a third of the way up. The molded band seems to be a revival of the similar ornament of Tudor times; and it was also used with Danish and other European tankards.

Mugs came into common use and remained popular through the

whole of the 18th century; and it was during this period that, while for a time the body of the mugs retained the straight sides, the base was occasionally incurved; an innovation which marks the transition from the early miniature tankard shape to the later pear-shaped mug, or cann as this type is called in America.

Under the influence of the Huguenot silversmiths, two-handled cups developed to the imposing affairs with a bell-shaped bowl and molded cover upwards of 10 inches high. Many of these large cups were intended as trophies for horse racing which became increasingly popular during the reign of Queen Anne. Some of the smaller-sized racing cups of this period were made of gold, but examples are rare; among the few surviving examples there is one which was given by Queen Anne as a prize for a race run at Newmarket in 1705.

Other and more magnificent vessels connected with drinking, such as the huge wine fountains and accompanying cisterns, found no favor in America; but a number of fine punch bowls based on English models of the early 18th century were made by different Colonial silversmiths.

Tankards

NEW ENGLAND. Influenced by the changes in England, the New England tankards of the early 18th century were more tapered; and while some of them were quite plain, as a general rule, the small molded band used in England was added round the body. The development of the lid to the eventual high dome shape was, however, more gradual. The New England beer drinker seems to have clung to the flat lid and it is possible to follow the stages of its "growing up": From the convex shoulder with the flat top, it developed another convex member, the flat top became smaller (FIG. 52) and occasionally a small insignificant finial was added (FIG. 52). Gradually the smaller flat top was domed and the body became more tapered (FIG. 53) to follow English tankards. Even so, with the larger number of New England tankards of this period the dome has a distinctly flattened top (FIG. 53), usually with a finial.

Finial ornaments were used with English tankards of this time but examples are rare. Some of the New England finials bear a resemblance to those of English Tudor tankards and the stoneware jugs with silver-gilt mounts popular in England during the reign of Elizabeth. Occasionally a New England silversmith would copy the New York handle ornamentation or the foliated band and wavy wire

43

above the base molding as in the tankard (FIG. 54) by Samuel Vernon of Newport, Rhode Island (1683-1735), now in the Worcester Art Museum; but that this tankard was a native of New England is clearly shown by the cover, the finial and the thumb-piece.

NEW YORK. New York seems to have been less ready to adopt the changes with their tankards. New England accepted the domed lid, but the silversmiths' patrons in New York preferred the flat lid almost through the 18th century. Their tankards, too, continued to be heavy and capacious and the elaborate ornamental forms used by the 17th-century men were repeated during the early years of the 18th century (see FIGS. 17 and 19). In fact, New York tankards, until the coming of the bulbous shape late in the 18th century, retained their distinctive character.

Finely cast and tooled cherub heads were more commonly used as ornaments to New York handle-tips, but many were plain disks. Another curious ornament which has been found on several New York tankards is composed of a mask flanked by two scrolls and the head of a large horned animal below. This might have been adopted from a coat of arms, but nothing is known of its origin. It is illustrated in the tankard by that little known maker, Peter Van Inburgh (1689-1740), which has the characteristic New York ornamentation on the back of the handle and the foliated band and zig-zag wire above the base molding (FIG. 19).

Two tankards which were among the silver from the Garvan collection sold in 1931 had a similar ornament on the handle-tip. One by Henricus Boelen (1697-1755) has a silver crown of Leopold I of Hungary inset in the lid, but apart from this and the ornament on the handle-tip the tankard is quite plain. The other is by Peter Van Dyck (1684-1750) but this is more freely decorated than the Boelen tankard: The lid is engraved with a monogram encircled by a wreath, the back of the handle is ornamented with a cast cherub mask and a formal pendant of foliage below and a band of serrated leaf forms and zigzag wire are applied above the base molding. Their rarity and the keen search by collectors for early New York tankards are reflected in the prices paid for the two here described, the one by Boelen bringing $8,500, and that by Van Dyck, $9,000.

Peter Van Dyck seems to have favored the serrated base band and he sometimes repeated the zigzag wire round the rim as in the one in Figure 17. This tankard also illustrates the row of gradated beads of the rat-tail order down the back of the handle and the excellent

44

modeling of the winged cherub mask on the handle-tip. With some, the handle grip is a plain spine or rat-tail (FIG. 18) and there is a tankard by Simeon Soumaine (1685-1750) in the Metropolitan Museum of Art which has a molded spine with a row of small beads down the entire handle.

It should not be assumed however that all early 18th-century New York tankards were as freely decorated. There are a number which are quite plain, except for an ornamental handle-tip. And it is noticeable that the double spiral thumb-piece was carried over from the previous century and used consistently until about 1730 after which time a variety of forms were adopted.

PENNSYLVANIA. Owing to the comparatively late establishment of any important group of silversmiths in Pennsylvania, certain articles, such as caudle cups, beakers and spout cups were by that time out of date; consequently even if any were made in Philadelphia or elsewhere in the Colony, as we know is the case with beakers, examples are extremely rare.

While a fairly representative number of early 18th-century Philadelphia straight-sided tankards are known, they are by no means plentiful. With some of these there is a decided Dutch influence which is specially noticeable in those made by Johannis Nys or John de Nys, as he is perhaps better known. De Nys who settled in Philadelphia early in the 18th century, had worked previously in New York and there, as would be natural, was strongly influenced by the Dutch forms. This is evident in such details as the addition of an ornamental band above the base molding and the use of the horizontal spiral or corkscrew thumb-piece (see FIG. 55).

It will also be noticed that this tankard has a cherub's head on the tip of the handle and that the flat lid, instead of having the projecting edge with the wavy front, follows the line of the molded rim after the manner of some German and Scandinavian tankards; a style De Nys may possibly have copied from a tankard brought to Pennsylvania from Europe. Most of the tankards known to be by or attributed to De Nys have the projecting rim to the lid with or without the ornamental band above the base molding.

While Pennsylvania tankards are fundamentally English, some have certain local features which when studied prove to be largely combinations of borrowings from New England and New York. If, for example, the tankard in Figure 56 is analyzed, we have the plain body with the more pronounced taper and the low molded domical

45

lid found in New England tankards; but the beaded rat-tail at the back and the cherub's head ornament on the tip of the handle suggest a borrowing from New York; and the domed member of the base is reminiscent of an English 17th-century drum-bodied tankard. The tall scroll-shaped thumb-piece is similar to but somewhat more elaborate than the style adopted in England at the end of the 17th century.

Other Pennsylvania tankards of this same type have a baluster ornament on the back of the handle and a plain shield-shaped disk on the tip; and with all of them there is a tendency to a more spreading base. Again, though the Pennsylvania silversmiths repeated the flattened domed lid of some New England tankards, unlike New England, they omitted the finial ornament.

Mugs and Canns

NEW ENGLAND. Cylindrical tapering mugs continued to be made to some extent through the 18th century, but a new shape which appeared in England during the High Standard period was adopted by the Colonial silversmiths. The body still tapered upward, but the sides had a slight incurve and, instead of the bottom being flat with a molded band (see FIGS. 23, 24 and 25), it was curved inward with a low molded foot as shown in Figure 59. It has some relation to the round bottom beaker since both retain something of the original horn outline, even if this is partially disguised by the incurved bottom. It does not seem to have attained any wide popularity in America, for examples are far less numerous than its offspring, the bulbous shape (FIGS. 57 and 58).

NEW YORK. There was a similar development in the New York mugs, but it is possible with these to mark that resistance to change in drinking vessels noticeable in the early 18th-century tankards. Admittedly, the New York silversmiths rounded the mugs at the base, but even in doing so they managed at first to retain the flat bottom.

These mugs with the rounded bottom mark the transition to the later and far more plentiful bulbous shape which date from about 1730. Examples of the former, however, were made after that date both in New England and New York and may usually be identified by a marked incurve below the rim with a plain molded lip (see FIG. 59).

46

Caudle and Two-handled Cups

NEW ENGLAND. During the early 18th century, there was an appreciable increase in the number of silversmiths in New England, particularly in Boston. These men produced a very considerable amount of fine work, and there are indications that the English models were accepted and copied soon after they appeared.

In their interpretations of the English forms, however, the Colonial silversmiths frequently introduced details which express their individual ideas. This is illustrated both in the large cup by John Coney (FIG. 60) and that by Edward Winslow (FIG. 61).

Both the shape and the embossed fluted decoration of these cups follow the general style of the English and Irish bell-shaped cups of the early years of the High Standard period. The Coney cup has the scroll handles surmounted by female terminal heads showing that the maker reached back and adapted a style of nearly half a century earlier; for this type of handle was used with English cups of the early Restoration period and with American bowls and caudle cups of the late 17th century (see FIGS. 10 and 33). The vertical flutes on the cover and foot are in every way similar to those of contemporary English and Irish large two-handled cups; but the fluting on the lower part of the bowl is much bolder and projects more noticeably beyond the line of the cup as if to suggest a calyx. This feature is often present in other New England pieces such as standing-cups and beakers.

To a lesser degree, the base fluting of the Winslow cup (FIG. 61) also suggests a calyx, though here the fluting is carried further up the cup and is not so deeply embossed; and the addition of the narrow fluted or cabled band just below the rim also tends to modify the projecting base fluting. The handles of this cup show a relationship to those of the late 17th-century tankards. Each of these two cups has a well-modeled melon-shaped finial which bears some resemblance to a finial used with some English two-handled cups; namely, acanthus leaves closed round a sphere to form a bud.

Smaller two-handled cups without covers, about 5 inches high, were also made in New England during the early 18th century. These were bell-shaped sometimes with bold fluting round the lower part with a cabled band below the rim. One such cup with simple scroll handles by William Cowell (1682-1736) was shown at the

47

exhibition held in 1911 at the Museum of Fine Arts, Boston, to which it was lent by the Church of the Unity, Neponset, Massachusetts. Another, in the same exhibition, by George Hanners (1697-1740) has a plain bowl with slightly more ornamental scroll handles; the Hanners cup was lent by the First Congregational Church of Christ, Woburn, Massachusetts.

NEW YORK. Large two-handled cups with covers are as rare among New York silver as they are among that of New England. In fact the only New York example of the earlier 18th century noted is one by Charles Le Roux (1689-1745), shown in Figure 62, which was exhibited at the Museum of the City of New York in 1937-8.

This cup was probably made about 1730 as a christening gift to Frederic de Peyster who was baptized in 1731. We are here including it in the pre-rococo period, because the shape and general style follow those introduced to England early in the 18th century; the same type of cup was popular in Scotland and even more so in Ireland where it remained fashionable for some years after it had been replaced by the elaborate rococo styles.

Like the Le Roux cup, those made in Ireland usually have the harp-shaped handles, which, though romantically thought to be of Irish origin, were actually introduced from France. It would therefore be natural that Le Roux, having worked under his father, Bartholomew, who was a Huguenot, should be directly influenced by French traditions, and this is shown in the use of the molded rib well up the bowl of the cup and the cut-card work on the base and cover, each of these features also having a French origin.

Small bell-shaped cups, similar to those of New England described above, were made by New York silversmiths of the early 18th century. Whether these were intended for domestic use or for churches is not certain, but most of the few known examples are now in churches. Two with quite plain bowls by Peter Van Dyck were referred to in the section on caudle cups in the previous chapter.

Punch Bowls and Monteiths

Punch, that formerly fashionable drink, was one of the various luxuries brought from the East. It was introduced from India to Europe in the early 17th century and is traditionally supposed to have derived its name from the Hindustani word *panch,* meaning "five," which is the number of the original ingredients; namely, spirit, sugar, water, spice and some acid fruit juice such as lemon. But Noah Webster suggests it is possibly a shortened form of "puncheon," a large cask which held from 72 to 120 gallons.

Silver bowls for mixing punch were among the various articles first made in England soon after the return of Charles II in 1660; but except for a few owned by some of the Livery Companies, most of the known examples date from about 1680 and after. There is one in the Pierpont Morgan Collection hall-marked 1685-6 with eight deep notches in the rim for taking the stems of glasses. This bowl is 11 inches in diameter and has no handles; it is of unusual rarity both for its date and the fact that it is decorated with flat-chased motifs of an Oriental character inspired by the decorations of the porcelain bowls imported from China.

By the end of the 17th century when the Huguenot silversmiths began to arrive from France, larger and elaborately decorated punch bowls made their appearance, though examples of these imposing pieces are by no means plentiful.

NEW ENGLAND. There is little doubt that large porcelain bowls for mixing punch were in fairly general use in America during the 18th century; but it might be assumed, judging from the few known examples, that similar bowls made of silver were among the extravagant luxuries ostracized by even the modified Puritan principles. It is therefore of considerable interest that the most ambitious piece of early American silverwork to come to light so far is a bowl of the monteith type decorated in the same ornate style as its English counterparts.

Incidentally, a monteith is a punch bowl fitted with a removable scalloped rim generally believed to have been designed by an eccentric Scotsman named Monteith who had a liking for cloaks with a scalloped border. The purpose of the removable rim was to allow the glasses to hang by the foot in the notches or depressions with the bowls inside the monteith.

Made by John Coney of Boston (1655-1722) this American punch bowl (FIG. 63) follows the shape and general form of those of the English High Standard period; the rim is fixed though scalloped and similar to that of a monteith. The lower part is fluted, there is a finely modeled lion's head in high relief with a heavy handle in its mouth on each side and the upper part is ornamented with applied cherubs' heads, scrolls, small floral blossoms and other forms in relief.

In addition to being unique, this bowl is of outstanding impor-

49

tance in the history of American silverwork as illustrating a phase of ornamental work which, because of its rarity, has not been widely recognized. Its rarity was emphasized when the bowl was offered for sale at auction in New York in June 1937, and brought the large sum of $30,000.

Another plain bowl with a scalloped rim (FIG. 64) also by John Coney was a true monteith, but the once removable rim has been fixed at a later date. The bowl itself without the scalloped rim is approximately the same height as, but slightly smaller in diameter than, the contemporary English bowls; but while the latter are hemispherical, the Coney bowl tends to have straighter sides and for that reason is deeper in proportion to its width. The molded scalloped rim, interesting as it may be, inspires the question as to whether it was an afterthought added by a craftsman less skilful than the maker of the bowl itself.

NEW YORK. Punch bowls made by New York silversmiths are even rarer than those of New England. Perhaps the conservatism of the still strong Dutch element in New York, especially among the early 18th-century silversmiths, would not allow the English style to replace the finely embossed and chased bowls described previously and illustrated in Figures 10 and 11 (see also PLATE I-A).

Punch bowls of the larger type such as were used in England were made in New York at about this time, but few seem to have survived. One (FIG. 65) came to the writer's notice some years ago. It is a plain hemispherical bowl about 10 inches in diameter with a slightly flaring rim on a molded domical foot. It was made by that little known silversmith, John Hutton, who was working in New York about 1720; and while it is an excellent example of fine hammerwork, it lacks the character of the shallow decorated bowls which are peculiar to New York.

OTHER DOMESTIC SILVER

Saltcellars

It is said that English is made up of mis-spelled and corrupted words from other languages, and the statement can be supported to an extent. Our term, saltcellar, is an example. This is a modern spelling of medieval *salte seller,* the seller being in turn the early English form of the French *salière* meaning a salt holder or salt box.

Our word salary has an equally "salty" origin, for it is derived from the Latin *salarium* which was an allowance of salt which the early Romans made to their soldiers and servants. Later when money was substituted for the ration of salt, the payment was known by the same name, though the word *salarium* continued to include rations. Possibly the phrase, "He's not worth his salt" has some connection with the ancient *salarium*.

NEW ENGLAND. Trencher salts continued in use both in Britain and America through the High Standard period and until the appearance, about 1735, of the now more familiar little bowls on three feet.

As previously remarked, many have long since disappeared into the melting pot, but enough Colonial trencher salts remain to show that several types of these small pieces were made by the silversmiths of both New England and New York; and that they were copied from those made in England in the late 17th and early 18th centuries.

There is evidence that the tall circular trencher-salt with the concave sides and fluted decoration mentioned previously (see FIG. 42) carried over to the early 18th century. Two were made for Sarah Middlecott who was married in 1702. One by John Coney is in the Museum of Fine Arts, Boston, and the other by Edward Winslow belongs to Mrs. Thomas M. Shepherd, a descendant of Sarah Middlecott. This Sarah was Winslow's cousin and it was for her mother that he made the sugar-box, mentioned in the previous chapter, which found its way to England and long afterward to the Edsel Ford Collection.

Early in the 18th century, the tall circular salt gave place to the small oval and octagonal trencher type. The latter (FIG. 66) are particularly fine examples of the symmetrical proportions and fine moldings achieved by skilled hammerwork. This may be said too of the oval shape, but it must be admitted the latter have not quite the same attraction. Like the octagonal, very few of the oval shape have survived, but two separate pairs are known: One pair by John Coney is in the Clearwater Collection at the Metropolitan Museum of Art and the other pair, which have a wide oval shape, 3⅝ inches by 3 inches, by John Burt (1692-1745) were exhibited at the Museum of Fine Arts, Boston, in 1911, lent by Miss Emily Sever.

NEW YORK. As in New England, the taller circular trencher salt (see FIG. 42) continued to be made in New York during the first few years of the 18th century. Most of the other trencher salts that have

51

survived follow the plain oval or octagonal styles, in every way similar to those made in New England.

New York silversmiths also made a small circular trencher salt (FIG. 67). These were similar to the English prototype which was in common use in the 17th and early 18th centuries. Some of the English salts of this type have been preserved in the London Livery Companies, but otherwise any examples, like the American counterparts, are extremely rare.

Miss C. Louise Avery, in her book, *Early American Silver,* mentions a pair belonging to Frederic Ashton de Peyster. These are 1¾ inches high and are attributed to Bartholomew Le Roux who was working in New York from about 1689 to 1713, and may have been made in the last ten years of the 17th century. Apart from their rarity, these salts are of very real interest as examples of small articles hammered up or raised from a small flat circle of silver—in other words, they were made in one piece.

PENNSYLVANIA. Even if some of the earlier Philadelphia silversmiths made the early 18th-century trencher salts, most of them must have gone to the melting pot later. Of course, there is always the possibility that some are still in the possession of descendants of the original holders, but unrecognized for what they really are, for even in these days of keen hunting small pieces still escape notice.

So far as we know, the only Philadelphia trencher salt is one made by Philip Syng the elder (1676-1739), which is in the Philadelphia Museum of Art. A typical example of this famous silversmith's skilful shaping and use of moldings with small pieces, it is octagonal in plan with incurved sides and three molded members both at the base and top. Knowing this salt, brings the wish that its former companion could be brought to light, for it undoubtedly was one of a pair at least.

Salvers or Tazze

NEW ENGLAND. From the number that have survived, it is clear that salvers on a low foot (FIG. 68), also known as tazze, were in fairly general use in New England during the early years of the 18th century. They were either quite plain with a simple molding or had gadrooning round the rim and the foot, as in the one illustrated; the latter follows the style which appeared in England at the end of the 17th century and was popular through the early part of the High Standard period.

Of the appreciable number exhibited at the Boston Museum in 1911, by far the larger proportion were lent by private collectors. We mention this point because these salvers are frequently described as patens, yet the fact that they are still in private possession would seem to indicate they were made for secular use.

They vary in size from about 5 inches to more than 10 inches in diameter and were sometimes made in pairs, though most of these "twins" have long since been separated. One pair made by Edward Winslow (1669-1753) were included in the Boston exhibition to which they were lent by King's Chapel, Boston. These are plain with the molded edge slightly over 6 inches in diameter on a molded trumpet-shaped foot, and were doubtless made originally for domestic use, because they were given to the King's Chapel in 1798 which was nearly fifty years after the maker, Edward Winslow, died.

That these salvers were regarded as important by their owners is clear from the fact that many of them bear the arms of early American families. One with the gadrooned edge, 9 inches in diameter by John Allen (1671-1760) and John Edwards (c. 1670-1746), was lent by Hermann F. Clarke to the exhibition at Yale University in 1939; this is engraved with the Coffin arms. Another, 10 inches in diameter, by John Edwards in the Mabel Brady Garvan Collection is engraved with the Walker arms. In the same exhibition, there was a very rare trefoil-shaped salver on a trumpet foot, slightly over 7 inches across, engraved with a crest (a unicorn's head) which was made by Edward Winslow; it was lent by Marcus Morton, Jr. Others similarly engraved with armorial insignia are owned by various private collectors.

NEW YORK. Very few circular salvers of the style described above were made in New York. The only one that has come to notice which can be attributed definitely to a New York maker is the example by Vanderspiegel described in the previous chapter.

One with a molded edge and trumpet foot bearing the maker's mark B R was included with the American silverwork exhibited at the Metropolitan Museum in 1911, to which it was lent by the Corporation of Trinity Church, New York—the mark, B R may be that of Bartholomew Le Roux.

Casters

Soon after the opening of the 18th century in England, the earlier cylindrical-shaped caster was replaced by the pear-shaped outline, sometimes called the vase shape. During the time the high standard of silver was enforced, casters were usually quite plain, though some examples were ornamented with cut-card work. There is, too, considerable decoration in the pierced designs of the perforated tops of both the pear-shaped and the small dredger type with a handle, which continued to be made; and with both styles the silversmiths often modified the plain outline by making the shape octagonal.

NEW ENGLAND. All the several styles of early 18th-century English casters were repeated by Colonial silversmiths. The small dredger type with the handle remained popular in New England after the middle of the century; and if today the plain cylindrical examples are more numerous, the octagonal shapes are still obtainable though few of the latter have come on the market in recent years. In fact, both the cylindrical and the octagonal made by Colonial silversmiths are more numerous than the English models from which they were copied.

Actually, these charming little pieces have retained their attraction since they first made their appearance; and modern reproductions serve as pepperpots on many a modern dining table.

Seeing different articles of silver on the table every day brings a familiarity with the various details and inspires a wish to discover the source of the shapes. This is so with small dredgers, and it is possible to see in them an association with tankards; for example, the plain cylindrical body of Figure 69 resembles that of the 17th-century English plain tankards with the S-shaped handle.

For the ancestry of the octagonal straight-sided dredger, we have to look further back in the Continental countries; this shape came to America through England from the German tapering hexagonal and octagonal tankards of the late 16th century. For even if some of the English and American octagonal dredgers have vertical sides, an appreciable number of the surviving examples have a decided taper, as is evident in Figure 70. There is a hexagonal tapering tankard with the maker's mark W E on loan at the Philadelphia Museum of Art.

English pear-shaped casters with high pierced tops were frequently made in sets of three, one large for sugar or salt and two smaller for Cayenne and Jamaica pepper or, as they are now more familiarly known, red pepper and allspice. Similar sets were produced by Colonial silversmiths and there is a pair by John Coney (FIG. 71) in

54

the Spalding Collection at the Museum of Fine Arts, Boston, that suggest they once had a larger companion.

Other casters of the pear-shaped outline were made octagonal in section: The lower rounded part of the pear on a spreading octagonal foot was used as the base, from the molded shoulder of which the straight sides curved sharply inward and tapered upward to a small rim. The cover was made to fit into the body and the lines of the body continued upward so as to form a series of eight panels which were pierced and chased with an elaborate pattern of delicate foliated scrolls. An example of this style is illustrated in Figure 117.

NEW YORK. Casters by New York silversmiths of the early 18th century are not numerous. The small plain cylindrical dredger type with the pierced dome top were undoubtedly in fairly common use as they were in New England, but few seem to have escaped the fate decreed by changing fashions; namely, being melted to furnish metal for articles in a later style. Some New York silversmiths would occasionally raise one of the little dredgers on three feet, possibly to give an air of greater importance (see FIG. 72).

A fair number of pear-shaped casters by New York men have been preserved. Several early 18th-century types were in the exhibition at the Museum of the City of New York in 1937-8. These included one of the octagonal pear shape, 7½ inches high, similar to the New England example illustrated in Figure 117.

One set of three casters in the same exhibition is of particular interest as showing that original sets by American silversmiths have remained together through the years. Two of the set (FIG. 73) are the same size and the other is somewhat larger. The bodies are the plain pyriform with a molded shoulder on the hemispherical lower part and the tapering upper part. The covers, which continue the tapered form, are pierced with quatrefoils and fitted with the bayonet fastening. These covers illustrate a somewhat unusual feature in the fact that the piercing is confined to the sides with a slightly domed plain top.

Bayonet fastening was introduced into England from France and is formed of two projecting lugs or ears fixed to the lower edge of the cover, the lugs passing two notches in the grooved molding round the rim of the body which, when given a half turn, engages firmly with the cover.

Like the bayonet fastening, each of the several types of caster originated in France. The pyriform shape was popularized in

55

England by the French Huguenot silversmiths during the High Standard period. But while inspired by the contemporary French casters, those made in America and England are more graceful. Paris pyriform casters are wider and the body from the shoulder has a decided concave in place of the taper; moreover the French covers are shorter and broader, with the result that they tend to appear top-heavy which is emphasized by the use of the bayonet fastening.

Candlesticks

At the dawn of the interest in American silver fifty years ago, virtually no candlestick by Colonial silversmiths was known, but some have come to light in the intervening years. With the exception of one by Cornelius Kierstede and the pair by Jeremiah Dummer referred to previously which have the clustered column, most of the later discoveries are of the cast baluster type which made its appearance in England at the end of the 17th century and remained popular until the coming of the neo-classic styles in the later 18th century. Perhaps the fact that they were cast accounts for few being made, because any cast object of the size of even a small candlestick calls for a fair amount of silver.

NEW ENGLAND. Most of the early American candlesticks were made by New England silversmiths who, while using the basic forms of the English models, never slavishly copied the details. Thus, in candlesticks as in other articles, they demonstrated both their skill in adapting and changing and their desire to create a design expressing something of their own ideas. It would have been an easy matter to cast a replica from an English candlestick, but it is clear that when an American silversmith made a candlestick of the baluster type, he set about it by the old-time method: This was to prepare a wax model of a design he had drawn and from this make a mold into which the molten silver was poured. After the metal had cooled, all that was necessary was to clean and sharpen the details of the casting and remove any marks of the mold.

Three cast baluster candlesticks (FIG. 46) by John Coney which we have had the temerity to attribute to the late 17th century were mentioned in the preceding chapter. Another style was made with an octagonal pear-shaped knop on a high molded foot and spreading octagonal base, of which there are a pair by John Burt (1692-1745) in the Fogg Museum at Harvard University. This type was doubtless suggested by similar English early 18th-century candlesticks, and those illustrated in Figure 74 are almost identical with a pair hallmarked 1710-11 in the Victoria and Albert Museum.

There are points in the Colonial candlesticks of this period indicating the silversmith's individual ideas and an ingenious bringing together of earlier forms: In one (FIG. 75) a wavy curve is introduced in the socket. The molded boss below the socket might well have been borrowed from the small member below the bowl of an early standing-cup and the conical foot follows the trumpet-shaped foot found in 17th-century salvers. For the base, however, we have to go back to the octagonal saucer-like base of the last few years of the 17th century (see FIGS. 46 and 47).

One adjunct to candlesticks of bygone times was a pair of snuffers usually accompanied by a small tray. The snuffers are similar to a pair of scissors with a small box or pan on one blade and a plate on the other. The plate which fits the box pinches off the charred wick of the candle and in closing presses it into the box. We moderns are accustomed to candlewicks which burn at the same rate as the wax, but in earlier times the wick burned more slowly with the result that it fell onto the side of the candle and the wax or tallow guttered over the side. To prevent this, the charred wick was clipped at intervals with the snuffers.

American silver snuffers do exist but they are even scarcer than the candlesticks. The only pair of snuffers complete with the tray we have met with were made by John Burt. The snuffers follow the traditional pattern common in England. The tray, however, is noticeably simpler than the contemporary English snuffer trays, although the shape, the scroll handle and the four hoof feet proclaim its immediate ancestor to have been of English origin.

These snuffers and tray together with a pair of candlesticks, also by John Burt, were shown as a lighting set at the exhibition of New England silver held at the Gallery of Fine Arts, Yale University, to which they were lent by Hermann F. Clarke. Each of the pieces is engraved D $\overset{W}{*}$ s denoting Daniel and Sarah (Hill) Warner who were married in 1720.

Among the extravagances introduced to England after the return of Charles II, silver wall brackets or sconces, as they are generally called, became widely popular. Unfortunately, like so much of the silverwork of that time they were of very light metal elaborately embossed to strengthen the metal and give an appearance of massiveness for which reason few have survived.

57

They continued to be made until the early years of the 18th century when they were replaced by the cut glass sconces and magnificent chandeliers which, with candlesticks, were described in contemporary advertisements as "lustres," a name which is applied to them at the present time. Large numbers of these same lustres were imported to America and many an original example remains in the Colonial mansion in which it was first installed; but only one pair of silver sconces by an American silversmith is known.

These American sconces were made by Knight Leverett of Boston (1703-53) and are illustrated in the catalogue of the Boston exhibition of 1911. They have a plain tubular scroll bracket and tall candle socket with a wide wax-pan and a small detachable wall plate. From the fact that they are engraved with a monogram RR and the date 1720, it may be assumed they were made in that year.

NEW YORK. Very few New York candlesticks dating before about the middle of the 18th century have so far come to light. Most of the known examples of the cast type show a rococo influence, as will be seen from the examples illustrated and for that reason we know they date after about 1730. One of the earlier cast octagonal pyriform baluster sticks with the plain molded octagonal base by Bartholomew Schaats of New York (1670-1758) is shown in Figure 76.

At first sight these resemble the similar sticks made by the Boston silversmiths (see FIG. 74) but when compared several differences are noticeable. The foot and base of that by Schaats (FIG. 76) lack the rhythmic grace of the Boston examples and a disproportionate deep nozzle is fitted to the socket—in fact, the manner of this nozzle would tend to suggest its being a later addition.

Teapots

Any list of silver articles that first came into general use during the early 18th century shows that the greatest stimulus to the silversmith's trade came from those now everyday drinks, tea, coffee and chocolate. The earliest English teapot bears the London hall-marks for 1670-1 and is plainly derived from the horn shape, for the body is similar to an inverted beaker with a high conical cover hinged to the socket, a short tubular spout and a leather-covered handle.

Tea was first brought to Europe from the East by the Dutch in about 1610 but was not introduced to England until some years later. Dr. Johnson mentions it was imported from Holland in 1666, but it was known in England before then, even if regarded as a medicine rather than a popular drink. In fact, as late as 1659 it was still valued more for its curative properties, as a broadsheet issued by Thomas Garway, the first London tea merchant shows. In a verbose advertisement he claims that tea is a cure for almost all human ills among them "lippitude distillations, hot liver, agues and surfeits."

All the first teaware, like tea itself, came from China. Most of it was the fine stoneware made at Ihing (formerly Yi-hsing) potteries. And the teapots brought from these ancient potteries were reproduced by European potters, first in Holland and later by John and David Elers in Staffordshire and Dwight at Fulham; the Elers being two Dutch silversmiths who came to England about 1690. After working at that trade for a time in London, they moved to Staffordshire and started a pottery where they produced a ware resembling the Chinese red stoneware.

NEW ENGLAND. When tea was first introduced from China the price ranged from the equivalent of $30 to $50 a pound, consequently it was beyond the reach of any but the wealthy. And even by the beginning of the 18th century, when larger quantities were being imported, it was still very costly. This fact probably accounts for the few American silver teapots before the early Georgian period. Had more than now exist been made, it is fairly safe to assume they would have been preserved, for any silver teapot would have been a treasured possession of the mistress of the house, carefully handed down from one generation to another, as we know many of the early ones were.

Unlike the pots for coffee and chocolate which retained the tall inverted beaker form, the teapot became a short pear shape with a duck-neck spout on a low ring foot and a high domical cover hinged to the upper handle socket—the earliest ones have the handle at right angles with the spout. This type in England dates from the early 18th century and reached America soon afterward, as there is a quite plain example in the Clearwater Collection at the Metropolitan Museum of Art which was made by John Coney of Boston (1655-1722).

This Coney teapot (FIG. 77) repeats the natural shape of a pear. The shape of the body follows the unbroken curve of the fruit which is completed by the high domical cover with a molded finial knob. There is a similar natural outline in the New York teapot illustrated in Figure 78, but this shows signs of the later more sophisticated

59

pear shape where the bulbous lower part is wider in proportion to the upper part of the body which takes a decided incurve tapering to the rim (FIG. 79). Another interesting feature with the Coney pot is the short cast spout rising almost vertically close to the body.

New England pear-shaped teapots, however, are considerably scarcer than those by New York makers. Most of the early 18th-century teapots bearing the marks of New England silversmiths are of the globular shape which was popular in England until about 1770. Like the English counterparts, the majority of the Colonial teapots of this type show influences derived from the rococo style and therefore belong in the following chapter.

NEW YORK. Like tankards and other silver articles, the New York pear-shaped teapots have certain distinctive features. That they derived from the English teapots of this shape is obvious; but a comparison shows that the New York interpretation of the pear shape is narrow in proportion to the height, the spouts are slightly smaller and longer, and there is a free use of moldings, all of which tend to make a more graceful outline. This is perhaps clearer when the relative heights are considered—the English teapots are about 5½ to 6½ inches high, while those made in New York are about 7 to 8 inches.

One English pear-shaped teapot made in about 1690 bears the mark of Sir Richard Hoare, goldsmith and banker. It is 5½ inches high, a rather immature affair with a small tubular spout, obviously inspired by the porcelain wine jugs imported from the East; the cover is domical with an ornamental thumb-piece hinged to a light silver scroll-shaped handle. This method of hinging the cover to the handle repeats that of the tankards, a relationship emphasized by the addition of the thumb-piece; and though the latter disappears, a relic of the tankard remains in the heavy hinges of the later pear-shaped teapots (see FIGS. 78, 79 and 80).

There is quite a similar but more advanced teapot by Peter Van Dyck (1684-1750) which, with its high domical cover, is a true pear shape. This example is in the collection of Mrs. Alexander Duer Harvey and on loan at the Metropolitan Museum of Art. Whether Van Dyck derived the idea of the teapot from an English or Continental source is debatable, but the use of cut-card work on the cover and the elaborate double scroll handle would suggest either a direct or indirect French influence (see PLATE IX-A).

This particular New York teapot is of more than usual interest as

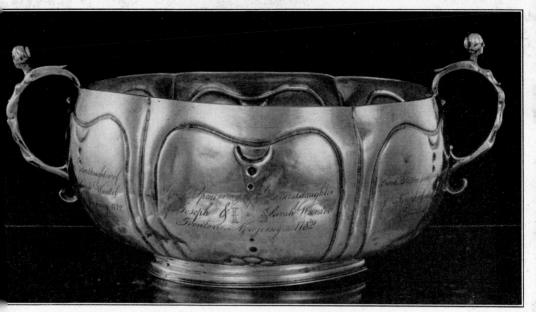

I-A: Two-handled punch bowl with shaped paneled sides and scroll handles with terminal female busts. By Bartholomew Le Roux, New York.

I-B: Two handled punch bowl with lobed rim and chased tulips and other flowers. This is the earliest punch bowl made in New England and is inscribed with the date *1692*, above which *No. 2, 1728* was inscribed later. By Jeremiah Dummer, Boston.

II: Beaker inscribed *Robert Sandersen 1685* and engraved with designs adapted from illustrations of the didactic poems of Jacobes Cats. By Cornelius Vanderburgh, New York.

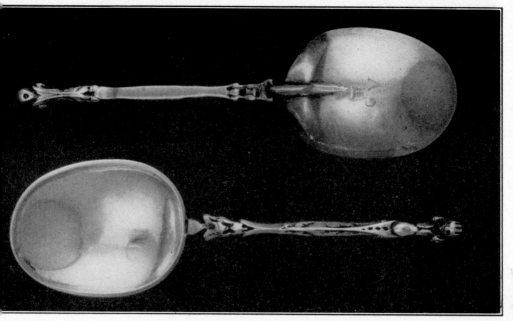

III-A: Spoon with elliptical bowl and cast and decorated stem finishing at the end as a scroll. Engraved *G. V.* on back of bowl. Belonged formerly to the Vechte family of Gowanus, Long Island. By Henricus Boelen, New York.

III-B: Pair of circular trencher salts with fluting round rim and base and a typical New York ornamental band above the base molding. By Jacobus Vanderspiegel, New York.

IV: Standing cup with lower part of the bowl fluted, short baluster stem and gadrooned foot. By Jeremiah Dummer, Boston.

V: Tankard with plain tapering body, flat lid, V-shaped tongue continuing down the
body from the upper joint of the handle, which finishes below in a shield shape;
the thumbpiece in the twisted volute known as the ram's horn type. By John
Coney, Boston.

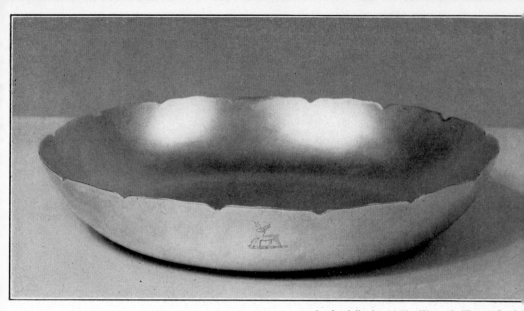

VI-A: Plain fruit dish by Daniel Christian Fueter, bearing his New York marks. This dish was found in England.

VI-B: Punch bowl decorated in the rococo style. By Richard Van Dyck, New York.

VII: Caudle cup and cover with spool-shaped handle and scroll handles each with a female terminal head. Engraved with the arms of Addington. By John Coney, Boston.

VIII: Two-handled cup and cover with the three brackets to serve as feet when cover is inverted as a stand for the cup. Engraved with the Bayard arms. Possibly a christening gift to Judith Bayard, baptized December 13, 1698. She was the daughter of Samuel and Margaret Van Cortland Bayard. By Gerrit Onkelbag, New York.

IX-A: Pear-shaped teapot with silver handle, engraved small flowers and leaves enclosing rectangular panel, and domical cover decorated with cut-card work. By Peter Van Dyck, New York.

In the Collection of Mrs. Alexander Duer Harvey and on loan at the Metropolitan Museum of Art

IX-B (below): Salver engraved with the arms of New York State. Diameter 21¾ inches. Inscribed: *This Piece of Plate is the Gift of His Excely, Govr. Tyron, the Genl Assembly of New York to Captn Sowers Engineer 13 Mar 1773.* By Lewis Fueter, N.Y.

X: Tea service of the Classic period: urn-shaped teapot and sugar bowl, and helmet-shaped cream jug with domed lid. By Abraham Dubois, Philadelphia.

XI: Tea service of oval fluted flat-bottom teapot with tapering spout, helmet-shaped cream jug on square plinth, and vase-shaped sugar bowl with spool-shaped cover, each decorated with bright-cut engraving. By Paul Revere, Boston.

XII: Cream jug showing rococo influence in the simple scrolled flutings. By Joseph Richardson, Sr.

XIII: Globular teapot chased with scrolls, flowers, foliage and shellwork in the rococo style. By Joseph Richardson, Sr.

XIV: Sugar bowl with cover chased with C-scrolls and flowers. Engraved *Wedding silver of Sara Shoemaker married to Edward Pennington, Nov. 26, 1754.* By Joseph Richardson, Sr.

XV: Coffee-pot chased with scrolls, shellwork, rose blossoms and other flowers in the rococo style. Engraved *Wedding silver of Sara Shoemaker married to Edward Pennington, Nov. 26, 1754.* By Joseph Richardson, Sr.

XVI: Two-handled cup and cover with baluster finial. Engraved with the arms of Rowe of Tolesbury Hall, Yorkshire. By Jacob Hurd, Boston.

it is possible to trace its rather primitive shape in the later splendid teapots by the same silversmith. Judging from those which have been handed down through many generations, Van Dyck seems to have made several essays to achieve a pear shape that really satisfied him, and his experiments to this end may be followed in several teapots of this type bearing his mark.

One, in the collection of Miss Elizabeth M. Bates, has a depressed bulbous lower part tapering upward to a narrow neck with a rather crude tubular spout (FIG. 79). The cover is a high dome decorated with cut-card work, like the one described above, and a tall wood finial knob, the handle being C-shaped and a relic of the tankard thumb-piece remaining in a small projecting scroll on the upper part of the handle.

Another teapot of the same form (FIG. 78) we may surmise is a more advanced "experiment" as it has a graceful faceted swan-neck spout with a bird's beak, the foot is molded and the shape of the handle improved. The outline has the more continuous curve and the high cover, which now has a silver baluster finial, is again decorated with cut-card work.

Van Dyck's eventual success in producing a perfect teapot is shown in such examples as that in Figure 80 and the one known American octagonal pear-shaped teapot (FIG. 81); the latter was found in England where, for some time, it was thought to be of Dutch origin. In form, this follows the similar English octagonal teapots which were made in appreciable numbers during the High Standard period.

That the pear shape was popular in New York is evident both from the number that have survived and the fact that these bear the marks of different silversmiths working in the early 18th century, among them Charles Le Roux, Thauvet Besley, John Brevoort, Jacob Gerittse Lansing and others.

But while this shape was preferred in New York even after it had been superseded by the globular teapots in England and New England, what is possibly the earliest American and certainly the first New York teapot (FIG. 82) is an ancestor of the globular shape with the straight tubular spout. It was made by Jacob Boelen (1654-1729) and was obviously inspired by the small porcelain teapots imported from China. The inset cover is domical, decorated with a band of spiral fluting and has a projecting edge which supports it on the rim of the body (as in the porringer FIG. 98). This interesting teapot is engraved with the arms of the Philipse family from whom it descended to Pierre Jay, who gave it to his daughter, Mrs. Lloyd

61

K. Garrison, the present owner. It is now on loan at the Metropolitan Museum of Art.

Coffee-pots and Chocolate-pots

It may sound strange today, but time was when coffee, like more potent beverages in recent times, came under the ban of prohibitionists. Coffee was first introduced from the Near East to Europe about the middle of the 17th century and as soon as it began to become more popular in Britain, it met with a host of objectors. One vociferous group insisted it would cause the nation "to dwindle into a succession of apes and pygmies" and housewives complained that, when on a domestic errand, a husband would dally at one of the houses where men gathered to drink coffee and gossip.

These coffee-houses became as popular as the ubiquitous saloon is today, and though they met with organized opposition and though Charles II tried to close them by royal proclamation on the grounds that they were centers of anti-government activities, both the number of coffee-houses and the coffee drinkers continued to multiply and flourish.

Incidentally, some of London's famous clubs sprang from those same coffee-houses and more than one still retains the name of the man who founded and ran a coffee-house in the long ago, as for example, Whites, Boodles and Brooks.

It is thought that Columbus was the first to bring word of the cocoa bean to Europe after one of his voyages to the Americas; but chocolate made from the bean was not introduced until about 1520. It was well over a century later, however, before it was used as a drink in England and within a short time it competed with coffee in the coffee-houses. Moreover, it was enthusiastically received in fashionable circles but its vogue lasted only a short time and, by the early Georgian period, chocolate as a drink had lost much of its former popularity.

NEW ENGLAND. Most of the earliest American coffee- and chocolate-pots were of the tall cylindrical form or the later pear shape copied from English models. The former was a refined form of the first "inverted beaker" type—in every way similar to the first English silver teapot heretofore described. For a time, the conical cover of the 17th-century pot remained in a plain high domical shape, but later this was replaced by a low molded cover. These several shapes and changes were all adopted with some local variations by the New England silversmiths.

With the straight-sided pots, the taper was sometimes more marked and the high cover molded instead of plain, as shown in Figure 83, or the body was almost cylindrical as in Figure 84 with the lower type of cover. The spouts in both the examples illustrated are the faceted swan-neck which was generally used in England. Another feature of these spouts is the suggestion of a bird's beak which occurs often with the English swan-neck shape of the early 18th century.

When the fashionable world demanded a suitable silver vessel for serving chocolate, the silversmiths met with some difficulty in producing a pot which would accommodate a stirring rod or molinet as it was formerly known, without chilling the chocolate. Some of the first experiments to this end were ingenious if somewhat quaint. One of the earliest known English chocolate-pots, hall-marked 1697-8, is like an Oriental pear-shaped vase, a form which was repeated in the chocolate-pot by John Coney of Boston (FIG. 85).

It is highly probable the latter was a direct copy: It is the same shape and size as the English pot, the spout is similar, the handle is at right angles with the spout and fitted to the cover it has a similar hollow cylinder surmounted by a finial to cover the hole for the stirring stick. The English pot is spirally fluted on the cover, shoulder and base, otherwise it is a counterpart of its New England offspring.

Another slightly later experimental chocolate-pot is the example (FIG. 86) by Edward Winslow of Boston (1669-1753) in the Metropolitan Museum of Art. If this is studied it is clear that the designer borrowed from several sources. The tankard furnished the heavy hinge and scroll thumb-piece; the cylinder for the stick on the cover came from an English chocolate-pot and the body and cover were inspired by the pear shape.

NEW YORK. From the scarcity of chocolate-pots, it may be assumed that New Yorkers had little liking for this beverage. Nor could coffee have been as popular in the Manhattan of Queen Anne's day as it became later; otherwise there surely would have been as many coffee-pots dating from that time as there are teapots.

Probably the earliest silver coffee-pot attributed to a New York maker is one (FIG. 87) now in the Metropolitan Museum of Art. Obviously copied from an English model, it has the plain tapering cylindrical body with the high molded domical cover and a pronounced swan-neck spout. Unlike any similar English pot, however, it has a high spiral or corkscrew thumb-piece, which is peculiar to New York tankards; another token of the period in which it was made is the handle at right angles with the spout, a feature common alike to the first English teapots, coffee- and chocolate-pots and also found in some pots by New England makers.

Tea-kettles

As more opportunities occur to study collections of American silver, it becomes apparent that larger pieces are few and far between. This may suggest that in the early years the amount of available metal was limited and explain why so few punch bowls, large two-handled cups and kettles have come to light. The writer has had the privilege of enjoying many pleasant hours studying American silver, but so far only three kettles dating from the 18th century have been noticed, the earliest of these being one by Cornelius Kierstede (1675-1757) who worked in New York until 1722 when he moved to New Haven (FIG. 88).

It shows a certain Dutch influence in a zig-zag wire round the rim and the spout has a Continental feeling; but the shape of the body and style of the bale handle are similar to what is probably the earliest known English kettle which was made by Anthony Nelme and is hall-marked London 1709-10. There is also one by Paul De Lamerie; this famous silversmith entered his first mark in 1712 and the kettle was hall-marked the following year. Each of these, like the one by Kierstede, has a flat bottom which fits in the ring of a stand holding a spirit lamp; and it is not impossible that the Kierstede kettle at one time had a stand or was used wtih a brazier. It should perhaps be pointed out that the spout is not as Kierstede made it; at some time it may have been necessary to repair it and the repairer added certain "improvements."

Braziers or Chafing Dishes

NEW ENGLAND. It is sometimes suggested that the brazier or chafing dish, as this once necessary article is also called, was not used in England and that it was introduced to America from France. A similar method of heating food was employed in France and Holland, but even if primarily it came from Europe, braziers of exactly

64

the same form as those bearing the marks of American silversmiths were made in England where a few exist to the present time.

Two dating from the end of the 17th century were sold at Christie's in 1934. Each of these has a long turned wood handle fitted in a silver socket and each is 6 inches in diameter (FIGS. 89 and 90). One, slightly earlier than the other, is cylindrical with a flaring lip and pierced round the sides and base. It rests on three bird's claw feet each holding a wooden ball, and the brackets rise from the feet ending above as scrolls similar to the "ram's horn" thumb-piece.

It is safe to say that this style of English brazier was the model used by John Coney for two braziers (compare FIGS. 91 and 89); for apart from the difference in the bracket finials, the pattern of the pierced work and the omission of the wooden handle and ball feet, the Coney braziers are virtually identical.

There is a similarly close resemblance between the other English brazier with the shallow pierced hemispherical bowl (FIG. 90) and the American braziers fitted with the long handle of which a number have been preserved and of which examples are illustrated here.

NEW YORK. Braziers bearing the mark of a New York silversmith are rare. Only two have come to our notice: one by Peter Van Dyck (FIG. 93) which has a pierced bowl with a molded edge, simple strap silver supports and a stout turned handle; and another the writer found in London which was later returned to its birthplace.

PENNSYLVANIA. Of the equally rare Pennsylvania braziers, there are two in the Philadelphia Museum of Art. The earlier of these (FIG. 94) was made by John de Nys and possibly dates from the late 17th century. This dating is supported by certain features similar to those of the English 17th-century brazier in Figure 90. The brackets are fixed to the rim of the bowl instead of being an integral part of the supports; the feet are similarly scrolled and the lower section is a convex shape with simple piercings instead of the more elaborately pierced ring that was used later.

In contrast to the usual finely pierced bowl, another Philadelphia brazier (FIG. 95) by Philip Syng is quite plain although the sides of the ring are finely pierced with a series of heart shapes. The bowl is supported on three stout legs with molded feet, rather suggestive of a cabriole leg, with a scroll above terminating in a scroll bracket with a flat tongue.

65

Porringers

It would be possible to prepare a genealogical tree showing the ancestry of the American porringer starting even before the days of Homer, three thousand years ago. Those who have visited Pompeii will recall the shallow vessel with a long flat handle for which the Greeks had the word *patera*. Thence the porringer could be traced through the various ancient metal, wood and pottery bowls, some of which have the flat handle, to the German, Dutch and French silver bowls with two flat chased handles and the plain shallow bowl with the single pierced handle of 17th-century England commonly (and we think erroneously) called a "bleeding bowl." And such a tree would include the porringer's more distant cousins, the ancient shallow drinking bowls, the mazer and the quaich.

NEW ENGLAND. But whatever its ancestry, there is little doubt that the first American porringer which was made in New England was the child of its immediate English ancestor. That many, either of pewter or silver, were brought to America by the early settlers is proved by references to porringers in wills dating as far back as the 17th century; and some of the earliest known English examples with the pierced handle have been preserved in America since they were brought here three hundred years ago.

Support for the suggestion that the American porringer was derived from English models is to be found in the relative sizes and the similarity of the pierced designs of the handles. There are some half dozen in the Victoria and Albert Museum, the earliest of which (1638-9) is about 3¼ inches in diameter, but those of the later 17th century are over 5 inches which is the average size of the New England bowls.

All have a wide circular boss in the center of the bowl (see FIG. 96) which is a carry-over of the boss or print or similar ornament in the ancient Greek patera, the English mazers and in rose-water dishes. Presumably the ornament was used with the early pottery pieces and the wood bowls to conceal any slight irregularity which might have been left by the potter in throwing or by the wood-turner's tool in turning the inside of a bowl.

Most bricks look alike to those who are unfamiliar with building and most American porringers are equally alike to the unobservant —excepting the two or three fitted with a cover. But if the bowls are

66

indistinguishable one from another, the pierced designs of the handles offer an interesting study both in their development and the ingenious combinations forming the various patterns (FIG. 97). The early handles are smaller with fewer and simpler pierced forms and the edges are noticeably square and solid-looking.

In the later pierced designs, there is a decided rococo influence in the free use of scrolls combined to form an intricate design. One such combination seems to have been used more or less consistently by New England silversmiths throughout the 18th century, the only difference being in the refining of the outline. The details of some are relatively flat and wide with square edges, with others the edges are rounded off and so appear less solid, while others are "whittled" by careful filing to offer a remarkably finished appearance.

In the representative collection of porringers at the Metropolitan Museum of Art there is one with a bowl larger than the average (about 6½ inches in diameter) and fitted with a cover. The bowl is of the usual plain character with the customary pierced handle, but the cover which is a low dome chased with a band of spiral flutes has a single ring handle in the center of a finely chased foliated ornament on a matted ground (FIG. 98)—a style of cover found with English two-handled cups of the late 17th century.

This covered porringer originally belonged to Thomas and Mary Burroughs of Boston whose names and the date 1680 are inscribed on the bowl and their initials on the cover. When their daughter, Mary, married Brinley Sylvester in 1718, it was probably given to the young couple, as their names and the date of their marriage are also inscribed below those of Thomas and Mary Burroughs. It bears no maker's mark, but as its original owners were prominent Boston citizens and from the fact that the pierced design of the handle closely resembles one favored by John Coney, it has been tentatively attributed to that well-known Boston silversmith.

Another Boston porringer with a cover by Paul Revere (1735-1818) appeared in a New York auction room some years ago. This has a quite plain domical cover with a small knob and the piercing of the handle is the attractive scroll design. According to the history furnished in the sale catalogue, it was given to Robert and Mary Hooper by Pauline Revere, a niece of Paul Revere.

Porringers were sometimes fitted with a cover at a later date by another silversmith. Several examples of this have come to light, one by Thomas Edwards (1701-55) being shown at the Boston exhibition in 1911, at which time it was loaned by Marshall Hopkins Gould.

NEW YORK. While porringers were doubtless one of the household articles used in early New York homes, they seem not to have been as generally popular as they were in New England. More than forty New England porringers were included in the exhibition held at the Boston Museum of Fine Arts in 1911 compared with ten by New York makers in the exhibition at the Metropolitan Museum of New York in the same year.

As the interest in American silver grew, however, more New York examples came to light and upward of twenty were shown in the exhibition at the Museum of the City of New York in 1937-8. These ranged in date from one by Benjamin Wynkoop (1675-1751) to one by Hugh Wishart who was working from 1784 to 1816. Two covered porringers were shown, both of which were less than 5 inches in diameter. One was made by Peter Van Dyck (1684-1750), the other by John Brevoort (1715-75); the latter is engraved H R, initials of Harriet Howland Roosevelt, third wife of James Roosevelt (1760-1847), the great-grandparents of the late President Roosevelt.

Another important porringer with cover (FIG. 99) in the Metropolitan Museum of Art is attributed to Jan Van Newkirke, also known as Joseph Newkirke (c. 1716); this has a deep bowl and plain domical cover with a baluster finial and two handles of an unusually elaborate pierced design.

Generally speaking, the New York handles have no particular features to distinguish them from those of New England, though patterns of a more intricate character occur with one or two of the known New York porringer handles; an example of this is shown in Figure 97-C, the handle from a porringer by Jacob Boelen (1654-1729) which was formerly in the collection of the late Joseph B. Brenauer.

PENNSYLVANIA. Porringers by Pennsylvania silversmiths are even scarcer than those by New York makers. The few known are mostly by men working in Philadelphia during the early 18th century such as Peter David, Philip Syng, Joseph Richardson. The most favored handle was the pattern composed of the clever use of scrolls shown in Figures 97-E and F; but the simple form with three large and one small pierced shape (as in FIG. 97-A) is also found with porringers by the earlier Philadelphia silversmiths.

THE SOUTH. It seems unlikely that porringers were used to any extent in the South. We know of only one example. This bears the mark of the Charleston, South Carolina, silversmith, Enos Reeves (1746-1807), and is noticeably smaller and lighter than those made in either New England, New York or Pennsylvania. The handle is of the design formed of scrolls (FIGS. 97-E and F) which is commonly referred to as the "keyhole" pattern for the reason that the balloon-shaped hole in the center at the top bears some resemblance to the small metal plate fastened over a keyhole.

CHAPTER THREE

The Rococo Period
About 1725 to 1770

WHEN THE OLD STANDARD OF SILVER, WHICH IS generally referred to as sterling, was re-established in Britain in 1720, the silversmiths were able to adopt the more elaborate ornamentation introduced by the French Huguenot craftsmen. Some number of these men had arrived in England and Ireland before 1720, and while their influence is apparent in the silverwork of the High Standard period (1697-1720), the ornamental forms were, as explained previously, restricted by the softer metal which was compulsory during those twenty-three years.

More decorative styles did not make their appearance immediately after the return of the old standard (harder) silver, for the plain designs associated with the High Standard are to be found dating at least to the end of George I's reign (1726). But from that time on, rococo replaced the simpler styles and, though the earlier rococo work is restrained, much that was produced later by the more prominent Huguenot silversmiths in London is often fantastic.

Fundamentally, the ornamental forms of the rococo are Oriental. They had been known in Italy before being developed to their eventual extravagance by Juste-Aurèle Meissonier of the royal furniture factory in Paris. Meissonier issued at least two volumes dealing with the style and, working with a French cabinetmaker named Gilles Oppenord, produced the furniture known as rococo.

Much of the decoration developed by the French designer is of that unnecessarily lavish and often grotesque character which caused Leigh Hunt to describe the style as a "jumble and worthy only of the tawdriness and incoherence of a parrot"; and there are numerous pieces of both furniture and silver produced in France and England which deserve this caustic definition.

Among the many decorative elements in English silver of the

rococo period, there is a marked prevalence of scrolls and marine objects. Shells are combined with scrolls or with gadroon for borderings; grotesque masks with sprays of flowers, sea monsters, tritons, animal heads, branches, bulrushes and ribbons, in addition to symbolic figures such as Hope and Despair were embossed and chased or cast and applied to articles whose fine outlines are frequently debased by superfluous ornamentation.

Upward of two hundred Huguenot silversmiths settled in England in addition to well over a hundred who settled in Ireland; and led by the more prominent men such as Platel, Willaume, Le Sage, Courtauld, Liger, Pantin and the more widely known Paul De Lamerie, they exercised a strong and lasting influence on English and Irish silverwork. A number of them came from France to America and though their original ancestry is now largely lost sight of, many of the names in the lists of American silversmiths working during the 18th century are those of Huguenot refugees: as for example, Poutreau, Le Roux, Boudinot, Letelier, Fueter, Mouliner, Huertin, Goelet, Pelletreau, Grignon, Quintard, Dubois and many others.

These skilled craftsmen left their imprint on early American silverwork, as they did upon the English and Irish; but there are very few instances in which the more pronounced rococo forms find expression in the ornamental treatment of pieces made in America either by men of Huguenot origin or by other American silversmiths.

DRINKING VESSELS

Beakers

NEW ENGLAND. As the 18th century advanced, beakers for domestic use gradually went out of fashion though they were still made for churches; the straight-sided tapering horn shape with the flat bottom, however, gave place in time to curves. At first the base of the bowl was curved inward slightly, the upper part retaining the straight sides and widening upward in a similar way to the horn shape but with a flaring lip, while a relic of the flat bottom remained in the use of a low molded foot.

New England beakers of this type were not unlike an inverted bell, and this later became more pronounced when the waist was drawn in and the lip given a more pronounced flare. Many of these bell-shaped beakers are fitted with two handles and raised on a trumpet-shaped foot, but whatever the historic or sentimental asso-

71

ciations attached to any of them, they are of little interest as examples of early American silverwork.

NEW YORK. Here the tall horn-shaped beaker which was derived from Holland continued to be popular during the second quarter of the 18th century, though, as a rule, it is a trifle smaller, often with a stout molding round the rim and base (see FIG. 100); but the engraved decoration, which is such an attractive feature in the early New York beakers, was largely discarded.

Later they assumed the bell shape similar to those of New England described above. This unattractive shape was introduced from France where it was fashionable quite early in the century. The French examples are wider and more distinctly bell shape and often extravagantly decorated with applied foliage and engraved designs.

PENNSYLVANIA. Beakers are known bearing the marks of Philadelphia silversmiths working before the Revolution but the number is so small as to offer little interest to collectors.

Tankards

NEW ENGLAND. By about 1740, the change in the style of the New England tankard which had made its appearance earlier in the century was complete; and the tapering shape with a rib round the body, and high domical lid and finial was firmly established. New England tankards of this type are noticeably taller than the average English prototype, but apart from this and some few minor features they are alike. For example, the New England silversmiths adopted a finial ornament such as an acorn, pineapple, flame and baluster (see FIGS. 101 and 102); their tankards had a somewhat more spreading base and many a slightly flattened top to the dome of the lid. Incidentally while they are unquestionably taller than the English, allowance must be made for the finial, which is included in the height given, because some of these finials are over an inch high.

There was no change in the handles which remained the S-shape, but the former ornamental thumb-pieces disappeared to be replaced by the stout stem topped by a scroll (FIG. 102) or the open type (FIGS. 101 and 103). Both these types of thumb-pieces were used with German and Scandinavian tankards of the 16th century and also with English tankards of Tudor times.

Such ornamentation as was applied to New England tankards of

72

this time was usually a cast baluster-shaped drop on the handle below the hinge; and while in some instances, a silversmith would use a cherub's head on the tip of the handle (FIG. 102), in most cases the tips had a circular, shield shape or oval boss or possibly were finished in a volute, as with the small tankard shown in Figure 103.

NEW YORK. Rococo influence in New York tankards, if not readily recognizable, is present in subtle changes which occurred in the second quarter of the 18th century. The straight-sided body with the slight taper and flat lid remained popular for some years after it had been superseded in England and New England by the more tapering shape and domical lid; but toward the middle of the century there are signs of the coming of the bulbous body.

In the meantime several features appear which to an appreciable degree distinguish the New York tankards of the second quarter of the 18th century from the earlier examples. And these features show clearly the strengthening of English influence.

This is noticeable in the gradual disappearance of the ornamental band above the base molding; the use of the baluster drop in place of the former elaborate ornamentation on the backs of the handles and the use of a disk (sometimes engraved) or volute on the tips (FIGS. 104 and 105); the acceptance of a variety of thumb-pieces copied or adapted from those of English tankards, and the double (sometimes called "recurving") scroll handle (FIG. 105). The last was not used to any great extent in the New York flat-top tankards and seems not to have been accepted until about 1750. At this time, the bulbous shape with the domical cover had begun to assert itself and with it the double scroll handle (FIG. 106).

PENNSYLVANIA. Pear-shaped or so-called "bulbous" tankards began to replace the straight-sided tapering type in England during the second quarter of the 18th century; and it would seem that this new shape found favor in Pennsylvania soon after it became popular in England. The first sign of the transition is illustrated in Figure 107 in which the body still has the straight tapering form but the bottom is rounded and the molded foot or base is smaller. The handle is the double scroll shape with a suggestion of a volute at the tip and a short beaded rat-tail down the back. This type which is, to an extent, peculiar to Pennsylvania shows one feature copied from the contemporary English tankards in the molded band applied round the body.

73

After the introduction of the curved bottom it was a short step to the complete pear-shape popular in England. With tankards of this shape the silversmiths reproduced even small details of the English models: The domical cover was given a wavy contour in three members (FIG. 108), the projecting rim rounded off and a simple shield or heart shape was added to the tip. The thumb-piece, too, was often of the simple cast open type as shown in Figure 108 and the base, while occasionally more domical, as a general rule followed the molded English prototype.

Mugs and Canns

In the various shapes of everyday articles, during the first half of the 18th century, the outstanding form is that of the pear. The same outline had been used in the previous century though it is not perhaps as quickly recognized in the ogee-shaped caudle cup as in the pear-shaped teapot and coffee-pot; nor is it generally realized that the shape was copied by the European silversmiths from Chinese porcelain and is almost as old as China itself.

Its graceful curves were adopted wherever possible and while straight-sided tankards were made in England until after 1760, and later in America, the pear-shaped or bulbous mug or cann, as it is referred to in America, was made in both countries at least thirty years before.

Apropos the word "cann": It was used in England in Shakespeare's time to denote a drinking cup and it has survived in America where it is still applied to the bulbous-shaped mugs such as are illustrated in Figures 57 and 58. In its modern spelling "can," it is used commonly to denote a container for preserved foods.

These canns were particularly popular in New England and a considerable number have come down through the years. They are all pear shape, about 4½ to 5½ inches high, some of the earlier examples having the simple scroll handle (FIG. 57) and others the tapering double scroll with the leaf form on the top and a volute at the tip (FIG. 58) copied from the large two-handled cups introduced to England by the French Huguenot silversmiths.

NEW YORK. If for some time New York resisted any change in the shape of their great tankards, no objection seems to have been offered to the introduction of the pear-shaped cann. There was a period of transition, which has been referred to in a previous chapter, when the early straight-sided shape was incurved at the base (FIG. 59) to be followed by the gracefully curved sides. And as with the tankards, there was a change in the style of the handle; the earlier examples retained the S-scroll which later gave place to the double scroll mentioned above (see FIG. 58).

These canns continued popular through the 18th and into the 19th centuries. It is possible many of them were christening gifts to children, as they were in Britain, though, it must be admitted, the fact that so few of the American canns are inscribed would tend to contradict this.

PENNSYLVANIA. Cylindrical mugs of heavy silver with reeded bands and plain handles were made by Philadelphia silversmiths during the second half of the 18th century. The cann type are far more numerous, however, and these follow the same evolution from the straight-sided tapering form to the pear shape as that of the canns of New England and New York described previously.

Two-handed Cups with Covers

NEW ENGLAND. That American silversmiths were quick to recognize the beauty of the rococo shapes and the incongruity of much of the ornamentation is shown in their adoption of many of the former and their general rejection of the latter. This selectiveness is noticeable alike in New England, New York and Pennsylvania silver. For instance, the large two-handled cups with covers introduced to England by the Huguenots were copied in America. But while many of the English models were excessively decorated (as for example, the one by Samuel Courtauld hall-marked 1760-61, in the Metropolitan Museum of Art) those by the American silversmiths were relatively plain.

These large cups while carrying on the tradition of the loving cup were often intended as trophies or presentation pieces both in Britain and America. Those made by New England silversmiths repeated the tall bell-shaped bowl with a molded band which appeared in England about the end of George I's reign. The cover was a similarly high molded domical shape and the handles had the small volute at the tip.

When, however, a New England cup is compared with a plain English prototype, several minor differences are observable: The English bowls have a slight downward taper while the New England

75

tend to be more vertical and the bottom wider and flatter. Again, the English handles are invariably the more elaborate double scroll type introduced from France, whereas the New England men retained the simpler tapering S-scroll with a plain scroll at the top instead of the leaf form (see FIG. 109). There is also a considerable difference in the foot which with the English cups is a low spreading molded type but the New England foot is relatively high with a deep domical member at the base. The features of the New England cups are shown in Figure 109.

We have said that these large cups were often presentation pieces and this is supported by the history associated with several of the known New England examples. The one illustrated (FIG. 109) was made by Jacob Hurd (1702-58) and, though not shown in the illustration, is engraved with the Rowe arms—three holy lambs with the crest also a holy lamb. These arms are registered as those of Charles Rowe, Tolesby Hall, Yorkshire, which suggests that the cup at one time belonged to a member of that family who settled in New England (see PLATE XVI).

Jacob Hurd made a similar cup which bears an inscription recording that it was presented to Captain Edward Tyng *As an Acknowledgement of his good Service done the Trade in Taking Ye First French Privateer on this Coast the 24th of June 1744*. This cup which is over 15 inches high and weighs 96¼ ounces is now in the Mabel Brady Garvan Collection, Yale University.

Another smaller cup by Peter Feurt, who worked both in New York and Boston during the early 18th century, is in the same collection. This is 9 inches high and has a bowl similar to the one by Hurd (FIG. 109). The foot, however, is of the flatter molded form and omits the rather high domical member and the handles have the curved voluted leaf instead of the plain scroll form, which features were copied from the English two-handled cups of the rococo period.

This cup by Feurt is engraved with the Mills arms and motto on one side; on the other side are those of Hope of Hopetown, quartering an unidentified arms with motto. It is mentioned in the will of Edward Mills, Jr., dated 1732: "I give to Henry Hope Esqr. a Silver cup with his Coat of Arms and mine engraved thereon."

There is a large two-handled cup of this same type by William Swan of Worcester (1715-74) in the Essex Institute, Salem. This is 10 inches high and closely resembles the one by Hurd and the foot has a similar deep domical member. According to the inscription, it was presented by the Province of Massachusetts Bay to Benjamin Pickman in 1749.

NEW YORK. There are fewer known large two-handled cups by New York makers. One by Charles Le Roux has already been noted in a previous chapter. Another by Elias Pelletreau (1726-1810) was exhibited at the Museum of the City of New York in 1937-8. It is nearly 13 inches high, engraved with the Van Courtland arms, and, though plain, shows the same French influence as is traceable in the contemporary English cups.

This is evident in certain well-defined features: The bowl has a more decided taper than the New England bowls; the molded rib is higher up the body; the foot is low and more finely molded; and the handles are of the type which was introduced to England by the Huguenot silversmiths and characteristic of the rococo style; namely, formed of two tapering voluted scrolls with a finely voluted leaf on the shoulder of the upper scroll.

Punch Bowls

NEW ENGLAND. We have already referred to the scarcity of American silver punch bowls. It would be natural to think that as the people of New England freed themselves from their Puritan traditions, more of these grand symbols of hospitality would have been made. Unfortunately that does not seem to have been the case, for they are as rare dating from the rococo period as they are before and after.

Several interesting New England examples were exhibited at the Museum of Fine Arts, Boston, in 1911. These included the plain bowl by William Homes (1717-83) shown in Figure 110 which was lent by Ambrose Dawes, a descendant of Thomas Dawes to whom the bowl was presented by the *Field Officers and Captains of the Regiment of the Town of Boston* in 1763.

Another of the monteith type with the removable rim (FIG. 111) by Daniel Henchman (1730-75) was in the same exhibition. This bowl shows the rococo influence in the fairly heavy C-scrolls applied to the rim; but the notches do not appear to be of a character suitable to hold the foot of a glass, so we may assume the removable rim was intended more for ornament than use. The bowl was presented by John Wentworth, Governor of New Hampshire, *to the*

77

Revd. Eleazer Wheelock, D.D., President And to his Successors in that Office at the first commencement, in 1771, of Dartmouth College where it has remained a treasured possession.

As this is being written, the spotlight of public interest is directed to the "Rescinders" or "Sons of Liberty" bowl which was made by Paul Revere and is without question the most historic piece of American silver—and incidentally the most valuable from a monetary point of view. This is a plain bowl of the same shape as the large porcelain bowls imported from China.

It is inscribed with the names of the fifteen Sons of Liberty for whom it was made. And no doubt it held many a good brew of punch during the years it was kept at the old Boston tavern, known as the "Bunch of Grapes," which was the meeting place of the Sons of Liberty. More than a century after those stirring times, it descended to Marian Lincoln Perry, a great-great-granddaughter of John Marston, one of the Sons of Liberty.

Charles Messer Stow in the New York *Sun* of August 27, 1948, gives an interesting insight into both its past and more recent history; he tells us that this famous bowl has now passed from the collection of the late Marsden Perry to the Museum of Fine Arts, Boston. But, he says, before Boston became the owner, it had been destined for the Metropolitan Museum of Art, adding, "Then followed on the part of the Metropolitan a bit of professional courtesy rare in Museum circles. It conceded that the Boston institution was the rightful repository for the bowl. . . ."

Reporting the presentation of the Revere bowl to the Museum of Fine Arts, Boston, by the citizens of the Commonwealth, the New York *Times* of February 16, 1949, mentions that Mrs. Marsden Perry is reputed to have refused an offer of $100,000 from J. Pierpont Morgan for the bowl and another of $150,000 from Francis P. Garvan. When Mrs. Perry's estate was being settled, it was offered to the Commonwealth of Massachusetts for $65,000; and though the Museum made the largest contribution to the fund-raising campaign, contributions were also made by no less than 55,000 Massachusetts school children.

All the large bowls are about 11 inches in diameter, but other quite similar, smaller ones were made by American silversmiths during the 18th century. Some, obviously too small for punch, were possibly used for holding sugar, or the dregs from teacups; others are of a size which might suggest their use for a small brew of punch, as for example, one by George Hanners (1697-1740) in the Spalding Collection at the Museum of Fine Arts, Boston, which is 7¼ inches in diameter.

NEW YORK. No large bowl by a New York maker dating from the rococo period or in the rococo style can be recorded; but a smaller plain bowl on a low foot which was made by Daniel Christian Fueter (c. 1756) is in the collection belonging to Victor A. Watson of London. Fueter worked in London before migrating to New York and his mark, DCF in an oval punch was registered in 1753. In the following year he came to America and in an advertisement in the New York *Gazette* describes himself as the maker of "all sorts of Gold and Silverwork." The bowl mentioned above and other silver made by Fueter in America bears two punches, DCF in an oval and N YORK in a separate punch following the outline.

PENNSYLVANIA. No 18th-century punch bowl by a Pennsylvania silversmith had been noted until about ten years ago when an important example was discovered in Annapolis by that tireless seeker, Stephen G. C. Ensko.

Like the one by Coney (FIG. 63) which it resembles, it is of the monteith type, though again like the Coney bowl, the rim is fixed. It has similar cast lions' head and ring handles and a similar gadrooned band round the foot, but the character of the remaining decoration is entirely different: The rim is scalloped and mounted with scrolling flutes enclosing pendants of foliage with other ornaments pendent from the cherubs' heads.

It was made by John Letelier of Philadelphia (c.1760-70) and was obviously inspired by an English punch bowl of the rococo period. But the style of the decoration on the bowl is unusual; the only English bowl showing the same arrangement of scrollings that the writer has seen was one by John Ward, hall-marked 1697-8, which appeared at Christie's in 1937. The London bowl is the same shape and has similar lions' head handles and gadrooned foot, but the rim is plain molded instead of being scalloped.

This rare American punch bowl was illustrated in an article by Millicent D. Stow in the New York *Sun* of October 16, 1937, when it was mentioned that it had joined the collection of Walter M. Jeffords.

79

OTHER DOMESTIC SILVER

Saltcellars

On balance, little was gained and much was lost by the introduction of the French rococo styles, for if the Huguenots increased the number of domestic silver articles, they were responsible for the disappearance of the simple forms of the preceding period. We lost, for example, the little trencher salts which, though they remained in use until 1740, were replaced by the small bowls on three legs. And English saltcellars of the rococo period were, like other objects, at times elaborately ornamented, though as a general rule relatively plain.

NEW ENGLAND. American saltcellars with the round bowl on legs were either plain or when some rococo ornament was used it was with few exceptions restricted to a gadrooned rim, scallop shells at the joints of the legs to the body and similar shells for feet.

Both plain and ornamented saltcellars of this style were made by New England silversmiths but existing examples are scarcer than might perhaps be expected. When compared with those of New York and Philadelphia, there is a certain studied simplicity observable in those of New England; the legs are sturdy, usually with hoof feet (FIGS. 112 and 113), showing a relationship with the legs and feet of contemporary furniture, for in the outline of the short legs there is something of the cabriole form and it is not difficult to see a resemblance in the foot to that of a goat.

In these smaller saltcellars, therefore, it is possible to trace something of ancient China: The cabriole shape was developed from the leg of an animal; the Dutch brought it from the East and later it found its way to England and America. The suggestion is that it was adopted from a goat's leg and this is probably correct as the French word *capriole* or *cabriole* is derived from *caper* (a goat) and means literally, a "goat's leap."

NEW YORK. Neither English nor American 18th-century saltcellars were noteworthy for their variety or design. The circular bowl on three legs became and remained fashionable until it was superseded by the formal Adam designs.

In New York saltcellars there is perhaps more evidence of rococo influence, but this is seldom pronounced. Such ornamental details as were adopted by the New York silversmiths were mostly restricted to the wavy gadrooned rim, a scallop shell at the joint of the leg to the bowl, and a scallop shell foot. One of the known exceptions is a pair of saltcellars by Charles Le Roux (1689-1745) who, as we have remarked, was trained by his French father and therefore influenced strongly by the rococo style. This expresses itself in the use of elaborate floral swags and finely modeled masks applied to the bowls and the dolphin feet (FIG. 114) so loved by the famous Huguenot silversmith Paul De Lamerie.

PENNSYLVANIA. Pre-Revolution saltcellars made in Philadelphia followed the conventional small bowl on three legs; and like those of New England and New York the silversmiths adopted the same modified rococo forms where any decoration is added. One minor feature which is sometimes noticeable is the use of a simple shell form at the top of the legs with hoof feet.

Sauceboats

Sauceboats with the long lip and single handle which came into use during the rococo period were an offspring of the earlier type which resembled an ancient boat and from which the name is derived. The early 18th-century sauceboat had a lip at each end and either a bale handle across the center or a small loop handle on either side for convenience in passing from one guest to another. Both the double-lipped and the later single-lipped boats were introduced from France where, as in England, some of them were, to say the least, fantastic in form and ornamental treatment.

NEW ENGLAND. At no time was an American silversmith tempted to repeat any of the fanciful sauceboats. He was satisfied to reproduce the simple type with the edge cut in a series of undulating curves and the long lip not unlike some of the cream jugs.

They were used in New England fairly early in the century; one by John Burt (1692-1745) is illustrated in the Boston exhibition catalogue of 1911. This has the usual oval body with the shaped edge and exceptionally long lip and the open double scroll handle; but in place of the more graceful legs with shell feet and a shell at the joint of the leg (FIG. 116), the sauceboat by John Burt has rather clumsily modeled stumpy legs with plain feet.

Legs with hoof feet were sometimes used by later New England men, and in such instances the modeling was invariably the work of a skilled hand.

As a rule, however, the feet were the rococo shell (FIG. 115), but though this same form was applied as an ornament at the joint of the leg to the body (see FIG. 116) many of the existing New England sauceboats have a somewhat heavy trefoil shape at the joint of the leg (see upper part of legs FIG. 115). In other instances, the ornament at the top of the leg was formed of a heavy circular button of silver fluted to suggest the striations of a shell and this was joined by a sturdy C-scroll to a similarly fluted button-like foot. There are a pair of sauceboats with legs of this type by Daniel Parker (1726-85) in the Spalding Collection at the Museum of Fine Arts, Boston.

One interesting sauceboat by Josiah Austin (1718-80) has a bowl with a plain unshaped rim and lip and a single loop handle set horizontally at the end. This is illustrated in the catalogue of the exhibition held at Boston, in 1911, to which it was loaned by Henry R. Dalton.

NEW YORK. Like those of New England, sauceboats made in New York were direct copies of English models; but it is to be regretted that any bearing the mark of a New York silversmith are rare indeed. Only three were in the exhibition at the Museum of the City of New York in 1937-8, and of these one by Peter Van Dyck (1684-1750) indicates that sauceboats were made there fairly early in the 18th century.

Very rarely does a New York sauceboat become available. The last instance when one appeared in the auction room that this writer can recall was in 1946. This example which was by George Ridout, who was working in New York about 1745, has the scalloped rim, but both the handle and the legs are unusual. The handle is a simple S-scroll with what is intended to be a volute at the tip, while the legs have a shell form at the joint to the body, but finish below in the form of a claw and ball foot.

PENNSYLVANIA. Philadelphia silversmiths followed the prevailing pattern with their sauceboats and it is noticeable that these show a skilled handling in both the modeling and tooling of the shell ornaments and shell feet which are bold with the details sharp and clear (FIG. 116). A somewhat plainer style made in Philadelphia was similar in shape and had the same double scroll handle, but the rim instead of being cut in a series of curves was punched with a row of beads and the feet were the simpler hoof type.

Casters

NEW ENGLAND. In the same way that the three-legged salts displaced the simpler trencher type, so the more sophisticated styles of casters introduced from France eventually superseded the little dredgers with the handle, though the latter continued to be made until about 1740 both in America and England.

In New England, the earlier cylindrical dredger seems to have been discarded for the octagonal form with a stout scroll handle and a molded domical top pierced with some simple design (type shown in FIG. 70).

Although examples are very rare, octagonal pyriform casters were made by New England silversmiths. The one illustrated (FIG. 117) follows the outline of the French casters which was copied in England and the style of the pierced work is essentially French in character.

Plain casters of this form were evidently popular in New England, as many made there during the second quarter of the 18th century have been found since American silver attracted the attention it was for so long denied. These show the rococo influence in the paneling of the tops pierced alternately with scroll and other designs, and the use of interlaced lines, usually of the lozenge or trellis-like pattern pierced with small holes (FIGS. 118 and 119).

During the later rococo period, the rounded base of the pear was extended in a tapering wavy line known technically as the "undulating pyriform" but more often called the "inverted pear shape." This type of caster was made in two sections, the upper one taking an incurve and tapering to the rim, and the joint of the two sections masked by a small molding (see FIG. 119).

NEW YORK. Many early New York families retained an affection for the simple little "kitchen dredger" type of caster after the several varieties of the pear shape had become fashionable. The rather small cylindrical type with the plain scroll handle was still made in the second quarter of the century, though most of the silversmiths had by then accepted the rococo influence to the extent of adopting the double scroll handle; also they adopted a baluster finial on the cover instead of the earlier insignificant "pimple" (FIG. 120).

Except for unimportant details, New York pear-shaped casters followed the same forms as those of New England. Both were based upon the French originals with such modifications as were made to the French designs by the English silversmiths of the rococo period; it is noticeable, however, that the American pierced work was seldom as ambitious as that of the English casters. Octagonal pear-shaped casters by New York silversmiths do exist but examples are very rare.

PENNSYLVANIA. Even though there was a greater development after about 1770, a considerable group of highly skilled silversmiths were working in Philadelphia prior to that date. In view of this, it is surprising to find such a marked scarcity of casters which were then in fairly general use both in New England and New York.

Candlesticks

NEW ENGLAND. Any known New England candlesticks of the early Georgian period—and like those of other periods they are few indeed—were copied from the contemporary English models of the simpler rococo style. By this time, the earlier baluster-shaped stem (FIGS. 46, 74 and 75) was discarded and all that remained of the knop was a projecting shoulder just below the socket joint (FIG. 121).

English candlesticks of this type were often ornamented on the shoulder and base, but the plainer ones were fluted in the same way as the known American examples. One other relic of the former knopped shaft survived in the small projecting member at the lower part immediately above the foot; and while the foot retained a resemblance to that of the earlier 18th century, the rococo influence was now introduced in the shaping and molding of the base as illustrated in Figure 121.

NEW YORK. Scarce as New England candlesticks of the rococo period are, even fewer are known bearing the mark of a New York silversmith; but those few show that the New Yorkers would at times give expression to the more elaborate rococo ornament. Although made early in the 19th century, one of a pair (FIG. 122) is included in this chapter to illustrate a style which repeats the fanciful forms found in French and English candlesticks of the third quarter of the 18th century. In fact so elaborate are these New York candlesticks, made by William Thomson (*w.* 1810-31), that they might well have been copied from a model by the famous Huguenot Paul De Lamerie in one of his more florid moments.

84

No part of either the shaft or base is plain: The socket has a calyx of large leaves, the shaft is decorated with flowers and scrolls which are repeated on the elaborate foot and base, and even the *bobèche* or loose socket is decorated. The method by which candlesticks of this character were made has been described in the preceding chapter; and if these more ornate types do not meet with universal favor, we still must recognize and admire the skill necessary to produce them.

Other New York candlesticks, such as that in Figure 123, are known in which the rococo influence is more subdued, even though slightly more pronounced than in the New England examples. This style shows the evolution from the plain baluster to the shaft with the shoulder; the base of the New York candlestick is ornamented at each corner with a definite shell shape which is repeated on the shoulder. This use of the shell is typical of the restrained rococo style adopted in English candlesticks of the second quarter of the 18th century.

One pair of New York candlesticks by William Anderson (*c*.1746), in the Museum of the City of New York, are of the same type as that in Figure 121 but quite plain. Both the shoulder and middle part of the shaft are hexagonal, tapering down to a small protruding member and short foot with a molded base which has four straight sides and recessed quadrant corners.

Teapots

NEW ENGLAND. Although, as remarked before, pear-shaped teapots were made in New England, the style more popular in Colonial homes throughout the first half of the 18th century was that derived from the globular shape. This shape was copied by the silversmiths from the small porcelain teapots made in China for the European market; it appeared first in England quite early in the 18th century, and there evolved from the almost complete sphere shape to that with the slight downward taper, which evolution is equally observable in New England.

Some of the earlier English and Scottish globular teapots have the plain tubular spout similar to that shown in Figure 82, but later the spout was a cast duck-neck shape ornamented with fluting and the teapot was decorated on the cover and shoulders with scrolls, shells and other rococo forms (FIG. 124). These features with some variations were reproduced by the New England silversmiths, together with a few characteristics that do not occur in the English prototypes.

85

Some of the latter were made almost spherical, but as a general rule, the shoulder was flattened slightly thus giving the body a depressed globe shape. The New England silversmiths, while flattening the top, retained the high shoulder curve and shaped the body with a more or less pronounced downward taper. The degree to which the tapering varies may be judged from the several teapots illustrated, as for example Figure 125 which has a close resemblance to the contemporary English shape and Figure 126 which resembles the outline of a pear.

Another New England characteristic was the domical lid (FIG. 126) which, on occasion, assumed a conical shape (FIG. 127) reminiscent of the lids of Cromwellian standing-cups. These are exceptional, however; the New England lids are mostly flat with a flush hinge such as was used with the English teapots, while the spouts also follow the English duck-neck shape ornamented with flutings (FIGS. 125 and 128).

It is possible to see in the variations of the New England globular teapots a transition to the slightly later inverted pear shape (FIG. 129), in some instances chased with rococo forms in the bolder style of the contemporary London teapots. And, some years ago, this writer came upon a Boston teapot of this shape raised on three rather rudely cast legs with shell feet in place of the customary spreading molded foot (see FIG. 130).

NEW YORK. Globular teapots would not seem to have been as popular in New York as they were in New England, yet one of the earliest known American teapots is a globular shape by Jacob Boelen (1654-1729) which was described in the previous chapter and illustrated in Figure 82.

One somewhat later example by Stephen Bourdett (c. 1730) tapers toward the bottom much in the same way as the New England pots; but the cast spout is less skilfully modeled and the cover is inset in the body instead of having the flush hinge (FIG. 131). It is only 4 inches high which is less than average size.

An interesting New York globular teapot (FIG. 132) by Thomas Hammersly or Hamersly (1727-81) is in the collection of American silver owned by Victor A. Watson of London. While its upper part has the globular outline, the lower part tapers more sharply than most of the New England pots, though it bears a resemblance to the one by Nathaniel Hurd in the Cleveland Museum of Art and shown in Figure 126.

There is little doubt that the inverted pear shape was as popular in New York during the second quarter of the 18th century as the pear shape had been previously. But where the earlier pear shape (FIG. 78) is quite plain apart from moldings, later teapots were often decorated in the rococo manner by New York silversmiths.

This is apparent in a number of the inverted pear shapes in which the ornamental design is apparently the silversmith's individual interpretation of the rococo style (for example, FIG. 133). The flower and leaf forms are considerably bolder than the similar French and English rococo elements, the scrollwork is subsidiary, and the ornamentation carried lower down the side of the body and extended to the spout.

New York silversmiths at no time lacked skill, but there are occasional signs of difficulty in reproducing the rococo forms; and there are a few instances where the ornamentation indicates lack of confidence, as in Figure 134. This pot shows clearly that the fine outline of the inverted pear shape is stultified by an unnecessary amount of rather immature chasing and embossing. Such examples are few, however, and are the more interesting because of their rarity.

This criticism is justified when the teapot in Figure 134 is compared with the splendid decoration of the tea service by Peter de Riemer (1738-1814) in Figure 135. The treatment of the various motifs in this service shows all the symmetrical balance of the French rococo in its more attractive style, and the chased flowers and scrolls —restricted to the shoulder and cover of the teapot—are in perfect proportion. From the fact that Peter de Riemer was baptized in the Reformed Dutch Church, New York, and that his father's given name was Steenwyck, it may be assumed he was of Dutch origin. Whether his father was also a silversmith is not certain, but it is clear that Peter had been apprenticed to a man who had learned his trade in Europe, for the work is worthy of the hand of a highly experienced Paris craftsman.

PENNSYLVANIA. Teapots of the early pear shape with the high domical cover had been relegated to the past by the time any appreciable amount of silverwork was made in Pennsylvania. Consequently, the first teapots were of the globular shape with the slight downward taper in every way similar to those of New England and the inverted pear shape which was favored in New York. From the scarcity of Pennsylvania teapots before, compared with the large number dating after, the Revolution, it seems clear that tea drinking in Philadelphia was not really popular until that city became the capital and so the center of social activities; but that it became fashionable then is indicated very clearly by the large number of silver things for the tea table that were produced in Philadelphia in the last quarter of the 18th century, and which are dealt with in the following chapter.

Coffee-pots and Chocolate-pots

NEW ENGLAND. Plain cylindrical coffee- and chocolate-pots with the flat bottom continued popular in New England for some years after they had gone out of fashion in England, though examples are rare; of the few that are known, some have almost vertical sides while others are tapered.

With the demand for curved lines, there came what might be termed a compromise between the tapering and the pear-shaped outline. The body was rounded at the base and raised on a low molded spreading foot, but the domical cover with baluster finial and the high swan-neck spout were unchanged. This variation (FIG. 136) was adopted by the New England silversmiths, though from the very few known examples this transitional shape appears not to have enjoyed any great vogue.

And it is doubtful whether it met with any greater favor in the more sophisticated circles of London, for by about 1750 it was outmoded by the plain pear shape which has since retained its popularity both in America and England. That the pear shape was quickly accepted by the New England families of the time is shown by the number that have come down through the years, some to take their place in collections while others remain in the possession of descendants of the families for whom they were made.

These New England pear-shaped pots differed little one from another or from the English models. They were usually quite plain on a simple molded foot (FIG. 137) such as was used by the English silversmith, and they had a similarly molded high domical cover and pineapple or other finial. Like the models, too, they show the rococo influence in the ornamental flutings and leaf forms of the cast spout and in the double scroll handle. This shape and style seems to have been a favorite with the famous Paul Revere (1735-1818) who, in at least one instance, replaced the molded foot by three legs with shell feet, though the result cannot be regarded as attractive as the normal foot.

New England men also adopted the inverted or undulating pear shape which in the case of coffee- and chocolate-pots might be defined as an elongated pear with the top inverted (FIG. 138). This shape is at times spoken of as "vase-shaped" thus suggesting it was derived from a vase, but we would be more inclined to give credit to some Anglo-French or English Georgian silversmith for evolving the outline from the pear shape in an effort to introduce more curves.

NEW YORK. There is the same transition from the straight sided to the pear shape in the New York pots and the later extension to the inverted pear shape. But with the New York inverted pear (FIG. 139) the wide part of the body tends to be more bulbous and the bottom undulating curve is usually shorter than in the New England pots. This would denote a direct English influence and that the New York men made little or no change in the shape; for the English pots are similarly broad and have the shorter curved section below. A like influence is seen in the use of a shorter foot but, unlike the English models which are often elaborately chased with rococo forms, those of New York are plain except for a band of gadrooning round the foot and cover and an ornamental spout.

PENNSYLVANIA. Though tea was not particularly favored as a drink in Pennsylvania during the first half of the 18th century, there can be little question as to the general popularity of coffee. Both the straight-sided and the pear-shaped coffee-pots were made, but by far the larger number of known examples are of the inverted pear shape (FIG. 140); and this last type remained popular well into the 19th century. As a rule, the shape favored by the Philadelphia silversmiths tends toward the more bulbous body of the New York pots, but the lower curved section is longer and the spouts rise above the level of the rim, both of the latter features being characteristic of the New England style.

Various types of finials, including the flame, pineapple and baluster, were used in Pennsylvania coffee-pots and the handles are mostly of the double scroll type. Some of the later pots have beading round the rim and foot and all are of heavy metal; the average weight of ten examples proved to be just short of 40 ounces.

Although it dates from the early 19th century, we might here refer to an interesting inverted pear-shaped coffee-pot by Edward Lownes of Philadelphia (c. 1817-33). Lownes copied it from an English original of 1760 and reproduced the chased flowers, scrolls and foliage

89

in the rococo style with which the English pot was ornamented. The pot is about 12½ inches high and weighs slightly more than 52½ ounces—thus being approximately the same size as similar Philadelphia coffee-pots but appreciably heavier. It was lent by Mr. John Cadwalader to the 1921 exhibition at the Philadelphia Museum of Art.

Tea-kettles

NEW ENGLAND. As noted before, only three American silver kettles seem to be known. The earliest, which is by Cornelius Kierstede, has already been described in the preceding chapter. The next in order of date is the globular example by Jacob Hurd of Boston (1702-58) illustrated in Figure 141, in the collection of Mrs. Stanley Cunningham. It has the slightly compressed globular body flattened at the top and bottom with a flush inset lid and turned ivory knob with a stout plain hinged handle, and cast faceted duck-neck spout, all of which are similar to the corresponding features of English kettles of this type.

While, however, it shows the rococo influence in the delicate engraved design on the lid and shoulder and in the ornamental work on the legs of the cast stand, these are noticeably less obvious than the ornamental work of English kettles; the latter, as a rule, have an elaborately pierced fringe between the legs which are of some fanciful scroll shape and have shell feet whereas Hurd used a simple lion foot.

It is engraved with the arms of Lowell quartering Leversedge, and descended from James Russell Lowell to his granddaughter Mrs. Stanley Cunningham, the present owner.

PENNSYLVANIA. Another notable kettle (FIG. 142) which was made by Joseph Richardson of Philadelphia (1711-84) belongs to the Gallery of Fine Arts, Yale University, by which it was lent to the Philadelphia Museum of Art. This, like the Coney monteith (FIG. 63) is one of the few instances where an American silversmith expressed the more elaborate rococo ornamentation in his work; and if it was copied from an English kettle then in America, one is given to speculate what became of the model.

Kettles of this shape enjoyed a considerable vogue in England from about 1745 to 1770 and were embossed and chased profusely with rococo motifs; but unusually free as the ornamentation of this Philadelphia kettle is, it in no way approaches the often fantastic

90

style adopted by some of the French Huguenot craftsmen and their English contemporaries working in London during the 18th century.

In its shape and many of the details, the kettle by Joseph Richardson shows a strong relationship to one by William Grundy, bearing the London hall-marks for 1753-4, now in the Victoria and Albert Museum. It has a similar handle with scrolls connecting it with the hinges and a similar domed cover and large knob, and there is an equally noticeable resemblance in the stand. On the other hand, there are interesting variations in the decoration particularly in the heavy spout and the arrangement of the chased scrolls and flowers to form a cartouche for the engraved coat of arms.

In the stand there is a more direct English influence in the interpretation of the rococo motifs. This is evident in the elaborate fringe between the legs and the scroll supports and shell feet, but here Richardson introduced a feature which again indicates his versatility, namely, the delicate tooled work on the ring of the stand and on the bowl of the spirit lamp. The rings of similar English kettle stands are either quite plain or unnecessarily ornate while the lamp is invariably plain.

Cream Jugs

When the English fashionable world first took to tea, it was used as the Chinese drink it, without milk. Apparently it had too strong a tang for the Western taste and milk or cream was added to soften it; and the silversmiths were called upon to add yet another article to the family plate. At that time, the only jug-like vessels familiar to them were the large helmet-shaped ewers which were used at the ceremony of washing hands at table, and the first cream jugs were helmet-shaped. Examples, however, are virtually non-existent; the only one seen by the writer appeared at a sale in London some twenty years ago.

NEW ENGLAND. At the time cream jugs came into general use, the pear shape was predominant; and the silversmiths first produced the sturdy little pear-shaped jugs with the beak-like spout on a molded foot (FIG. 143) which were copied from the early Georgian models. This was the forerunner of the later variations of the same outline that were evolved and popular until superseded by the conical shape on a square plinth of the classic style.

In New England, cream jugs with some few minor differences, followed the English shapes. The earlier plain pear-shaped jug with

91

the low molded foot (FIG. 143) does not seem to have been made by the American silversmiths to any great extent; but there still exist an appreciable number, slightly larger, of this shape on three feet. These, like the English models, have the long wide lip and the rim cut in a series of wavy curves (FIG. 144) similar to the rims of the sauceboats.

This same type of jug was sometimes chased in the rococo manner when the small curious scroll-like legs would be replaced by some more advanced shape, such as those shown in Figure 145, which have the rococo shell ornament at the joint and claw and ball feet.

With the change to the inverted pear-shaped teapots, the cream jugs were also made in that shape, the three cast legs being replaced by a low stem and spreading molded foot. The rim is almost always a plain curve instead of being shaped as before, and is ornamented occasionally with a row of bead-like punches (FIG. 146) to stiffen the metal. New England cream jugs of this type, however, are relatively scarce, which suggests a preference for the plain pear shape on legs.

NEW YORK. As a group, the New York cream jugs were all copies of English models and therefore allied closely to those of New England. At the same time, some of the surviving examples show variations largely peculiar to New York. As with New England, examples of the earlier small pear shape of the chubby type with applied lip and molded foot (as in FIG. 143) are rare; but there are more of this shape raised on three legs (FIG. 147).

The cast handles and legs of the New York pear-shaped jugs with the wavy rim were finely modeled and tooled, as is shown in the one illustrated in Figure 148. This has the double scroll handle and the shell ornament at the joint of the leg and shell feet and, when compared with similar New England jugs, it will be noticed that the long lip rises above the level of the handle. The latter feature occurs also in the inverted pear shape in some of which the lip was made almost vertical, as in Figure 149.

PENNSYLVANIA. While teapots made by the silversmiths in Philadelphia or elsewhere in Pennsylvania are scarce dating before the Revolution, both cream jugs and sugar bowls are relatively numerous. The cream jugs followed the styles prevailing in New England and New York. Local features are, however, noticeable in the inverted pear shape which is often more bulbous (FIGS. 150 and

151), and the shaping of the rim varies from the usual curves and notches to a series of small scallop shapes (compare the rim of FIG. 151). Most of the known examples are plain, but there is one by Abraham Dubois (c. 1777) in the Philadelphia Museum of Art which is decorated with floral motifs in the rococo style (FIG. 151).

Sugar Bowls

NEW ENGLAND. Like other articles connected with tea drinking, New England sugar bowls were direct copies of the English patterns and developed similar changes during the 18th century. Some of the earlier bowls were fitted with a cover and their resemblance to the small Chinese porcelain bowls with covers indicates their origin. The bowl itself was quite plain with a low molded foot, and the cover a low dome with a stout ring applied to serve as a handle, or the cover could be inverted, when the ring served as a foot and the cover as a stand for the bowl or as a separate dish (FIG. 152).

Later, in keeping with the change in the shapes of teapots and coffee-pots, the plain hemispherical bowl gave place to the inverted pear shape. This type seems to have remained popular in New England until the late 18th century and several by Paul Revere (1735-1818) are now in different collections; and there are examples ornamented on the bowl and cover with boldly embossed and chased scrolls, festoons of flowers and fruit in the rococo style (FIG. 153).

Most of the sugar bowls had the simple molded foot, but a few made in New England were raised on three short scroll legs with hoof feet (FIG. 154) common with sauceboats and cream jugs. And though rare, examples were also made octagonal with a plain domical cover shaped to follow the lines of the bowl.

NEW YORK. As might be expected in view of the greater popularity of the inverted pear shape in New York, many covered sugar bowls of that shape bear the marks of New York silversmiths. The bowls of the earlier rococo period retained the rather high cover with the ring handle which, as mentioned above, serves as a foot when the cover is inverted—this has been called a "foot-handle," a combination aptly describing it.

Somewhat later, the cover was inset and the foot-handle was then generally replaced by an ornamental finial knob. A few of the known examples are chased in the rococo manner both on the body and cover

93

(FIG. 155), and some of the designs suggest a silversmith's own more poetic concept rather than the formal rococo forms. But at no time did the New York silversmiths indulge in the profuse ornamentation which is typical of the English inverted pear-shaped bowls, and which is specially noticeable in English bowls that are part of a set with two equally ornate tea caddies. Though of little real use today, an appreciable number of these sets in their original silver-mounted cases have been preserved to the present time.

PENNSYLVANIA. Hemispherical sugar bowls with the domical cover and ring foot-handle by Philadelphia silversmiths are known, but the larger number are the inverted pear shape with the high domical cover and finial. Some of these bowls and other pieces for the tea table have a feature associated with Philadelphia and repeated to some extent later by the Baltimore and other Southern silversmiths; it is a shallow pierced plinth under the foot, and a similarly pierced band or gallery frequently applied to a beaded edge round the rim as in Figure 156.

There is some question as to the exact origin of this pierced ornament. The source which suggests itself is the pierced band used for the plinths of old Sheffield plate tea urns of about 1770. Or it may have been an adaptation from the plainer pierced designs found in some contemporary English silverwork. But even so, the general arrangement of the piercing recalls the early Roman colonnades such as the columns and arches of the Colosseum, suggesting a classic origin.

Salvers and Trays

Today the names "salver" and "tray" are largely interchangeable, but, strictly speaking, they have different meanings: Salver is derived from the Spanish *salvar*—meaning literally tasting the food or drink before serving it. Later the word came to denote a tray used by a servant when presenting anything to a superior. In more modern times, smaller ones are usually known as card trays or waiters, but the name "salver" is still applied to the larger ones.

"Tray" was probably adopted in its present sense to distinguish it from the smaller salver when tea services became popular in the time of George III. The meaning, now almost obsolete, of "tray" is a long trough-like shallow basket made of strips of wood and used in gardens, still referred to in English country districts as a "trug" from the Anglo-Saxon *treg*.

94

NEW ENGLAND. Even if they must be counted with the rarities, there are sufficient American salvers in the rococo style to show that the various modified English patterns were copied. The circular salver with the rococo molding and an applied ornament was apparently more generally favored in New England, but the octagonal form with the curved and angular molding was also made.

Three of the octagonal type on four small feet (FIG. 157) by Jacob Hurd were in the Boston exhibition of 1911. One of these, lent by William S. Townsend, is 11¾ inches in diameter and a pair, lent by Hollis French, 6¼ inches. Each has the shaped border of the type often called "Chippendale," probably from the fact that small tables of that period were similarly shaped and molded. The border is formed of four convex and four shorter concave sections joined by angles and is one of the styles introduced into England by the Huguenot silversmiths.

English salvers of this type are more often plain, apart from an engraved coat of arms, but each of the New England examples has a finely engraved band following the shape of the border in addition to a coat of arms.

Even when they used the ornate borders, the New England silversmiths were obviously influenced by the traditional preference for simplicity; for in adapting various rococo forms, they avoided at the same time the often florid decorations of the English prototypes. The plain molding bordered with unobtrusive scrolls and shell forms (FIG. 158) was used by Paul Revere and may have been developed by him; two salvers by Revere each about 13 inches in diameter with this border were in the exhibition at Yale University in 1939.

Another simple border was formed by a pair of plain scrolls and arranged as what is known as the double cyma (〰) and each pair joined by a shell ornament; an excellent example by Samuel Edwards (1705-62) is in the Museum of Fine Arts, Boston.

With the large oval tray (FIG. 159) Revere made another effective adaptation of the rococo ornament. Instead of the continuous oval curve, it has a scalloped (technically known as "multifoil") border with a shell applied to each of the curves, but here again the desire for simple lines is evident.

This tray which is now in the Mabel Brady Garvan Collection was exhibited at Boston in 1911 and is illustrated in the catalogue with many other examples of Revere's work. It was made in 1797 for Elias Hasket Derby of Salem, the famous merchant whose ship, the *Grand Turk,* in 1786, made the first trading voyage to Canton, China.

95

NEW YORK. As would be natural, the salvers in the rococo style by the New York silversmiths are, in the main, similar to those of New England. When existing examples are compared, however, it is clear that some of the features can be regarded as peculiar to New York.

No example of the octagonal type as illustrated in Figure 157 is known bearing a New York maker's mark, but a fair number of circular salvers are in various collections. One by Simeon Soumaine (1685-1750) in the Metropolitan Museum of Art has a plain molded border with twelve small incurves to vary the outline.

New York silversmiths adopted the scroll and shell border and sometimes added a leaf form, but the indications are that the gadrooned border was more popular. A pair of salvers with the scroll, shell and leaf by Samuel Tingley (*c.* 1767) were in the exhibition at the Museum of the City of New York, 1937-8, and are illustrated in the catalogue. In other instances, the scrolls were slightly larger and more definite with a single shell applied at fairly wide intervals round the edge. There is one by Myer Myers (1723-95) in the Museum of Fine Arts, Boston, which is bordered with eighteen scrolls in series of three and a shell between each series; this salver has a somewhat unusual feature—the middle scroll of each three has two small projecting "tails."

New York salvers with the gadrooned border varied little from the style shown in Figure 160, one of a pair on ball and claw feet by John Le Roux (*c.* 1723), which appeared at an auction sale in 1931. A similar pair by Myer Myers were found in England and are in the collection of Victor A. Watson of London.

Occasionally a New York silversmith would introduce a variation to the gadrooned border, replacing the inside plain molding by one of gadroon interrupted at intervals by a small cinquefoil. This style seems to be peculiar to New York and is illustrated in the Museum of the City of New York catalogue of 1937-8 by a 15-inch salver by John Heath (*c.* 1761) and one of 7¾ inches diameter by Andrew Underhill (*c.* 1780).

PENNSYLVANIA. Both the scroll and shell ornaments and the gadroon were applied to Philadelphia salvers and the general styles of the known examples follow those of New York. Earlier men, such as Joseph Richardson, sometimes used the plain molding without any ornament on the rim or a modified rococo ornamental border. One salver by Joseph Richardson (1711-84) in the Mabel Brady

Garvan Collection, Yale University, has a singularly attractive adaptation: two small scrolls joined in the center by a larger C-scroll form, as it were, a section; this combination is repeated round the rim and each section is joined by a small fan-like shell which is rounded off at the top. All these ornaments are strongly modeled and have the effect of a series of continuing reversed curves giving a distinctive shape to the circular salver.

Those with the gadroon have the plain molding, usually shaped as in Figure 161. As with all salvers of this type, the applied border has two members, one plain and the other gadrooned; in the example illustrated, which was made by Joseph and Nathaniel Richardson (c. 1785), small shell ornaments are introduced and it has three well-modeled legs with claw and ball feet.

HISTORICAL SOCIETY OF PENNSYLVANIA

The conclusion of this chapter is intentionally in supplementary form because it deals with a group of American silver which though of outstanding importance is by no means widely known.

This group, which is owned by the Historical Society of Pennsylvania, comprises six examples of Philadelphia silverwork ornamented in the more extravagant rococo style. Three of the pieces—a small salver by Philip Syng, Jr., and a coffee-pot and covered sugar bowl by Joseph Richardson, Sr.—were unquestionably made to order as each is engraved, *Wedding silver of Sara Shoemaker married to Edward Penington, Nov. 26, 1754;* the others are a globular teapot and a cream jug by Joseph Richardson, Sr., and a covered sugar bowl by his son, Joseph (PLATES XII-XV).

At first sight they resemble the English rococo, but the ornamentation shows differences in the smaller motifs, and originality in the arrangement. The treatment of all the pieces, except the cream jug, reflects something of the Irish rococo decoration combined with certain ornaments borrowed from the Anglo-French silversmiths and their English contemporaries.

If, for instance, the salver by Philip Syng is analyzed, the relationship to the Irish work is evident: It has the deep undulating molding with an applied scroll, shell and foliated border, a broad band chased with C-scrolls interspersed with flowers round the outer part of the tray, an escutcheon in the center, and it has scroll feet, all of which features are found in Irish salvers. A larger salver showing similar features, including the scroll legs, which was made in Dublin about

97

1750-60 is illustrated in Jackson's book on English plate *(Figure 329)*.

With the coffee-pot and sugar bowl of Sara Shoemaker's wedding silver, the finial is in the form of a flower and leaf on a short stem. This finial was doubtless copied from some piece by De Lamerie or one of his contemporaries, as a similar ornament is found on the lids of the more ornate English tea caddies and other objects of the rococo period. A silver-gilt coffee jug by De Lamerie with a finial in the form of a five-petaled flower and foliage was sold at the Swaythling sale in 1924 and a pair of caddies with similar finials by Samuel Taylor were formerly in the Hearst Collection.

Further Anglo-French influence is present in the coffee-pot and sugar bowl by Joseph Richardson, Sr., in the boldly chased rose blossoms and others flowers combined with the scrolls below the rim; the striated fringe-like bordering to the scrolls; the scrolls at the base of the cast spout and the shellwork on the body round the joint of the spout; and the ornaments on the foot. The accompanying sugar bowl is embossed and chased with similar forms, but with this there is an Irish feeling in the arrangement of the C-scrolls and flowers which bear a resemblance to the ornamentation of some Irish dish rings (or "potato rings," as they are erroneously called).

Both the teapot by Joseph Richardson, Sr., and the covered sugar bowl by his son, Joseph, are embossed and chased in the more extravagant rococo style, but the interpretation is strongly individualistic: The teapot, which is of the globular shape with a slight taper downward, is ornamented with scrolls, large blossoms and foliage round the shoulder and smaller scrolls and floral forms at the base of the spout. Shellwork is applied to the lower part of the spout and, like the coffee-pot, a wide striated fringe encircles the spout where it joins the body (see PLATES XIII and XV).

In the decoration of the covered sugar bowl by Joseph Richardson, Jr., the traditional C-scrolls are largely replaced by foliated scrolls combined with shellwork and small flowers and the upper part of the domical cover is embossed and chased with large swirling leaves radiating from a finely modeled finial. The small cream jug is simpler and, it must be admitted, less interesting, because the decoration is restricted to somewhat immature scrolled flutings (see PLATE XII).

Another example of Philadelphia silverwork showing a full acceptance of the rococo style of decoration, the kettle by Joseph Richardson, Sr., has been referred to earlier in this chapter and illustrated in Figure 142.

CHAPTER FOUR

The Classic Period
About 1765 to 1825

WE MAY NOT ALWAYS RECOGNIZE OR BE WILLING TO admit it, but the fact remains that all true designs of later eras were based on those of earlier civilizations. For as those of the first half of the 18th century stemmed from China, so those of the second half were inspired by the art of the ancient Greeks and Romans.

After about 1757, by which time various books on the discoveries at Herculaneum and Pompeii had been published, Europe came to acknowledge more fully the beauty of the classic forms; and within a few years the rococo was superseded by the style we refer to as the classic. This radical change appeared in Continental countries some time before it was accepted in England where the rococo was not finally displaced by the classic forms until about 1765.

The period we have titled "The Classic," which covers some sixty years from its inception until about the end of the 18th century, is generally referred to in Britain as the Adam style. This name derives from Robert Adam who was one of four sons of a Scottish architect. Adam spent some years studying ancient architecture in Italy where he became absorbed in all that was classic. Later, he and his brother James established themselves as architects in London where Robert soon became dictator to the world of fashion in architecture and interior decoration.

English silver of this style is labeled by its particular ornamental forms: medallions, festoons of fruit and foliage, the Greek fret meander, rosettes, swags of drapery, pendent husks, rams' heads, lions' heads, winged sphinxes, laurel, lanceolate and acanthus leaves, the anthemion (the honeysuckle ornament), griffins and other details which Adam and other students had seen and sketched from the ancient architecture, vases and articles of silver and bronze discovered in the classic ruins.

In America, the Revolutionary War had caused a hiatus in the development of all the crafts and when the wheels of industry were restarted, the classic designs were in full blossom in Europe. And it is not unreasonable to suppose that the American designers saw in the new forms something that would symbolize the Young Republic; or that they could be adapted to represent what might be largely an "American" style. For though based upon the English and to a lesser extent the French classic models, the American late 18th-century silver does show a marked individuality; and if minor differences are apparent in the work of the several schools of silversmiths, the general style is similar whether of Boston or Baltimore.

In the early part of the 19th century, the classic was merged with the so-called "Empire" designs which were introduced from France. The new style that resulted gained considerable popularity and was adopted widely for furniture; but being less suitable for metal, relatively little American, and probably less English, silverwork of the Empire style was made.

Basically, the Empire designs emerged from those of the French Louis XVI period as a combination of Egyptian, Greek and Roman classic forms. In France, the style developed to an extravagance which, if at times repeated in England, found no acceptance in America. Several prominent English artists, among them John Flaxman, devoted their attention to producing designs for silverwork in the Empire style; but unfortunately, most of these designs when translated into silver suggest that these artists' skill in drawing was in inverse ratio to their understanding of silver as a medium to express their ideas.

French Empire silver is pompous and the English which follows the French designs fairly closely is patently foreign. The American silversmith, however, generally succeeded in toning down both the ostentation and the exotic feeling; though, if the results he achieved were more attractive than those of his English confrères, they were not notable for their beauty nor for the character we associate with American silverwork. But at least his shapes and ornamentation were intelligible, which cannot be said of the French and English counterparts.

DRINKING VESSELS

By this time, silver drinking cups had been superseded by glasses. Tall cups of the standing type, some showing a classic influence in the ovoid-shaped bowls, were used as chalices in churches; beakers and tumblers and two-handled cups were still made although in smaller numbers; but tankards, mugs and canns continued and large pitchers such as would be used for holding beer drawn from the family cask or for serving punch were in fairly general use in the late 18th and early 19th centuries.

Beakers

NEW ENGLAND. Beakers made in New England during the late 18th and early 19th centuries developed no outstanding characteristics. The early plain horn-shape with the slightly flaring lip and molded foot about 5½ inches high was continued but, as a general rule, the beakers were about 3½ inches high with plain flat bottoms; and while the general outline was basically that of the original horn, the straight sides were given a curved outline.

With the straight-sided beakers, a stout reeded band was applied round the rim and the foot, probably to strengthen the sides and at the same time relieve the otherwise extreme plainness of these rather insignificant little vessels. In their efforts to satisfy the demand for curved forms, the New England silversmiths also repeated the inverted bell shape with the low spreading foot which originated in France during the preceding, rococo, period.

NEW YORK. Straight-sided beakers that had been introduced into New York by the Dutch settlers held their place through the 18th and into the early 19th centuries. Those intended for church use retained most of their former height, but others for domestic use were reduced to less than 4 inches. Most of the latter have a somewhat squat appearance, owing to the width being greater in proportion to the height. In some instances, a stout molding was applied round the base and rim, or round the base only, and occasionally the small beakers were decorated with bright-cut engraving.

Incidentally bright-cut consists of zigzag lines and is generally regarded as a classic decoration, but it was known and used on silverwork in England before the Norman Conquest.

PENNSYLVANIA. Beakers are rare among Pennsylvania silver but beaker-shaped cups were made in Philadelphia in the last quarter of the 18th century. A set of twelve were made by Edmund Milne in 1777 for George Washington as camp cups. These are flat-bottomed and almost cylindrical, 3¼ inches high of quite stout silver reinforced by a fairly heavy molding round the rim and base, doubtless to withstand the rough usage they would meet with in a military camp. According to Milne's bill, Washington supplied him with sixteen silver dollars which weighed about 14 ounces, to melt and use for making the beakers or "camp cups," as Milne calls them; the actual charge for the making was £8 8s. ($42) but a small surplus of metal was credited by the silversmith and the net cost was the equivalent of $33.25.

Discussing these cups, Dr. John Marshall Phillips told the writer that he had learned recently that eleven of them were eventually melted and added to other silver for a tea service for George Washington's adopted daughter (Martha Washington's grand-daughter) Nellie Custis, who married George's nephew. This information will probably surprise a number of students of American silver.

Smaller beaker-shaped cups, known as toddy cups, also seem to have enjoyed some popularity and examples appear at intervals when an important collection is dispersed. A pair came into the auction room a few years ago at the sale of the American silver belonging to Herbert Lawton. These are 1¾ inches high and 1⅞ inches in diameter and for that reason of a somewhat squat appearance. They were originally owned by General Nathaniel Greene, who was first in command under Washington, and were used during the Revolutionary War.

Most of these Philadelphia beaker-shaped cups are plain, but they were occasionally decorated with bright-cut and other engraved work of the type introduced during the classic period.

THE SOUTH. Beaker-shaped cups similar in size to those of Philadelphia were made in Maryland, Virginia and other parts of the South. There is a pair of camp cups in the United States Naval Museum which were made by Charles Burnett of Alexandria, Maryland, for George Washington. These are of the same shape and sturdy character as those by Edmund Milne mentioned above and being of a later date may well have been copied from them.

Beakers with more tapering sides, about 3½ inches high, made in the South usually have a reeded band round the rim and base. Others of about the same size, but with slightly convex sides strengthened by a reeded band round the rim and halfway down the body, on a ring foot, were made in Maryland at the beginning of the 19th century. And it might seem that the sturdy cups made by Milne for

102

Washington set a fashion, as almost identical beaker-shaped cups were popular in the South for some years after.

Tumblers

These round-bottomed wine cups were used in England until at least the reign of George III, but while they are known to have been made in America during the late 17th and early 18th centuries, no later examples of the traditional small tumblers (see FIG. 7) have apparently come to light.

There were, however, two pairs of larger ones in the 1921 exhibition at the Philadelphia Museum of Art, to which they were lent by Mrs. George McCall. These are 3½ inches high (approximately twice the size of the early tumblers) and are engraved with flowers and bright-cut bands.

Tankards

NEW ENGLAND. Bulbous-shaped tankards modeled on those which appeared in England in the second half of the 18th century attained some popularity in New York and Philadelphia, but New England remained faithful to the straight-sided tapering shape.

New England tankards of this period tend to be taller, some of them being nearly 12 inches high. The molded rib round the body and the same slightly spreading molded foot, sometimes with the deep convex member, as shown in Figure 101, continued to be used. The handles remained the simple S-scroll, generally with a cast ornamental drop from the hinge on the upper part of the handle, and a plain oval or other shaped disk on the tip.

The covers developed a more definitely domed top and are therefore higher than the flattened dome described in the previous chapter. The thumb-pieces were usually of the scroll type on a long shank such as is illustrated in Figure 102; but the open scroll thumb-piece was also used, sometimes reversed as shown in Figure 101—that is, the thumb-piece of the tankard curves inward toward the cover instead of outward as in Figure 103. A feature with New England tankards of this period is the consistent use of an imposing finial such as a spiral (sometimes called a flame) rising from a baluster, a pine cone, and sometimes a plain baluster.

Apropos the pine cone: This is not infrequently described as a pineapple or as an artichoke; where this style of finial was made

103

more ornamental by the addition of a calyx, as in Figure 101, it has an unquestionable resemblance to either of these fruits, but even so, its ancestor in America was probably the pine cone.

NEW YORK. Change of fashion had little effect on the New York tankards through the 18th century. The generous straight-sided shape which had been adopted in the 17th century resisted successfully all attempts to oust it from favor. During the second half of the century the body became slightly more tapered, the double scroll replaced the more simple S-scroll handle and ornamentation on the handle was restricted to a cast baluster drop, sometimes halfway down the handle (as in FIG. 105) but more often quite short.

After the middle of the century both the bulbous (FIG. 106) and the straight-sided tapered shapes with domed covers were made, but neither attained any great vogue and examples are few. There is one of the bulbous shape by Jacob Gerittse Lansing of Albany, New York (1736-1803), in the Clearwater Collection at the Metropolitan Museum of Art. Like the similar tankards made in Philadelphia, the one by Lansing follows closely the English prototype: It has a molded domical cover and a thumb-piece formed of intersecting bands, a double scroll handle with a rather flat drop on the upper part, and a spreading foot. And it repeats the New York tradition that tankards should be generous, and of heavy metal, for it is 9 inches high and weighs over 41 ounces.

Barrel-shaped tankards which had a short vogue in England during the later 18th and early 19th centuries were made by New York silversmiths, but again examples are scarce. One by Hugh Wishart of New York (*w.* 1784-1816) was in the exhibition at the Philadelphia Museum in 1921, lent by Mrs. George Biddle. This tankard which has a flat lid is less than 6 inches high and has four reeded bands round the body, a form of ornament which supposedly simulated the metal bands round wooden barrels. Unfortunately a short open spout has been added at a later date.

PENNSYLVANIA. Bulbous-shaped tankards became popular in England about 1750 and the shape was adopted by the Philadelphia silversmiths; and though other shapes were made during the late 18th and early 19th centuries, the massive bulbous type retained its popularity.

Judging from existing examples, few variations were made in the shape. It is of interest therefore to refer to a bulbous tankard illustrated by Mr. Bigelow. It has the typical Philadelphia body with the spreading foot and double scroll handle, but the cover is considerably higher and certainly less symmetrical; the lower member of the cover is a deep convex with the usual small member and a high domed top instead of the graceful low dome of the tankard in Figure 107. Moreover, the cast thumb-piece, while of the open type, has a shell-like ornament at the top and there is a band of ovolos round the rim of the cover and the foot.

Mr. Bigelow mentions that the tankard was presented to the First Presbyterian Church of Trenton, New Jersey, in 1857 and though questioning its American origin, suggests that the maker's mark J A in script is possibly that of a Boston silversmith. Since that book was published, we have had the list of marks prepared by Mr. Ensko which records a J A in script as the mark of Joseph Anthony of Philadelphia (*c.* 1783).

Although very few are known, cylindrical tankards ornamented with reeded bands were made in Philadelphia. One by Joseph Lownes (*c.* 1780-*c.* 1816), which was in the exhibition of 1921 when it was lent by Charles P. Humphreys, is slightly less than 5 inches high, has two reeded bands and flat cover similar to the English prototypes.

Another with a cylindrical body and reeded bands by Samuel Williamson of Philadelphia (*c.* 1794) belongs to the First Congregational Church, Deerfield, Massachusetts, and is illustrated in *The Old Silver of American Churches* by the late E. Alfred Jones. This example is over 8 inches high and has a low domed cover with an eagle finial.

THE SOUTH. In view of the late development of Southern silverwork, it is natural that few tankards were made by men working in Maryland and other parts of the South. Any that are known date from the end of the 18th or beginning of the 19th centuries. The shape that seems to have been favored is the straight-sided tapered body about 8 inches high with the domical cover and S-scroll handle. In form they followed the similar New England tankards, but in place of the small molded rib round the body and the molded foot the Maryland silversmiths applied a wide reeded band and a similar band round the base.

In some instances the reeded band round the body was omitted when a narrow one was used round the base. Some of the domical covers have a small finial but judging from available specimens, the finial was more often omitted.

105

Mugs and Canns

NEW ENGLAND. Bulbous-shaped mugs of the type known as canns, which have been referred to in the previous chapter, remained the most popular type through the late 18th and early 19th centuries. This is evident from the large number that have survived bearing the marks of New England silversmiths of that period. They vary slightly in height but otherwise they all follow the same general pattern except in certain rare instances when the body is more definitely pear shape and encircled by a small rib.

At the same time, the bulbous shape did not entirely replace the straight-sided tapering mug similar to those of the early part of the century (see FIGS. 23 and 24), which continued to be made in England especially in the outlying sections. The New England straight-sided mugs of the late 18th century are by no means plentiful but an example does appear now and then. They were invariably flat-bottomed usually without any molding, though the rim was moulded; the body was either plain or had two bands of reeding with a stout handle generally of the double scroll shape.

NEW YORK. As in New England, the bulbous cann was the more common type of small cup in New York during the late 18th and early 19th centuries, but again the straight-sided type was also made and a number of them are still preserved in different collections. Such examples of the latter as are known show features in every way similar to those of New England including the reeded bands round the body. But while this similarity exists the New York mugs are generally smaller, the average height being 3 inches while that of the New England mugs is about 4 inches.

Another type of New York mug, examples of which are available occasionally, has a cover and is known as an ale cann. One came up at an auction sale a few years ago. This has a plain cylindrical body about 5 inches high, with a double scroll handle and spreading foot. The cover is similar to that of an earlier flat-top tankard except that it has a large finial knob.

PENNSYLVANIA. Canns made by the Philadelphia silversmiths are to all intents facsimiles of those by other schools; but if a representative group of American canns is studied, two small special features may be found in some of the Philadelphia examples: one is fairly consistent, namely, the pronounced curl to the scroll of the leaf on the shoulder of the handle; the other less consistent feature is in the double scroll handle.

With most double scroll handles of canns the joint of the upper and lower (smaller) scroll is clearly visible (see FIG. 58), but with some made in Philadelphia the joint was mitered and the line of the handle is unbroken. An analogy is the joint of a picture frame, the two miters of which ensure a perfect right angle and virtually conceal the joint.

Late 18th century Philadelphia cylindrical mugs were either plain with a molded rim and base or had the two reeded bands round the body. They were usually about 4½ inches high and made of heavy metal, some of the known examples weighing nearly 16 ounces.

Ale canns with covers, similar to those of New York, were also made by Philadelphia silversmiths. One 4¾ inches high by Joseph Lownes has a slightly tapering body with two reeded bands, a simple loop handle and flat cover with a pierced thumb-piece and is, to all intents, a miniature tankard.

THE SOUTH. Mugs and canns made in the South followed the shapes and general styles prevailing in other parts of America during the late 18th and early 19th centuries. The first bulbous-shaped canns were somewhat smaller, about 4½ inches high, but in the early years of the 19th century the size increased to about 5½ inches high.

Influenced by those of Philadelphia, the Southern tapering cylindrical mugs were either plain or decorated with two or three reeded bands round the body; as a rule the handle was the sturdy double scroll shape, but the simple strap form was used by some silversmiths. Like the bulbous cann, the cylindrical mugs vary in height from about 4 inches to 5½ inches, the taller mostly dating from the early 19th century.

Punch Bowls

NEW ENGLAND. Only one New England punch bowl showing classic influence is known and, like others already referred to, this has historic associations. It was made by Paul Revere and has the sloping sides and plain ring foot of the Chinese porcelain bowls, from which it was probably copied. The classic influence, while not pronounced, is present in a narrow bright-cut band on both the outside and inside of the rim, a style of ornament which would date the bowl after the Revolution if the date were in question.

107

But its age and history are established by the inscription which records that the bowl was presented to General William Shepard by the Militia of Springfield in recognition of his quelling Shay's Rebellion at Springfield Arsenal in 1787. The bowl is now in the Mabel Brady Garvan Collection and was exhibited at Yale University in 1939.

NEW YORK. Bowls of a size suitable for a large "brew" of punch, bearing the marks of New York silversmiths working during the classic period, are as rare as those dating before that time. One by Ephraim Brasher (c. 1786-1805), now in the Museum of the City of New York, is 9¾ inches in diameter and like the bowl made by Paul Revere in 1787 follows the general shape of the Chinese porcelain bowls; and again like the Revere bowl, it is decorated with a band of bright-cut engraving round the rim (FIG. 162).

Another plain bowl on a molded foot, also by Brasher, is in the Clearwater Collection at the Metropolitan Museum of Art. This, however, is less than 8 inches in diameter, a size which suggests it was intended for a smaller brew. In the catalogue of the Clearwater Collection, reference is made to the tradition that this bowl formerly belonged to Commodore Isaac Hull who commanded the *Constitution* in the War of 1812.

Pitchers

In Britain, a deep vessel with a handle and pouring lip is generally referred to as a "jug," but in the United States the older name, "pitcher," is still retained. The latter is a first cousin to beaker for it is likely that both originated from the Old English word *biker* (a jar).

The ancestry of the word "jug," however, is doubtful. It was used in the 16th century and one etymologist suggests that in earlier times, the name Jug was a pet form of Joan or Jane. Webster also mentions this use of the word as applied formerly to a woman, a servant or a mistress—in early times a soldier's wench was called a jug or jugge. And it is possible that as the great drinking vessel of polished leather known as a black-jack was intended for Jack, a smaller one for Jack's Joan or Jane came to be known as a jug.

NEW ENGLAND. Large pitchers, with or without covers, to hold water or beer were made in America during the late 18th and early 19th centuries though apparently in no large number. They vary both in shape and size and were quite frequently used as presentation or commemorative pieces.

One shape which seems to have been favored in New England was that of a barrel with two reeded bands round the body and one round the bottom. An interesting presentation pitcher of this type by William Moulton (1772-1861) is in the Boston Museum of Fine Arts; it is slightly over 10 inches high with a hinged domical lid and wide spout fitted with a strainer. One side is engraved with the inscription, *To Mr. Isaac Harris For his intrepid and successful exertions on the roof of the Old South Church when on fire December 29th 1810* . . . and on the other side is a picture of the actual fire.

A similar barrel-shaped covered pitcher, but with a scrolled thumb-piece, marked "D. Moseley" in script, in the Mabel Brady Garvan Collection, is engraved, *Henry Barney Smith,* and may well have been presented to him to commemorate his graduating from Harvard College in 1809.

Another type was made in New England with a plain bulbous-shaped body tapering both upward to the rim and downward to a flat bottom; both the rim and base were molded and the handle was of the hollow type with a pronounced downward taper and a plain disk applied to the end. The example illustrated (FIG. 163) is inscribed, *In remembrance of the Family Estate in Federal Street,* and the monogram PR. It is 7½ inches high and was formerly in the collection of Herbert Lawton.

NEW YORK. Pitchers of the shape shown in Figure 163 were also made in New York; one by John and Peter Targee (c. 1798-1820) being sold at auction in 1946. This example has a high domical cover with an angular strap handle and is considerably larger than the one made in Boston.

One of the more conventional pitchers adopted by the New York silversmiths from a Chinese vase had a pear-shaped body and deep neck about 9 inches high often with gadrooning round the rim, a flat bottom and a quite simple S-shaped handle. One of these with historical associations was exhibited at the Museum of the City of New York in 1937-8. It was made by William Thomson (*w.* 1810-31) and is inscribed, *To Capt. Sam C. Reid from his fellow Citizens of New York in testimony of his gallant defence of the Private Armed Brig. General Armstrong at Fayal 26th Sept. 1814;* the other side of the pitcher is engraved with a pictorial map of naval operations.

Pitchers seem to have been presented as gifts of appreciation as well as to commemorate some event, as is shown by a pair by Hugh Wishart (*w.* 1784-1816), which are inscribed, *The Heirs of William Irving to John Thomson, Esq., the friend of their father and executor of his estate, 1793.*

PENNSYLVANIA. Plain pear-shaped pitchers with the deep neck and double scroll handle were made by the Philadelphia silversmiths, and others were influenced by English classic or Empire forms.

Those pitchers which were obviously inspired by the English Adam designs had the conical body and long concave neck copied from the classic vases and a rim with a wide lip of the type known as helmet shape. The joint of the upper and lower sections was masked with a molding, generally a simple beaded band which is repeated round the rim and foot.

There is a like classic influence in the shapes of the pitchers developed from the French Empire style; but in place of the former plain outline various ornamental forms are introduced: Handles were made in the form of a dragon or a serpent, plinths raised on four animal paw feet and the body decorated with wreaths of vine and acanthus leaves, anthemion and garlands enclosing an eagle, a ram's head or other symbol.

During the last few years of the 18th and the early part of the 19th centuries, there was a considerable vogue in England for various types of pottery pitchers mounted with a Sheffield plate rim and hinged lid, or rim only. In view of the popularity of Sheffield plate in America at that time, some of these jugs were doubtless imported from England, and perhaps similar jugs were fitted with silver mounts by American silversmiths. But that any appreciable number of pottery jugs were mounted in America appears very unlikely, though the writer did once see an English small stoneware jug decorated with figures in relief with a silver rim and hinged cover bearing the mark of a Philadelphia silversmith.

THE SOUTH. The Maryland silversmiths seem to have retained an affection for the pear-shaped pitcher with the deep neck. As a general rule these pitchers were ornamented with the reeded bands round the neck, the body and the foot, but others were fluted round the lower part as well as having the reeded bands on the body above the fluting.

Some were fitted with a domical cover, but without a finial, and such a pitcher usually had a thumb-piece. The handles were stoutly made either of the double scroll shape or in a somewhat curious

110

form which seems to be largely peculiar to Maryland. It is formed of an angular section which is the actual grip joined to the pitcher at the top by a single scroll and continuing below in the form of a double scroll—actually a combination of something from the rococo double scroll with the angular handle used with some cream jugs of the early 19th century.

OTHER DOMESTIC SILVER

Saltcellars

NEW ENGLAND. None of the pierced or other rather fancy saltcellars of the English classic period found favor in New England or elsewhere in America. The boat shape with two loop handles on a spreading foot as illustrated in Figure 164 was made in New England, but the rarity of examples suggests that it was not widely popular.

Most of the New England saltcellars made in the late 18th century were the circular bowl on three feet which were introduced during the rococo period and which are dealt with in the preceding chapter. They are, however, by no means plentiful and it is seldom that a pair or even a single one comes on offer.

NEW YORK. Saltcellars of this period by New York silversmiths are similarly scarce. The style with the blue glass liner was made, though existing examples are so few that it is highly probable they were made to order rather than having been in general use.

Some experimental novelties appeared during the early 19th century, but none of these contributed anything to American silverwork; as for instance, a type with a shallow circular bowl on a spreading trumpet foot ornamented with foliage, specimens of which occasionally find their way to the auction room. This particular "design" might well have been copied from some English 16th century font-shaped cup.

PENNSYLVANIA. As Philadelphia was the social center during the early years of the Young Republic, it is natural to expect that a larger number of saltcellars would be produced there at that time. But this does not seem to have happened, for existing examples are no more plentiful than those made by other groups of American silversmiths. Moreover, despite the acceptance of the classic forms with other articles, the small round saltcellars on three feet remained popular.

111

THE SOUTH. Various styles of saltcellars were made in Baltimore and other Southern centers during the classic period. The boat shape with loop handles similar to the New England example illustrated in Figure 164 was favored to an extent, and there is a pair evolved from this shape by Samuel Kirk of Baltimore (1792-1872) in the Metropolitan Museum of Art which are sufficiently individual to suggest the design was entirely local. The bowl is plain and fitted in a gadrooned rim supported by a frame on four silver legs of an architectural character, joined together at the bottom by shaped braces reminiscent of the flat understretchers of some late 17th-century tables.

Circular saltcellars were sometimes made in sets of four. As a rule the bowls were fairly plain, but some were ornamented in the exuberant rococo style found in English saltcellars. This form or ornamentation was particularly popular in Baltimore during the early 19th century and is illustrated by a pair of saltcellars by Andrew E. Warner (1786-1870) in the Clearwater Collection at the Metropolitan Museum of Art.

These have the usual shallow circular bowl but the rim has a decided flare and is ribbed and scalloped to suggest shell work. The bowl is boldly embossed with flowers and leaves on a somewhat roughly matted ground and the short legs have a shell above and hoof feet. Actually they resemble the now rare English saltcellars of pierced rococo work fitted with a glass liner, which date from about 1765.

Sauceboats

NEW ENGLAND. During the classic period in England, the sauceboat with the long lip was replaced by the small covered tureen. These English sauce tureens were designed after the shape of the classic vase and have two loop handles and a spreading foot on a square plinth. There is no indication, however, that the tureens were accepted in America where the less formal sauceboat on three legs remained popular. The New England late 18th-century sauceboats were in every way similar to those described and illustrated in the preceding chapter.

NEW YORK. There was a like absence of classic influence in the New York sauceboats dating after the Revolution; and as in New England, the type introduced during the rococo period continued to be made.

112

PENNSYLVANIA. Most of the Philadelphia sauceboats of the classic period were the long-lipped type on three legs; but others were made in which rococo elements were combined with the classic, as the one shown in Figure 165. This has the boat-shaped body with the shorter lip, and the rococo influence is evident in the gadrooned bands round the rim and foot, while the suggestion of a plinth resembles that of the English classic sauce tureens. The handle is formed as two distinct scrolls, the larger joined to a smaller one fastened to the body.

THE SOUTH. Maryland and other groups of silversmiths in the South repeated the boat-shaped sauceboats with either the plain shaped rim (see FIG. 115) or the gadrooned rim. The legs were finely modeled and cast with the usual shell form where they join to the body, and hoof feet, though the foot was sometimes a plain disk. The handles are, as a rule, of the double scroll shape, but the Philadelphia handle shown in Figure 165 was sometimes used.

Casters

NEW ENGLAND. None of the various insignificant tawdry little casters with pierced sides and glass liners of the English classic period attracted any notice in America; and though the shape based on the classic urn was made, the larger number of American late 18th-century casters were the inverted pear shape. The latter also remained popular in England despite efforts to introduce the fanciful designs of Robert Adam.

New England inverted pear-shaped casters of this period had pierced tops similar to that shown in Figure 119. The plain type with the rounded bottom (see FIG. 118) which had been popular before the Revolution was also continued, but there is no evidence that the urn-shaped caster was accepted in New England.

NEW YORK. Casters with the conical body and concave neck, which had a considerable vogue in England in the last decade of the 18th century, were made in New York. However, while similar in form, the New York pieces developed certain minor differences: The English casters of this type had a much taller concave neck and top, and the foot, instead of having the circular molded base as in the New York example illustrated (FIG. 166), was raised on a square plinth.

113

Another style of late 18th-century New York caster was the plain pear shape in two sections with the joint masked by a molding. These were relatively simple with a domical top pierced with concentric circles of small holes in place of the more elaborately pierced panels of the tall tops.

PENNSYLVANIA AND THE SOUTH. Pear-shaped casters retained their popularity in Philadelphia after the Revolution, though examples are rare. It is possible other types will come to light as time goes on and some of these will tell us whether the classic urn shape with the square plinth was also made.

And there is an absence of evidence to show whether the classic styles of casters were made in the South.

Candlesticks

With the coming of the classic vogue, baluster candlesticks in England were superseded by various types with columnar shafts inspired by ancient architecture and often ornamented with festoons, rams' and lions' heads, bands of laurel leaves and similar classic forms. None of these was repeated by American silversmiths though there are American candlesticks of the late 18th century which indicate a classic influence, even if their number is all too few.

NEW ENGLAND. No candlestick of the columnar or other type, popular in Europe during the classic period of the late 18th century, bearing the mark of a New England silversmith has so far come to light.

NEW YORK. One of a pair of columnar candlesticks made by Isaac Hutton of Albany (1767-1855) is illustrated in Figure 167. These are interesting for several reasons: Instead of the ambitious shaft in the form of a Corinthian column and capital which was popular in England, Hutton used the simpler Doric column; and the care with which he reproduced the proportions is evident from the measurements of the candlesticks; for example, the height of the fluted shaft is slightly more than four times its diameter at the base which accords with ancient architecture; and there is a careful observance of such details as the upward tapering of the shaft, and the shape of the capital.

A pair of New York candlesticks which came to the writer's notice some years ago (FIG. 168) were made by Joel Sayre (1778-1818). They

114

are of interest not so much for their artistic qualities as for their similarity to a typical Sheffield plate pattern of the early 19th century. Most of the various English columnar and other styles of candlesticks of the late 18th and early 19th centuries were made in Sheffield plate and these were as handsome as, yet less costly than, their solid silver counterparts.

Obviously, in view of the number required for lighting a large house, it would be more economical to use Sheffield plate candlesticks; and there is little doubt that an appreciable number of these were imported to America during the early days of the Republic; and many have been preserved across the years to the present day. Frederick Bradbury in his book on Sheffield plate refers to a columnar candlestick reproduced from one bought in America in 1777, which was brought to Sheffield about fifty years ago by a descendant of the original purchaser.

By the second decade of the 19th century, candlesticks began to show that debasement in design which resulted from the futile efforts to combine rococo and classic motifs. But these and other "novelties" are of small importance either from an artistic point of view or as specimens of silverwork.

PENNSYLVANIA AND THE SOUTH. From the almost entire absence of any bearing the marks of silversmiths working in Philadelphia or the Southern States during the classic period, we can only assume that candlesticks of silver or Sheffield plate were imported. Large rooms for important social gatherings were lighted by dozens of candles in the magnificent crystal chandeliers, but, as one account of the time puts it, "Four candles on the table make the room luminous and Splendid" at an informal dinner.

Teapots and Tea Services

Inverted pear-shaped teapots continued to be made both in England and America after the classic designs had been introduced, but by the last quarter of the 18th century, they gave place to the more fashionable straight-sided style which marks the classic period. Actually there is little that is classic in these teapots, apart from the engraved decoration. They first appeared in England about 1780 and the various shapes were evolved probably from the small cylindrical or drum shape copied from teapots imported from the East. While the cylindrical type was made in England, there are considerably more bearing

115

the marks of different American silversmiths, particularly those of Philadelphia.

These forerunners of the more sophisticated straight-sided teapots are all much alike. Most of them are quite plain except for an occasional engraved design on the shoulder and a beaded band round the edge of the shoulder and above the base molding. The covers are inset and either flat or slightly domed as in the one illustrated (FIG. 169) and the spout is invariably a tapering tube extending above the level of the rim.

None of the various straight-sided teapots offered any great difficulty to a skilled craftsman, nor did they take as long to make as the pear-shaped and globular pots. The last two had to be raised by patient hammerwork from stout sheet metal and then planished, but the straight-sided styles were of quite thin silver shaped to the desired outline and the two ends soldered together, after which the flat bottom was soldered on.

NEW ENGLAND. While accepting the straight-sided teapots, New England apparently refused to consider the vase shape or urn shape, as it is also called, with the tall concave cover which is rather like the outline of a spool (see FIG. 174); but sugar urns of this shape were made by New England silversmiths who doubtless copied them from English models. It is evident, too, that the straight tapering tubular spout persisted in New England even after the swan-neck spout was adopted. The latter was used, but not to the same extent as in New York and Philadelphia.

Though the small cylindrical teapot (see FIG. 169) was made in New England the scarcity of surviving examples suggests that the shape was not generally popular.

Most of the New England teapots of the classic period are oval in plan, but distinction was added to the simple oval by shaping the sides; and the various shapes are a tribute to the skill and versatility of the different silversmiths.

One of the several graceful outlines was achieved by a series of concave flutes of equal width round the entire body of the teapot; in other instances, the flutes were restricted to each end of the oval thus forming a serpentine shape. These teapots were made with either flat or low domical covers which had wood knobs fastened by a small silver bolt and thumbscrew; the thumbscrew to allow the knob to be detached when cleaning.

Sometimes the plain oval outline was retained and the straight sides

116

given a slight convex curve or the body was made to taper downward; with these, the flat shoulder was replaced by a concave and, as a rule, a domical inset cover, though the domed cover with a flush hinge was also used.

As all the teapots of this period had flat bottoms, they were accompanied usually by a small tray or stand on feet to prevent the heat marring the table top. Some of them still have their original stands, but in many instances the two pieces have become separated. At the same time, flat-bottom teapots were, to their disadvantage, fitted with ball feet instead of being supplied with the small stand.

Whether Paul Revere himself made all the splendid silverwork produced in his shop or whether, like his Anglo-French namesake, Paul De Lamerie, he was gifted with the ability to select clever journeymen does not affect the fact that some of the finest teapots and tea services in the classic style bear the magic stamp REVERE (PLATE XI).

One service which was exhibited at the Museum of Fine Arts, Boston, in 1911 and which belongs to that museum comprises an oval teapot of the style with the slightly tapering body and a small tray on four feet, a conical or as it is called, helmet-shaped, cream jug on a circular foot with a square plinth, and a vase-shaped sugar bowl with a high cover of the spool type which finishes in a small dome surmounted by a finial; each piece is engraved with a wide bright-cut band round the rim. This service was presented to Edmund Hartt, who was responsible for the building of the frigate *Boston,* launched in 1799.

A superb fluted service by Revere shown at, and illustrated in the catalogue of, the same exhibition, consists of a teapot and stand, a vase-shaped sugar bowl and cover and a vase-shaped urn fitted with a spigot. The urn, which is 18 inches high, has two loop handles and both it and the sugar bowl have the classic spool-shaped cover and square plinth. The stand is shaped to follow the fluted outline of the teapot which has the tapered tubular spout and an unusually high wood handle with a prominent projection on the top which is a hang-over of the early thumb-piece. It is natural to assume that these three pieces were formerly accompanied by a creamer, which has in the years been separated from its companions.

Another plainer urn (FIG. 170) by this famous New England silversmith, belonging to the Massachusetts Historical Society, bears the inscription: *To Perpeutate The Gallant defence Made by Cpa*^{t}*. Gamaliel Bradford in the Ship Industry on the 8th July 1800 when Attacked by four French Privateers* . . .

117

Tea urns more or less replaced silver teakettles toward the end of the 18th century. They were generally intended to hold hot water for refilling the teapot, but at large gatherings were sometimes filled with properly made strained tea which was drawn off into the cups through the spigot. Most of the urns were fitted with a socket fixed in the center of the inside in which a fairly large round piece of hot iron was placed to keep the heat in the contents; others were made to take a spirit lamp underneath.

NEW YORK. In view of the English origin of the basic forms of all the straight-sided teapots, there is naturally a close resemblance between those made in different parts of America; but there are certain features which to a greater or lesser extent distinguish the teapots by the various groups of silversmiths.

Several such features are observable in the New York teapots of this period, namely: A prevalence of the concave shoulder, the domical and the bell-shaped cover, the urn finial invariably of silver, absence of fluted sides and the designs of the engraved decoration.

Some of the New York teapots follow the English prototypes more closely, as for example one by William Gilbert (*w.* 1772) which we last saw at the sale of some of the Garvan Collection in 1931. This teapot is plain oval engraved with narrow bright-cut bands round the top and bottom and engraved decoration on the tubular spout. The shoulder is flat and the lid rises in a graceful curve to a low dome with a pineapple finial.

Judging from the larger number with the concave shoulder, it would seem that this was preferred to the flat style. And there is one by J. Schanck (*c.* 1792) which illustrates this and other features mentioned above. It has the plain oval shape with the concave shoulder and high bell-shaped cover with a silver urn finial, the body is ornamented with the horizontal bordering of bright-cut and an engraved shield flanked by floral festoons on each side with beading round the rim and the bottom. This teapot is in the Clearwater Collection at the Metropolitan Museum of Art.

Engraved shields and medallions were intended for the monogram or arms of the owner, following the English custom. The English form, however, was usually a simple square or other geometrical panel without the additional ornamentation.

New York silversmiths adapted the octagonal outline to their straight-sided teapots with particularly graceful results. This shape has a wide section on either side and three narrower ones at each end.

In some cases, the sides are quite flat, but in others the various sections are formed of convex and concave curves thus producing a sinuous curve; it could be described as an oval with deep vertical depressions hammered in at each side near the ends.

At times, the engraved band at the top of the body is wider than the one at the bottom and it is noticeable that the designs of these decorations have no counterpart either in England or New England. One of the designs is a series of trefoil motifs which are reminiscent of the foliated bands above the base molding of early New York tankards and Dutch beakers.

Regarding the origin of the high, rather pointed, cover which we have termed bell-shaped: this in fact has a relation to the classic spool shape which was occasionally used by New York silversmiths in its original form as shown in Figure 171. This teapot with a stand and a covered sugar bowl to match were made by Daniel Van Voorhis who worked first in Philadelphia and later in New York, but we are unable to determine in which city they were made. The three pieces are now in the Clearwater Collection at the Metropolitan Museum of Art.

Tea parties must have been fashionable in New York during the late 18th century, judging from the number of tea services alone, and without taking into account the more numerous "unattached" teapots, cream jugs and sugar bowls that have been preserved.

Some fifteen services were shown at the exhibition held at the Museum of the City of New York, in 1937-8. These, and others in different collections covering the period from about 1785 to 1825, show that in the first part of that time the New York silversmiths tended to rely more upon the English designs with such modifications as were necessary to suit the taste of their patrons or which might occur to the silversmith himself. And for that reason, a tea service will sometimes include one piece of which no prototype is found among English silver.

An example of this may be noted in the exhibition mentioned, namely a service of three pieces by Daniel Coen (*w*. 1787). The teapot is the familiar oval and the cream jug conical or helmet shape, but the sugar bowl, while classical to the extent of having a conical bowl on a foot and square plinth, has a high domical cover with a silver pineapple finial.

It was, however, in their adaptations of the classic forms that some of the New York men expressed their skill and individual ideas. An illustration is a service made by Hugh Wishart (*w*. 1784-1818) which was formerly in the Brenauer Collection. All the pieces are

119

octagonal in plan, paneled in convex and concave curves, described previously as suggesting an oval with two deep depressions at each end. The body of the teapot tapers downward and has the concave shoulder and a cover rising in the classical spool shape with a small domical top and urn finial. In place of the usual flat bottom, it has a plain stout foot to correspond with the classic plinths of the other pieces.

The cream jug, waste bowl and sugar bowl are each on a spreading foot with an octagonal plinth and the cover of the sugar bowl repeats the concave shoulder and spool-shaped cover of the teapot. Each piece is engraved with a band of trefoils round the upper part of the body and the teapot has another similar band round the bottom. The fact that the teapot has a swan-neck spout dates the service in the early 19th century, as at that time the straight tubular spout was being discarded.

Up to the present, American silverwork of the first quarter of the 19th century has aroused no marked enthusiasm; but as time passes, it is not improbable that more attention will be paid by future collectors to the designs developed from the French Empire by American silversmiths.

All the indications point to the Empire style being more popular in New York than elsewhere in America. It is also obvious that where the English Empire pieces were slavishly reproduced from the French conceptions, the New York designs show an adaptive originality. Admittedly, the style departs from the traditional American simplicity of outline in the freer use of applied ornament, but it exhibits none of that formal stiffness which is present in the French and English Empire designs.

Like others that preceded it, the Empire style is labeled by distinctive ornamental features, the principal of which are the lion, the eagle, torch, winged victory, sphinx, lotus, acanthus, scrolls, cornucopia with fruit, and claw feet, some of which in modified forms were adapted in America.

Some of the early 19th-century silversmiths achieved an essentially American style; and it may be that this was the outcome of concessions to the prevailing vogue for ornamentation restrained by the inherent preference for simplicity. The outcome of this "compromise" is apparent in most of the existing pieces which were influenced by the Empire forms, particularly in the tea services (see FIG. 172).

When the several articles of the service illustrated in Figure 172 are compared with the tall teapots and coffee-pots which were fashionable

120

in Philadelphia and the South (see FIGS. 174 and 176) it is obvious that the shapes had the same classic source, even if the sugar bowl is widened and depressed and so loses something of the original conical outline.

This service is an excellent illustration of the skill exercised by American silversmiths in adapting the Empire ornamental forms. Acanthus leaves are applied round the rims and foliated scrolls round the shoulders; the eagle motif appears in the bird claw feet holding a ball and again in the spout of the teapot which finishes in the form of an eagle's head; the legs continue upward as a large leaf and the handles of the sugar bowl and cream jug are formed of scrolls. And the large floral knobs on the covers may quite well have been inspired by the Empire cornucopia.

PENNSYLVANIA. At this period Philadelphia held first place as the commercial and social hub of the United States; for being the cradle of the Republic and the national capital from 1790 to 1800, the city attracted wealth, learning and the best craftsmen in the country. During this time, there was considerable entertaining, with the result that silverwork was in wide demand and the Philadelphia silversmiths enjoyed a period of prosperity.

Evidence of this remains in the large number of teapots and other articles connected with tea drinking, which were made during the late 18th century in Philadelphia and other localities in Pennsylvania.

Straight-sided teapots following the English oval and octagonal shapes were made in Philadelphia, but surviving examples seem to be fewer than in New England and New York. The oval shape, which was sometimes fluted, usually has the low domed cover; and the symmetrical proportions achieved with both the fluted oval and the octagonal shape are a tribute to the men who made them.

Among the writer's notes of the yesterdays is one of an oval fluted straight-sided teapot he saw in the Philadelphia Museum of Art. The note does not record the name of the maker, but it does recall a remarkable example of his work. The teapot is oval in plan with two vertical flutes at either end and two on each side. The resulting shape is slightly convex sides flanked by two narrow vertical planes and serpentine ends. It has a tubular spout which, like the handle sockets, is flattened on two sides to conform with the narrow planes of the body.

This same style of spout was used with the splendid octagonal teapot in Figure 173, the shape of which resembles that of a London

121

teapot in the Victoria and Albert Museum. Bands of foliated forms are engraved round the upper and lower parts of the body; each of the small sides is engraved with flowers and the larger sides with a shield pendent from foliated scrolls. The cover of this teapot is of unusual interest because it does, in fact, show an ingenious adaptation of the spool shape to a straight-sided octagonal teapot.

Of the straight-sided teapots produced in Philadelphia, the cylindrical or drum-shaped, as it is called (FIG. 169), was unquestionably the more popular and is very largely distinctive of that group of silversmiths. The shape is similar to that of the stoneware teapots that came from the Ihing (formerly Yi-hsing) potteries at the end of the 17th century. These were the models for the earliest European teapots which were made first by the Dutch potters and later by Elers in Staffordshire and Dwight at Fulham.

Like the stoneware, the silver pots were made with the tapering tubular spout which was usually straight, though on occasion it was given a slight curve. The Philadelphia teapots of this shape were ornamented on the edge of the shoulder and the base with the small beaded molding which was more consistently used in Philadelphia than elsewhere.

While all these teapots follow the same basic form, certain variations were introduced to the shoulder and the cover. The one illustrated (FIG. 169) rises in a gentle curve which is continued by the low domical cover and the baluster finial with a wooden insulating disk. A similarly curved shoulder was sometimes fitted with a flat cover, or the shoulder would be flat with a collar on the rim and a flat cover.

Occasionally, this style of teapot was ornamented with the pierced gallery round the rim and a similarly pierced plinth, as shown with the sugar basin in Figure 156, but examples of this are not numerous.

One teapot (FIG. 174) which may be regarded as a Philadelphia design was evolved from the shape of a Roman vase. Like the coffeepots of the same style, the teapot shows a relationship to the English coffee-pots and jugs of the classic period which have the conical body and tall concave neck as well as the trumpet-shaped foot; but, as a rule, the English silversmiths omitted the plinth.

When, however, the Philadelphia pots are compared with the English, it is clear that apart from the outline of the body and foot, there is little resemblance between them. With the Philadelphia shape, the long neck disappeared and was replaced by a concave shoulder rising to a rim; but the contour of the English neck is present in the high spool-shaped cover with a small domed top surmounted by a vase-shaped finial—the finial incidentally repeats in miniature the shape of the teapot.

The outline of the cover re-occurs with the foot which is raised on a square plinth and the spout, while longer, resembles the duck-neck shape of the early 18th-century teapots rather than the swan-neck.

Tea services evolved from the classic vase had a considerable vogue in Philadelphia after the Revolution and an appreciable number comprising three or four pieces are today in the possession of descendants of the original owners. The teapot (FIG. 174) with a waste bowl and sugar bowl of the same style are owned by Miss Ella Parsons and some of the services include a coffee-pot, at least 16 inches high. Nor did the Philadelphia silversmiths spare the metal when making these services, as is evident from the fact that one of four pieces will weigh upward of 120 ounces (PLATE X).

One service by John Letelier (c. 1760-70), which was exhibited at the Philadelphia Museum of Art from the collection of Miss Mary Mills, has a cylindrical teapot with a domed cover and the Philadelphia pierced gallery round the rim and the pierced plinth, an inverted pear-shaped sugar bowl with a similar domed cover and pierced ornaments, and a cream jug which was achieved by combining something of the cylindrical with something of the pear shape. The bowl of the jug is straight sided and tapers toward the bottom where it extends in a small rounded shape which repeats the bottom of the inverted pear; it has a molded spreading foot on a pierced plinth similar to that of the sugar bowl (see FIG. 156) and a handle formed of four scrolls.

Philadelphia tea services dating from the end of the 18th and the early years of the 19th centuries were mostly of the straight-sided styles following the English patterns. The various examples now in different collections indicate a preference for the paneled octagonal shape and the outline achieved by fluting. The latter is illustrated in Figure 175, which is a service made by Joseph Lownes (c. 1780-c. 1816) and exhibited at the Philadelphia Museum of Art from the collection of Mrs. W. Logan McCoy.

This service has features which assist in deciding the period in which silverwork was made within the working career of a silversmith. The style of each of the pieces would suggest the late 18th century, but the fact that the teapot has the swan-neck spout indicates that it dates from the early 19th century for, as mentioned earlier, the straight tubular spout was used with straight-sided teapots until about 1800.

And it is plain from other services that the straight-sided flat-bottomed teapots with the swan-neck spout remained popular in

123

Philadelphia well into the 19th century. This can be determined from the fact that some of them are accompanied by one of the oval sugar bowls with light strap handles and a domical cover and a rather squat oval cream jug with a helmet-shaped rim and flat bottom, both of which made their appearance about 1805 and continued fashionable for some years.

At least one Philadelphia large urn fitted with a spigot is known. It was made by Christian Wiltberger (1770-1851) and is in the later classic style. It has a wide fluted conical body, of a more squat character than those made by Paul Revere (see FIG. 170), on a spreading foot supported by a shaped plinth on four ball feet. On each side of the bowl there is a cast lion's head holding a ring handle, a form of ornament used with English urns of the early 19th century. The shoulder is concave and rises to a rim with a high plain domical cover.

This rare example was included in an exhibition of silver owned by Virginia families held at the Virginia Museum of Fine Arts, Richmond, and was illustrated in *American Collector* with an account of the exhibition by Edward Morris Davis, III. He mentions that this urn was formerly at Westover which was long the family mansion of the Byrd family. Miss Edith Tunis Sale in her book on Virginia houses says that the estate was bought in 1688 by William Byrd, the first of the name in Virginia, and describes the mansion, built by his son in 1730, as the finest example of existing Colonial architecture.

THE SOUTH. Baltimore silverwork and that by other groups working in the South shows a marked reliance upon the Philadelphia designs. This is particularly noticeable with the teapots and services which repeat both the shapes and the applied ornaments such as the pierced gallery and beaded molding favored by the Philadelphia silversmiths.

From about 1780 to 1790, the small cylindrical teapot was the most popular style particularly in Maryland, and this differed in no essential feature from the Philadelphia prototype. Some of the known examples are slightly smaller, but the Southern silversmith, like his Pennsylvania contemporary, always used quite stout silver.

Shaped straight-sided teapots similar to those illustrated seem to have largely replaced the cylindrical type during the last ten years of the 18th century. And the Baltimore silversmiths also attempted to adapt the vase shape to a low teapot, though the results were no more successful than similar efforts by their English contemporaries.

These by no means pleasing teapots were made of thin silver; the body was a squat conical shape with deep flutes radiating from the bottom, the shoulder a wide concave also fluted, and the cover a high dome with a vase finial. And bearing in mind the classic origin of the vase, both the English and the Baltimore silversmiths used a foot with a plinth shaped to follow the outline of the fluted body.

But however negative some may feel toward this depressed shape, it undoubtedly enjoyed a certain vogue during the later 18th century and there still exist a few services of this design comprising a teapot, vase-shaped sugar bowl, cream jug and waste bowl.

Numerous other services dating from the late 18th and early 19th centuries are still owned by different families in Maryland and other parts of the South, and these include many of the tall vase shape, which were copied from the Philadelphia tea services of that style.

Toward the end of the first quarter of the 19th century, the Baltimore silversmiths produced teapots and other teaware of various shapes on a low foot which were evolved from the vase shape. These, however, are neither of importance in the history of American design and craftsmanship nor of interest to collectors except to illustrate the unpleasing forms which made their appearance both in America and Europe.

Coffee-pots and Chocolate-pots

English coffee- and chocolate-pots of the classic period have the conical body and high concave neck derived from the Roman vase. As a general rule, the English pots are elaborately chased with various classic forms; but, as remarked previously, while the shape was adopted in the United States during the early Republican period, the American interpretations are invariably quite plain apart from small moldings and engraved work.

NEW ENGLAND. Judging from the extreme rarity of vase-shaped coffee- and chocolate-pots bearing the marks of New England silversmiths, we may safely assume that the tall classic pots found little or no favor in social circles of Boston or elsewhere in the New England States; but it is of interest to note that the silver of several churches includes flagons which were obviously copied from the English classic jugs and chocolate-pots.

Several of these flagons were exhibited at the Museum of Fine Arts, Boston, in 1911, among them a pair by Jesse Churchill (1773-1819) which belong to the Church of West Boston. They are 15½ inches high (the English jugs are about 8 inches) with the conical body and tall concave neck rising to a helmet-shaped rim fitted with a hinged domical cover and a tall finial. They are invariably plain except for a simple reeded band round the rim, the foot and the shoulder, the last, in some instances, having a narrow bright-cut band below.

There is no question but that these "classic" flagons were made solely for use in churches. The Clearwater Collection at the Metropolitan Museum of Art includes one by Rufus and Henry Farnam of Boston (c. 1807), which was shown in the Boston exhibition of 1911, at which time it belonged to the First Baptist Church, Salem. This example is 16½ inches high.

Actually, New England coffee- and chocolate-pots of any type dating from the early Republican period are few and far between, and those which do exist show that the classic styles failed to replace the inverted pear shape. Several examples of the latter in different collections are known to have been made in the last quarter of the 18th century: One by Paul Revere in the collection of Mrs. Nathaniel Thayer has been traced in Revere's accounts of 1781; and there is another made by him about 1796 in the Worcester Art Museum. Both these pots have the low spreading gadrooned foot, but in some instances, a classic touch would be introduced to pots of this shape by using a slightly taller stem and domical foot on a square plinth—that seems to have been the only concession allowed in New England to the classic fashion with coffee- and chocolate-pots of the late 18th century.

NEW YORK. There was a similar persistence of the inverted pear shape in New York through the 18th century, though there is evidence that the tall classic vase type enjoyed slightly more popularity than in New England. In their use of the classic shape, the New York silversmiths would sometimes embody features borrowed from the rococo style; and in such pieces they not infrequently achieved a design which shows a marked individuality.

These features occur in a coffee-pot by Phillip Dally (c. 1779). The body is conical with the tall concave neck and, while the circular foot is similarly classic in form, the plinth is omitted. The cover is a plain high dome with a cone finial which was a carry-over from the rococo, an influence again evident in the double scroll handle with a volute socket below, as well as in the cast spout decorated with scrolls. This coffee-pot which is about 13 inches high and quite heavy (it weighs 44½ ounces) was exhibited at the Museum of the City of New York in 1937-8.

PENNSYLVANIA. While the tall vase-shaped coffee-pots, such as shown in Figure 176, were popular in Philadelphia for some years after the Revolution, and an appreciable number have been preserved, this classic type by no means superseded the inverted pear shape. There are examples of the latter bearing the marks of different silver-smiths who were not working in Philadelphia before about 1775, though a tentative classic influence may show itself in a beaded orna-ment and in the use of the urn finial.

That preference for simplicity noticeable with the silverwork of Colonial times, remained equally strong after the Revolution and until the coming of the ornate styles of the 19th century. Admittedly, silver was used to an increasing extent, especially in Philadelphia, but most of it was plain.

Details of the tall teapots evolved by the Philadelphia silversmiths from the classic vase have been discussed earlier in this chapter. And the comments made there apply equally to the coffee-pots of this type (see FIG. 176) which are in every way similar to the teapots except that they are taller and heavier—for example, of a coffee-pot and a teapot in a service made by Joseph Lownes the former is 16 inches high and weighs 48 ounces, whereas the teapot is 10¼ inches and 25¾ ounces.

THE SOUTH. As mentioned previously, the designs adopted by the Baltimore and other groups of silversmiths in the South were very largely borrowed from Philadelphia. At the same time, there are certain minor features which tend to identify the Southern work. The vase-shaped coffee-pot and other pieces of that shape are, to all intents, replicas of the Philadelphia prototypes even to the use of the pierced gallery (see FIG. 176). But a comparison shows that the conical body of the Southern pots often has a more decided downward taper and there is a tendency for the spool-shaped section of the cover to be slightly taller; in some instances too, the square plinth is larger and not as deep as the plinth of the Philadelphia pots.

Some of the vase-shaped services made in the South, like those made in Philadelphia, include both a coffee-pot and a teapot. Others have only one pot; and there are signs that in the latter instances, the pot was of a size suitable for coffee or tea and could, with its accom-panying sugar vase and cream jug be used as a service for either.

In addition to what may be called orthodox coffee-pots, i.e. the vase shape or the inverted pear shape which was equally popular, several experimental shapes were evolved by different Baltimore silversmiths; unfortunately these were merely the grafting of classic elements upon

127

some earlier form, or abortive attempts to vary the classic vase shape.

Where the inverted pear shape was merely raised on the taller circular foot with a plinth, there was no disturbance of the symmetrical outline or any suggestion of incongruity. But when this same shape was given a tall classic spool-shaped cover in place of the natural dome, and the swan-neck spout ornamented with a row of small beads on both the upper and lower sides, the result was far from harmonious.

One of the Southern variations of the classic vase shape was a rather bulbous conical body on a plain spreading molded foot with a clumsy duck-neck spout and high domical cover with an ornamental finial. Other similar experiments might be mentioned but none of them would offer any interest.

Small Jugs for Milk and Cream

Three styles of small jugs connected with the things for the tea table superseded the pear shape after the Revolution. Two of these were inspired directly by the classic forms, one of which followed the designs borrowed by Robert Adam from the Roman vase and was similar in outline to the coffee-pot shown in Figure 176; the lower part being somewhat suggestive of an eggcup on a trumpet-shaped foot and plinth and the neck concave rising to a helmet-shaped rim with a wide lip. The second and much more familiar cream jug of this period had the deep conical body without a neck but with a similarly shaped rim and this is generally called the helmet shape (see FIG. 177).

The third variety made its appearance in England about 1800. This was a rather squat flat-bottomed jug with bulging sides and helmet-shaped rim which, during the early 19th century, very largely replaced the more graceful conical shape both in America and Britain.

NEW ENGLAND. Cream jugs of the type referred to as helmet shape, bearing the marks of New England silversmiths are by no means numerous, most of the known examples being the work of Paul Revere.

Although copied from English models his cream jugs with the conical body show certain distinctive characteristics: They were slightly taller, the body was longer and gracefully tapered and the foot somewhat shorter; again, the lip was longer with a somewhat pronounced downward curve at the end. These attractive cream jugs were invariably decorated with delicate engraved work and some of them were finely fluted and engraved.

The early 19th-century squat oval shape with the flat bottom was made in New England, but it does not seem to have found much favor; and the same comment applies to the examples of this type which still exist, if one may judge from the small value placed on them at auction.

NEW YORK. Excellent engraved work was executed by New York silversmiths on the helmet-shaped cream jugs, but fluting does not seem to have been used to any extent. The New York style is shown with a cream jug by William Gilbert (*w*. 1772) in the Metropolitan Museum of Art. This has the small beaded molding round the rim and, immediately below this, a narrow engraved band; the body is engraved with floral festoons and a ribbon knot with a shield pendent from the knot. The plinth of this jug is eight sided, each side taking a concave curved form.

With the passing of the classic styles, the squat cream jug, described above, replaced the graceful helmet shape in New York as it did in other parts of America and in England.

PENNSYLVANIA. Customs and manners of bygone generations are recorded in the household articles they used and have left behind them. And we need no better illustration of this than the silver things for the tea table which were made and used in Philadelphia during the time that city was the capital of the United States.

Familiarity with even a few representative collections of American silver shows that the amount of Philadelphia silverwork associated with tea drinking is noticeably larger than that bearing the marks of New England and New York silversmiths.

Philadelphia teapots and services which have been dealt with earlier in this chapter, are themselves numerous, but there are in addition the many cream jugs and sugar bowls of the classic period, which may have, in other days, been accompanied by a silver teapot or coffee-pot—on the other hand, they may have been used with a porcelain pot or even with a silver one of an earlier period which was a family heirloom.

There are various types of cream jugs dating from the last quarter of the 18th and the early years of the 19th centuries. Upward of forty were in the exhibition at the Philadelphia Museum of Art as long ago as 1921; of these about twelve were the type with the conical body or

129

helmet shape, and a like number were of the inverted pear shape which indicates that this earlier shape was by no means displaced by the classic designs. The remainder were mostly the later squat type.

Certain features of the Philadelphia helmet shape seem to have been largely peculiar to that city. Frequently the body was made unusually wide at the rim and in some instances the lip was shortened; with others, the body was shaped rather like a flattened oval instead of the usual circular outline and the foot and plinth were also oval. Fluted examples were made and with these the plinth is invariably shaped to follow the line of the fluting as illustrated in Figure 177 which is one of the rare twelve-sided cream jugs.

Another characteristic occurs with the engraved decorations which seldom follow the traditional patterns. This, too, is illustrated in Figure 177 which has a deep band formed as panels by the ribs of the sides, each panel enclosing an elaborate rayed motif within a double circle of tiny punched dots; the band of panels has a double horizontal row of the small dots above and below and these are repeated on each side of the vertical ribs of the body; similar punched decoration is applied round the foot and the edge of the plinth.

An interesting cream jug illustrating the Philadelphia engraved work appeared in the Garvan sale some eighteen years ago. It is eight sided and oval in plan, the rim has a stout plain molding and immediately below is a wide bright-cut band of simple leaf forms; and like the one in Figure 177 the band has a double horizontal row of punched dots above and below. The body is engraved with a conventional ornament of running scrolls with small flowers and leaves pendent from either end; the foot which is oval and the plinth which is eight sided are quite plain.

THE SOUTH. Both the plain pear shape on three legs and the inverted pear shape were made in Baltimore and other centers during the classic period. Some interesting local variations were introduced, however, particularly with the Baltimore jugs: An unusually long lip was sometimes used, handles were formed of four scrolls, the short legs would be twisted corkscrew fashion to strengthen the metal, and the inverted pear shape was sometimes made with three legs instead of the usual spreading foot.

Helmet-shaped cream jugs were made in the South, but it is rare that one comes on offer. There are two by J. Adam of Alexandria, Virginia (c. 1800), in the Metropolitan Museum of Art, one of which has a plain molded rim without any decoration. The other has bead-

130

ing round the lip and foot which, with both jugs, is the trumpet shape on a square plinth. Another example by the same maker was formerly in the collection of Mrs. Miles White, Jr. This has a plain molded rim but the body is fluted and the plinth shaped to follow the lines of the flutes.

Sugar Bowls

No sugar bowl of the fanciful styles with a glass liner fashionable in England during the late 18th century seems to have been made in America. It was popularly believed that glass was more suitable than silver for sugar holders; and bowls were made of colored glass and fitted in elaborately pierced silver casings, chased and embossed with classic foliage, garlands and other motifs in keeping with the designs of Robert Adam.

Most of the glass bowls were conical shape; some were without a cover, and the silver casing, about 6 inches high was fitted with a swing handle to form a basket-like bowl. These were sometimes made in sets of three, but while of interest as specimens of pierced work, it cannot be denied that they tend to be somewhat tawdry.

Glass bowls were also fitted in tall vase-shaped holders with the spool-shaped cover elaborately pierced and embossed. These holders are similar in outline to the American classic vase-shaped sugar bowls. The English bowls usually had two high loop handles, which, with the decorative treatment, deprives them of the simple dignity which is so attractive a feature of those made by American silversmiths.

NEW ENGLAND. Few of the New England silversmiths seem to have made the vase-shaped sugar bowls. Most of the known examples bear the mark of Paul Revere and these, like his other classic designs, are distinctive both for their rhythmic lines and their decorative treatment.

Revere achieved a remarkable sense of light and shade with the style of the fluting he introduced with this shape. Each flute is fairly narrow and tapers down to the bottom of the conical bowl with the result that the flutes radiate from the point where the bowl joins the foot.

One such bowl accompanied by a fluted helmet-shaped cream jug is in the Clearwater Collection at the Metropolitan Museum of Art. This bowl is engraved with a narrow band and festoons on the upper part. The cover is almost flat, rising rather sharply to the spool-shaped section which has the small domed top and a flame finial.

131

An unusual sugar bowl by Revere was lent by Mrs. Samuel Cabot to the Boston exhibition of 1911 and is illustrated in the catalogue. It is slightly more than 7 inches high and has a plain bowl with two loop handles raised on a molded spreading foot; the cover is a high bell shape with a tall finial.

This bowl is of interest because, while the loop handles and high cover were used in England, no English prototype suggests itself and it was therefore probably one of Revere's own designs.

Boat-shaped sugar bowls with the bail handle on a high spreading foot by New England makers are slightly more numerous, but are far from plentiful. These are about 4½ inches high and occasionally fluted, in which case the foot is either shaped to follow the outline of the flutes or is a plain molded oval. As a rule they were made without covers, though a fluted boat-shaped sugar bowl with a cover by David Tyler (c. 1760-1804) was in the Boston exhibition referred to above.

One unusual sugar bowl by David Vinton of Boston, and Providence, Rhode Island (c. 1790), has a plain deep globular bowl and domical cover on a molded spreading foot. At first sight it might appear to date before the Revolution, but an urn-shaped finial on the cover and small beaded bands round the cover and the foot, indicate the classic influence.

NEW YORK. There are clear signs that the inverted pear-shaped sugar bowl and cover fitted with the foot-handle remained popular for some years after the Revolution, and was made concurrently with the vase shape and boat shape.

At times the influence of the inverted pear would make itself evident even in the classic vase-shaped sugar bowls made by New York silversmiths. This influence is present in one by William Gilbert (w. 1772), which is in the Museum of the City of New York. The bowl instead of having the conical form, contracts suddenly near the bottom in a way similar to the inverted pear-shaped coffee-pots (see FIG. 139). The cover is formed of a deep concave section supporting the spool-shaped top with an urn finial and the foot is circular and domed without the usual square plinth which again shows something of the inverted pear shape.

One vase-shaped sugar bowl by Gilbert in the same museum has a conical bowl tapering sharply downward. The cover is similar to the one described above, but in place of the classic trumpet shape it has a spool-shaped stem with a high domical foot raised on a square plinth. A third example, also by Gilbert, which is in the Metropolitan

Museum of Art shows a distinct English influence: The conical body is rounder at the bottom, the foot and plinth follow the English classic style and the tall cover is a continuous concave outline.

Each of these bowls has the beaded molding round the top and shoulder of the cover, the rim and foot, and each is engraved with what might be called a typically "Gilbertian" design of running tendrils and tiny leaves.

Apart from the variation in the engraved decoration, New York vase-shaped sugar bowls follow the same general pattern, and though most of them are now in different collections an example does become available at intervals.

Oval boat-shaped sugar bowls by New York makers are known, but they rank with the rarities. An example by Alexander S. Gordon (c. 1795) was in the exhibition at the Museum of the City of New York, 1937-8; this has a fluted bowl with a wide engraved band round the rim, a high bell-shaped cover and pineapple finial, the flat spreading foot being shaped to follow the outline of the fluted body.

PENNSYLVANIA. Sugar bowls, like other teaware, are considerably more numerous among Philadelphia silver of the late 18th century than among that of New England or New York.

Philadelphia vase-shaped sugar bowls are basically the same as those made by other groups of American silversmiths. When they are studied, however, it is not difficult to find details which are largely peculiar to the Philadelphia designs—remembering always that these same details were borrowed and used by the Baltimore and other silversmiths in the South.

Probably the most readily recognized of these details is the pierced gallery round the rim and occasionally round the base, though this ornament is not as prevalent as may be generally supposed—of some twenty-five by Philadelphia silversmiths in the 1921 exhibition, only eight had the pierced ornament.

Fluting was used fairly freely and bowls are known with as many as twelve flutes. In some instances both engraving and applied ornament were omitted from the fluted bowls as in the one illustrated with the tea service in Figure 175. This bowl is shaped by wide flutes radiating from the bottom and the plinth is shaped to conform to the outline of the body, but it is neither engraved nor has it the customary applied beaded ornament.

Several other types of sugar bowls were made in Philadelphia during the classic period, among them the conical bowl with the spreading foot and square plinth similar to the tall vase shape, but without the cover, the graceful boat shape and the inverted pear shape with the domed cover—the last sometimes ornamented with the pierced gallery round the rim and pierced plinth as shown in Figure 156.

Salvers and Trays

When tea drinking first became fashionable, the various articles, spoken of as the tea equipage, were placed on the "tea table" which was the early 18th-century name for what we now call a tea tray. Until about the middle of the century, it was customary for the tea tray to stand on a wooden table much as it does in our time. In many larger houses, the massive tray was often placed on a wooden stand, the top of which was the same size as the tray with sockets cut in the wood to take the feet and hold it firmly. These convenient stands are mentioned in early inventories as "mahogany stands to set the silver tea and coffee tables on."

In England during the late 18th century, larger oval trays were introduced to replace the circular type; and some of the ovals have a pierced vertical rim to conform to the classic fashion, with the bottom made either of silver, wood or papier-mâché.

NEW ENGLAND. No American tray with the pierced vertical rim is known; in fact oval trays by American makers are virtually non-existent, and any others are very scarce. From those that have come to light, it seems that silver trays large enough to hold a complete tea service were rarely made in America.

Of those known to have been made at this time in New England, the largest is the oval example by Paul Revere illustrated in Figure 159. It is 17 inches long and was described in the previous chapter for though made in the classic period it is essentially rococo in character.

NEW YORK. None of the few salvers or trays by New York silversmiths shows any marked classic influence. All of them reveal clearly that the makers and their patrons were content with the rococo designs both in the shaping and in the applied ornaments.

The few known larger examples were presentation pieces. One salver nearly 22 inches in diameter with wavy gadrooned border made by Lewis Fueter (c. 1775) is owned by the New York Historical Society. It is engraved with the arms of New York and inscribed, *This Piece of Plate is the Gift of His Excely. Govr. Tryon, the Genl*

134

Assembly of New York. to Captn Sowers Engineer. 13 Mar 1773; and around the border of the tray there is a finely engraved garland of leaves and flowers. But though it was made after the Revolution, it is rococo in form and ornament. Thomas Sowers was the engineer in charge of repairing the battery at lower Manhattan (PLATE IX-B).

PENNSYLVANIA. The largest American silver tray and the only one which shows distinct classic influence in its treatment was made by John McMullin of Philadelphia in 1799. It is octagonal in shape, 30½ inches long and 20½ inches wide with a reeded rim and chased leaf forms at the angles and is engraved with bright-cut floral designs.

According to the inscription it was presented by the board of managers of the Marine and City Hospitals to Philip Syng, M.D.—presumably a connection, possibly a nephew of the famous Philadelphia silversmith. This Philip Syng was resident physician at the City Hospital and the tray was in recognition of his work during the epidemic of yellow fever in 1798—incidentally, the second epidemic of the fever in five years. The tray was shown in the exhibition at Philadelphia in 1921, lent by Mr. Edward Conner.

All other Philadelphia late 18th-century trays that have come to notice are circular and small, ranging from about 6 inches to 13 inches in diameter and with a few exceptions they follow the English rococo style. Classic influence is noticeable in the few with a reeded or beaded border; but the latter are rare and it is safe to say that by far the larger number differ very little from those made before the classic had replaced the rococo designs.

THE SOUTH. Any post-Revolution salvers or trays made in Baltimore or elsewhere in the South follow closely the patterns adopted by the Philadelphia silversmiths, that is, the rococo forms or the classic bead or reed border.

One tray by Andrew E. Warner of Baltimore (1786-1870) now in the Clearwater Collection at the Metropolitan Museum of Art is of more interest for its historical associations than for its beauty. It is oval, 17½ inches long, mounted with a massive cast border representing the biblical leviathan and roses in high relief, and inscribed, *The Citizens of Baltimore to Commodore Stephen Decatur. Rebus gestis insigni: ob virtutes dilecto* (Illustrious for his deeds: beloved for his virtues). Stephen Decatur commanded the American squadron against the Dey of Algiers in 1815; on his return in the following year he was

135

appointed by President Madison to formulate a plan for the creation of the United States Navy.

In America as in Britain, the tradition of using a tray to commemorate some important event has persisted, but one could wish the donors would restrict the often lengthy inscriptions to the underside.

CHAPTER FIVE

Spoons and Forks

WE WILL NOT HERE TRACE THE EVOLUTION OF THE
spoon from the original shell used by primitive man, but join it at the
point where it began its Colonial life. From that time, the spoon followed the same path in America as in England; and so closely do
those made by the Colonial silversmiths resemble the English models
of the late 17th and the 18th centuries that, except for the marks, it is
not easy for a layman to distinguish one from the other, though after
experience and study that same layman will readily recognize the
latent differences.

Seventeenth-century Spoons

NEW ENGLAND. Even though the possessions brought to New
England by the early settlers were perforce limited by the available
accommodation on shipboard, those which they were able to carry
with them naturally included small and valuable articles such as
spoons and other silver which had been used in the homes from which
they came.

It is highly probable that some of the spoons were the so-called "seal-
top" type which were popular in England during the later 16th and
the 17th centuries. The earlier seal top had a fig-shaped bowl, which
changed to the elliptical shape around 1650. They were used frequently as christening gifts and for that reason it is suggested that
some came to America.

All the known New England 17th-century spoons except two have
the true elliptical bowl; and this allows us to think that the two may
have been made before or soon after 1650.

The two exceptions are one by John Hull (FIG. 178-A) which is in
the Essex Institute, Salem, and one by Hull and Sanderson which was
acquired in 1948 by Robert Ensko, Inc. The bowls of both these
spoons might be termed transitional. At first sight, they would be

137

accepted as elliptical, but when studied there is an obvious relic of the fig shape in the more pointed outline where the bowl joins the stem (compare FIGS. 178-A and B).

And we might venture to suggest that the spoon by John Hull is slightly earlier than the other which was illustrated with a note by Millicent D. Stow in The New York *Sun* of April 23, 1948. This in- ferred from the difference between the stems: The Hull spoon has a narrow stem slightly rounded off at the end, both of which features relate to the slipped end type; the stem of the one by Hull and Sanderson is wider and stouter and the end is rectangular (similar to the spoon in FIG. 178-B). We have rather stressed these minor differ- ences, because such details add considerably to the interest of studying early silver.

All these early spoons with the simple flat stems belong in the category known as Puritan spoons. It is sometimes thought that this form was developed in England, but it was probably introduced from France where plain flat stem spoons with elliptical bowls were made some years before they were known in England.

These austere spoons appeared in England about 1655 and continued fashionable for a short time after the return of Charles II to the throne in 1660, when the more attractive trifid shape made its appearance. Perhaps the fact is not easily recognized, but the trifid was a child of the Puritan spoon, and of French origin. About 1643, three small notches were cut in the end of the plain flat stem of the French spoons and in this it is possible to see the forerunner of the cleft end of the later trifid, and so on to the so-called "wavy end."

This evolution is as easily traceable in New England spoons as in those of the then Mother Country: Using the New England Puritan spoon with the elliptical bowl (FIG. 178-B) as the basic shape, it is possible to see from the Irish spoon in Figure 178-C that by making the stem thinner, widening and rounding the end and filing two small notches, the embryo trifid made its appearance. Then the end of the stem was given a graceful pear-shaped outline which was notched in two places, leaving a small tongue-like section which was turned up toward the bowl which is known as the trifid (see FIG. 178-D).

Toward the end of the 17th century, the notches became less notice- able or were concealed as part of decoration added to the end of the stem as in Figure 178-E; and eventually the notches were discon- tinued and the stem assumed the wavy end, as in Figure 178-F.

If examples of the Puritan spoons bearing the marks of New Eng- land silversmiths are few, there are a very considerable number of the

138

trifid and wavy end in different collections; and examples become available often when a representative collection is disposed of.

NEW YORK. It is unfortunate that the optimistic note in the preceding paragraph cannot be applied to New York spoons of this period, for very few have come to light.

It is not to be expected that the simple Puritan spoon would hold any attraction for the first New York silversmiths who were almost all of Dutch extraction. But there is one spoon by Henricus Boelin (1697-1755) similar to a pattern which was fashionable in France at the same time as, or possibly before, the Puritan. This Boelen spoon, which was shown in the Museum of the City of New York in 1937-38, has the elliptical bowl with a cast stem ending in a scroll (PLATE III-A).

Trifid and wavy end patterns were made in New York and one bearing the mark of Jacob Boelen (1654-1729) came into the auction room in 1946. Two trifid spoons in the exhibition at the Museum of the City of New York in 1937-8 indicate that the early English custom of distributing spoons to mourners in memory of a dead person was observed in America.

These two spoons were made by Cornelius Vanderburgh (1653-99); the bowl of one is inscribed, *O S V Cort^{lt} ob^t: A^o 1684: Ap^r: 4.* and the Van Cortlandt arms flanked by O and S. It was one of the spoons distributed at the funeral of Oloff Stevenszen Van Courtlandt, the founder of the family in America. The other spoon which was also inscribed was one given out at the funeral of Henricus Van Deursen in 1692. A similar spoon by an unknown maker in the Metropolitan Museum of Art is engraved, *Maria V Renselaer Obit 24 Jann 1688/9.*

Eighteenth-century Spoons

By the opening of the 18th century, spoons had developed several changes all leading up to the various patterns that were made through the next hundred years. The bowl while still elliptical was narrower, the lower part of the stem was rounded, but both the triangular tongue or rat-tail at the back of the bowl, which was used with all 17th-century spoons, and the wavy end were retained. And English spoons of this time are known with the small projecting top of the wavy end turned over and hammered down toward the front of the bowl.

In this last feature it is possible to see the inception of the rounded end turned up toward the face of the bowl with the pronounced ridge

139

running well down the stem which is known as the Old English pattern. But while this pattern differed in all other respects from the late 17th-century spoons, the rat-tail survived until about 1730.

There was the same transition with American spoons, even though examples showing all the several changes at the end of the 17th century are lacking. The evolution of the stem from the wavy end to the rounded top with the long ridge, as well as the change in the shape of the bowl are illustrated in the American spoon in Figure 179-A.

After the disappearance of the rat-tail in about 1730, a small molded section with a rounded end was added below the drop where the rat-tail had been previously. Spoons with this feature are often referred to as the double drop type. A few years later the ridge down the face of the stem disappeared, except for a trace of it just below where the end turns, as shown in Figure 179-B. The only other change that occurred in this pattern was the turning down of the end of the stem as is shown in the later engraved spoons illustrated in Figures 179-C and D.

NEW ENGLAND. All the changes mentioned above were adopted in New England very soon after they appeared in England. In addition to plain spoons, the New England silversmiths produced spoons with an ornament on the back of the bowl; these became popular in England about 1740 when they were introduced from France. The various ornamental forms were borrowed from the rococo style and the one most favored by the New England silversmiths seems to have been the shell, although the more elaborate foliated scroll ornament was also used.

Several varieties of long-stemmed spoons seem to have been made in New England. One made by Ezekiel Burr of Providence, Rhode Island (1764-1846), described as a mote spoon, was in the Boston Exhibition of 1911 and is illustrated in the catalogue. It is 10 inches long with a rounded top, Old English stem and a small bowl which has three slits running lengthwise. It is somewhat reminiscent of the early 18th-century English spoons with similarly long stems which were known as hash spoons, although the bowls of these were without the slits, though some have a pierced "gate" dividing the bowl lengthwise.

Another spoon by Benjamin Burt illustrated in the same catalogue is over 16 inches long. This has a tapering tubular handle and resembles closely the large spoons with similar handles that were used

140

in the time of Queen Anne for serving hash and quite possibly for ladling punch from the bowl into a jug for serving.

Late 18th-century New England spoons are to all intents replicas of the contemporary English and are similarly ornamented with bright-cut engraved work (FIGS. 179-C and E) or have an engraved pattern known as feather edge (FIG. 179-D) or the beaded ornament.

One pattern which is peculiar to America was evolved from the Old English pattern by cutting the sides of the rounded top at an oblique angle (see FIG. 179-F), thus causing the top of the stem to resemble the shape of the end of a coffin, from which is derived the name "coffin spoon."

These were made in New England during the last ten years of the 18th and the early 19th centuries. Mr. Bigelow in his book suggests that the pattern may have been introduced as a funeral spoon and he lends support to this by citing two made by Daniel Rogers of Newport, Rhode Island (c. 1750—). One of these is inscribed to commemorate the death of Joanna Good in 1775, and the other, the death of Samuel Gidds in 1777.

NEW YORK. All the various 18th-century patterns of spoons were produced in New York but the number of known examples would suggest that spoon making was not as important a branch of the trade in New York as in New England.

Ornaments on the back of New York spoon bowls show a decided versatility in the adaptation of the shell which might be combined with a flower, a wheat sheaf or a scroll; and occasionally an ornament was applied to the bowl of a spoon which was engraved with bright-cut on the front of the stem.

One teaspoon made by Ephraim Brasher, which was in the exhibition at the Museum of the City of New York in 1937-8, is an exact copy of the little known English spoon sometimes called the Liberty spoon.

These had a political significance and were made in England during the later 18th century. They are invariably teaspoon size and the back of the bowl is decorated with a large old-fashioned wicker bird cage hanging, as it were, from the drop at the bottom of the stem. A small bird is flying from the open door of the cage and below is the motto, *I Love Liberty,* which was adopted by the English politician John Wilkes whose lasting fame rests upon his undaunted and successful fight for the freedom of the press and for the rights of electors to choose their representative without restriction.

141

Some unusually fine long-stemmed spoons with large bowls were made in New York, and a number of the surviving examples bear the mark of Simeon Soumaine (1685-1750). They vary in length from 12 inches to 15 inches and have the elliptical bowl and the ridged stem with the end turned up toward the face of the bowl. Although referred to as basting spoons, it is hard to imagine a careful housewife allowing one of these fine pieces of silverwork to be damaged by scooping up fat from an iron cooking pan. Any that had been used for that purpose for any length of time could not fail to show very decided wear on one side of the bowl—dependent upon whether the cook was right- or left-handed. This writer has seen at least two English large silver spoons of this type which had at some time taken the fancy of the Queen of the Kitchen—each bowl was worn to a straight line on one side.

The most important American spoons are a set of eight teaspoons with a strainer spoon made of gold by Simeon Soumaine. The teaspoons are 4 inches long and the one with a perforated bowl 4½ inches. The stems are the early 18th-century pattern known as Old English, with the ridge down the length of the face and the bowls a slightly pointed elliptical shape with the tongue or rat-tail at the back. These rarities were included in a sale in October 1932 at the former American Art Association (now the Parke-Bernet Galleries), and the writer clearly recalls the exciting battle of bids caused by those little spoons.

They were catalogued as "Swiss XVIII century," but there were a few among the audience who had recognized their true nationality. When they were offered, someone bid ten dollars; slowly the bidding rose to fifty dollars, after which the few who knew their real value joined the conversation and the last word, spoken by Stephen G. C. Ensko, was $1,000—a figure which would be far exceeded today.

Spoons with the coffin end stem, which have been described previously, enjoyed some popularity in New York during the last few years of the 18th and the early 19th centuries and though the larger number are plain, they were occasionally decorated on the stem with bright-cut engraved work.

PENNSYLVANIA. Spoons by the 18th-century Philadelphia school of silversmiths are of the same patterns as those already described. Nor is there any outstanding difference in the ornaments on the backs of the bowls or the later decorated stems which are illustrated in Figures 179-C, D and E.

142

Long-stemmed spoons with the large bowls were in every way similar to those made in New York and while the coffin end style was made, apparently it did not enjoy any wide popularity in Philadelphia.

One English pattern, the Onslow, seems to have found its way to America and have attracted at least some passing notice in Philadelphia. Whether spoons and forks were made remains doubtful, but a ladle by Joseph and Nathaniel Richardson (c. 1785) was clearly inspired by the Onslow pattern. This interesting piece is in the Clearwater Collection at the Metropolitan Museum of Art.

Known technically as scroll-headed, the pattern was named after Arthur Onslow, Speaker of the House of Commons from 1728 to 1761. It appeared first about 1745-48 and was popular to a certain extent until the later 18th century. The original bowls were elliptical with the double drop at the back and the stem differs from that of any other known pattern. Instead of the familiar rounded top turning up toward the face of the bowl, it turns down in the form of a volute and the face of the stem at the top is ornamented with a series of ribs. And the bowls sometimes have an ornament below the drop on the back.

Even if the Onslow pattern itself went out of fashion, it left its influence on later spoons. At that time, the ends of the stems turned up toward the face, but the greater convenience of the Onslow turned-down end was recognized and adopted; by about 1780 the turned-up end was discontinued.

Flatware of the Onslow pattern is by no means plentiful. One of the few services seen by the writer was among the silver belonging to Mrs. Elizabeth M. Baldwin, which was sold at the Parke-Bernet Galleries in November 1946. The spoons and forks in this service, however, were by different English makers and of different dates in the last half of the 18th century, but it included a ladle with a shell bowl similar to the one made in Philadelphia.

Sugar Tongs

Loaf sugar, which was invented in Venice four centuries ago, was then made in the form of a cone and cut into small pieces and three sugar loaves pendent were used as a grocer's shop-sign until the early part of the last century. The convenient little cubes of the present day are of quite modern origin.

Sugar tongs do not seem to have been introduced until the early years of the 18th century; unfortunately the English silver examples

143

of that time are not hall-marked, consequently it cannot be said definitely when they were first used. The earliest sugar tongs were similar to a pair of scissors with shell or spoon-shaped ends, and examples of these bearing the marks of American silversmiths have been preserved (FIG. 180).

Other scissor sugar tongs were in the form of a stork with a long beak opening to grip the sugar, but no American example of this type is known. Some of these suggest that sugar in olden times was associated with the legendary duty of the stork. The body of the bird is hollow and inside there is the figure of a baby which is revealed when the tongs are opened, and English sugar tongs of this romantic form are known which have a snake coiled round the neck of the bird. But no satisfactory explanation of the connection between the stork, the baby and the snake has yet offered itself.

The more familiar bow shape is closely related to the spoon, for it is two small spoon bowls on long stems joined by an arch which has been hammered and tempered to give a springy flexibility. This type appeared during the second half of the 18th century and was made in fairly large numbers and of different patterns by American silversmiths.

The earlier bow-shaped sugar tongs were variously pierced and chased and are undoubtedly the more attractive—and also the more difficult to find. Later styles were engraved with bright-cut and other decoration to match the contemporary spoons; those of the early 19th century are plain and shaped to match the fiddle pattern.

Forks

When the first settlers sailed for America and for some time after, forks were virtually unknown as an eating tool in England. As late as 1669, an Italian count writing of his visit to Britain remarks:

> On the English table, there are no forks nor vessels to supply water for the hands, which are washed in a basin full of water, that serves for all the company or perhaps at the conclusion of dinner, they dip the end of a napkin into the beaker which is set before each of the guests filled with water and with this they clean their teeth and wash their hands.

And according to the contemporary authorities, it was etiquette that "each guest attending a banquet should provide himself with a knife."

144

The "basin full of water" mentioned by the count refers probably to the large rose-water dish or basin which, with an accompanying ewer, was essential to the dining table in olden days. Before the days of forks, meat was held with the fingers on the trencher, cut into pieces and carried to the mouth with the fingers; any guest who was served a bone grabbed it with both hands and pulled the meat off with his teeth.

When the feast was finished, the hands of the company would be somewhat soiled. So a servant carrying a large ewer and another carrying a basin passed round the table and—starting with the master of the house—poured rose-water from the ewer over the hands of each guest and caught it in the basin; after this ceremony, the hands were dried on a towel, presumably carried by another servant.

At formal banquets such as are held at the Halls of Livery Companies, this washing of hands ceremony is still observed, though today it is merely symbolized by each guest dipping the napkin in the basin and wiping his mouth.

Forks for table use were adopted first in Italy and from there found their way through France to England, and it has been suggested that this more delicate manner of eating stemmed from the ivory chopsticks of the Chinese. A 17th-century English traveler wrote that "the use of silver forks with us by some of our spruce [overnice] fastidious gallants taken up of late, came from China to Italy and thence to England."

By about 1655, a three-pronged fork with the flat stem and stump-end of the Puritan spoon was introduced to England from France. After the Commonwealth, the end of the stem became trifid in keeping with the spoons. Forks with three or four prongs were made from that time, though examples with two prongs have survived. The changes which occurred in the stems of spoons were repeated in forks and by the end of the 17th century forks with the wavy end stem were made.

Even after forks came into fairly general use, it was still customary for guests to provide their own table tools. Reminders of this remain in the late 17th-century sharkskin cases containing a small two-pronged fork, a spoon and a knife which could be carried in the pocket or the "hand-bag" of the time. This same custom prevailed in early Colonial days and there is in the Boston Museum of Fine Arts, a small fork and spoon by John Coney (see FIGS. 178-F and 181-C) which in both size and design are similar to the English "pocket tools."

145

Forks by American silversmiths of this early period are very rare. One of a pair with two prongs and wavy end by John Noyes of Boston (1674-1749), which are in the Museum at Boston, is illustrated in Figure 181-B. Two others with three prongs and stems with the wavy end were recognized last year by Stephen G. C. Ensko as the work of Joseph Goldthwaite of Boston (1706-80); these were described and illustrated by Millicent D. Stowe in the New York *Sun,* October 17, 1947.

In the early years of the 18th century, forks were small with three prongs similar to the American example in Figure 181-D. Slightly later, the distinction was made between table and dessert forks with the result that large heavy forks came into being and the former three prongs changed to four prongs.

Several of the rather crude two-prong forks with a spoon bowl at the other end of the stem, bearing the marks of different American silversmiths, have come to light (see FIG. 181-A). These are singularly interesting as they resemble those described in early 16th-century inventories as a "Suckett Spone wt. a forke Joyned together." There is one in the British Museum which dates probably from the early part of the 16th century; this is 6 inches long (about the same size as the American sucket forks) and has a flat stem of stout silver with a small spoon bowl at one end and two short rude prongs at the other.

From the fact that they were made in America, it would seem that some were brought from England by the early settlers and that a form of sucket was popular in Colonial times until at least the beginning of the 18th century. The word "sucket" which is now obsolete is doubtless a corruption of the French *succade* (a sweetmeat) and in English Tudor times denoted such dainties as ginger, plums or similar fruit in a heavy syrup—presumably the fruit was "speared" from a dish with the forked end and the syrup dipped with the spoon bowl.

Even toward the end of the 19th century, steel forks with bone, ivory or porcelain handles were in more general use both in America and England than the present generation might suppose. And some of us can recall the steel forks and knives fitted into thin silver handles shaped rather like an old-fashioned pistol butt and filled with a composition made largely of resin. The larger sizes of both the pistol handle forks and knives were truly awesome weapons, though the knives, which are some 12 inches long, today serve as excellent bread knives. These pistol-handled knives and forks were made by the silversmiths of New York and Philadelphia toward the end of the 18th century, and a few are still preserved in private collections.

If not highly important, skewers, butter tasters and marrow scoops should be included with domestic silver hand-tools.

In earlier days, every kitchen was supplied with a number of iron skewers rather like large bodkin needles. These were used to fasten a joint of meat to the spit so that it kept its shape while turning and roasting before the great open fire; when the joint was sent to table, the iron skewers were replaced by silver ones the earlier examples of which are also shaped like a large bodkin with a slot in the end.

Later silver skewers such as were made by American silversmiths were larger and flat or slightly convex; while perhaps rarely used today for their intended purpose, many of them have chamfered edges and make attractive paper knives.

Butter or cheese tasters (sometimes called testers) are similar in shape to an apple corer. American silver tasters are extremely rare; there are two which formerly belonged to Judge Clearwater's great-grandmother in the Metropolitan Museum of Art.

Marrow scoops, which are related to the spoon family, were used to extract the marrow from bones when that delicacy was enjoyed in fashionable circles—it is still a delicacy but no longer fashionable. There are a few American examples (FIG. 179-G) copied from the English scoop with the long narrow spoon-like bowl and a channeled stem. Another type made in England was a fairly large spoon bowl with a narrow channeled stem.

CHAPTER SIX

Bygones

Argyles

TO MANY PEOPLE, AN ARGYLE IS A MYSTERY EVEN when they see one. Actually, it is a gravy holder invented about 1775 by a practical man who objected to cold gravy.

Argyles were made in various shapes, many of them rather like small teapots; others might well be mistaken for spout cups, as for example the one illustrated (FIG. 182), but there is considerable difference in the construction. With the teapot-shaped argyles, a small cylinder with a separate cover was fitted in the center of the body to hold a heated billet of iron which kept the heat in the gravy.

Most of them, however, were fitted with an inside lining to form a jacket into which hot water was poured through a small lip which had a hinged cover; the gravy being surrounded by a wall of hot water. Broadly speaking, the arrangement has some relationship to a modern thermos flask.

The argyle shown in Figure 182 was made by Seril Dodge of Providence, Rhode Island (1765-1803), and was among the silver from the Genevieve Garvan Brady Collection which was sold in May 1937.

Buckles

In the yesterdays, as in our time, a change of fashion invariably met with more or less opposition. So it was in 1665 when King Charles the Gay adopted a new style of dress to which the diarist Evelyn refers as the Eastern Fashion. On October 18 of that year, Evelyn notes: "It being the first time his Majesty put himself solemnly into the Eastern Fashion of vest, changeing doublet, stiff collare band and cloake, into comely vest, after the Persian mode with girdle or straps and shoe strings and garters into boukles of which some were set with

148

precious stones. . . ." And Evelyn himself had adopted the mode by the end of that month, for he writes, "I had on the vest and surcoat or tunic as 'twas call'd after his Majesty had brought the whole court to it. It was a comely and manly habit. . . ."

King Charles "changeing . . . shoe strings and garters into boukles" marks the introduction of buckles to England, but, so consistently did the many objectors lampoon those who wore buckles, they were not adopted generally until early in the 18th century. An instance of the scornful ire the new fashion aroused appears in a newspaper of 1693 which is worth quoting somewhat fully:

> Certain foolish young men have lately brought about a new change in fashion. They have begun to fasten their shoes and knee bands with buckles, instead of ribands, wherewith their forefathers were content, and moreover, found them more easy and convenient; and surely every reasonable man will own they were more decent and modest, than those new-fangled, unseemly clasps or buckles, as they call them, which will gall and vex the bones of these vain coxcombs beyond sufferance and make them repent of their pride and folly. We hope all grave and honourable persons will withhold their countenance from such effeminate and immodest ornaments. It belongeth to the reverend clergy to tell these thoughtless youths, in a solemn manner, that such things are forbidden in scripture.

Admonition had little or no effect for shoe buckles became increasingly popular around 1700. Portraits of various periods show that the earliest were quite small and oval but, by the end of the 17th century, the large, square style shaped to fit the instep, was adopted and this continued in vogue until about 1750. In the meantime, however, the larger oval shape was introduced and was fashionable both with shoes and, in smaller sizes, as knee buckles from about 1730 to 1780. Just before they went out of fashion those worn at the knee were still the small oval shape, but those for shoes were the square type which often were unnecessarily large.

After remaining popular for a century, buckles eventually gave way to shoestrings or laces in about 1791. And their departure aroused almost as much resentment as their arrival, for the introduction of shoestrings naturally brought an end to buckle making and unemployment to thousands of people. The buckle makers asked the Prince of Wales (afterward George IV) to help in reviving the trade, but though he himself continued to wear buckles and ordered all his

149

household to do the same, the fashionable world refused to follow the royal example and shoe buckles gradually passed to the limbo of forgotten things.

That they were equally fashionable in America is shown by the number now in various private and public collections, one of the most representative being in the Metropolitan Museum of Art which includes the many examples assembled by the late Judge A. T. Clearwater. These illustrate the various styles of shoe buckles and those used for fastening the breeches at the knee and for stocks—the broad stiff band of material which was the collar and cravat of that time.

It is clear they were the work of trained and experienced craftsmen, for such ornaments as small bow-knots, medallions, pierced and interlaced work and the attractive faceting all suggest the hand of a skilled jeweler rather than an average silversmith. For example, one pair of shoe buckles in the Metropolitan Museum of Art have pierced and shaped edges with two rows of facets separated by a gold wire.

In addition to those of silver, a number of plated examples have been found in America, and while it has been suggested that the latter were made in America from imported fused or Sheffield plate, as it is better known, this seems doubtful. As the late Frederick Bradbury points out in his *History of Old Sheffield Plate,* buckles of fused plate are conspicuously absent even in the quite early days of Sheffield plate, because this method of making them presented three difficulties. The copper base was too soft and pliable to withstand the rough usage; to achieve the thickness necessary for the arch of the buckle and at the same time to taper it toward the ends called for infinitely careful hammerwork; and cutting the shape and the pierced designs would leave raw copper showing along the edges which it would be extremely difficult to hide by side-plating.

It is safe to say, therefore, that plated buckles were made by close plating rather than the fused process and without trespassing too far into the fields of technicalities, we might here indulge in a brief description of each of these methods.

Fused plating consists of an ingot of copper, slightly alloyed with zinc, and a sheet of silver. The copper is planed to ensure a smooth surface and then filed and scraped until the face to be plated is free of any imperfections. A piece of silver is cut nearly the size of the surface to be plated and this too is cleaned thoroughly. Then the two prepared surfaces are placed together and hammered or pressed, thus embedding the silver in the copper. A copper plate, treated with a solution of chalk to prevent its sticking, is placed on the silver to protect it from the fire and the three pieces of metal are bound together with iron wire. Borax is applied to the edges of the silver and copper where they touch each other and the copper and silver "sandwich" put on a coke fire in a furnace. When properly "cooked" it is taken out and allowed to cool, the protecting copper plate removed, when it is sent to the rolling mill to be turned into plated sheets from which various articles can be made.

Close plating, on the other hand, is used for covering steel and is as simple though quite different from fusion plating. First, the article to be plated is thoroughly cleaned, then dipped in sal ammoniac which acts as a flux, and afterward dipped in melted tin. Thin silver foil is fitted as evenly as possible to the article and a hot soldering iron passed lightly over the surface. This melts the tin which forms a solder between and joins the steel and the silver-foil covering, after which the surface is carefully smoothed with another hot iron, the rough edges or fash, as it is called, clipped away and the edges made smooth with a burnisher.

There are many more aspects of these two forms of plating, but these will be sufficient to illustrate how the one differs from the other, and how buckles, spurs, bits, knives and other steel objects were made to appear like silver.

Coasters

Today, the original use of coasters or decanter stands, as they are sometimes called, is almost forgotten, but time was, in the late 18th and early 19th centuries, when they were essential to any well-appointed dining table. They were first introduced when it became customary to remove the cloth from the table for dessert, and we can only suppose some ingenious humorist conceived the idea of placing the decanter in one of these stands and "coasting" it along the polished surface. This explains why the fairly deep silver or Sheffield plate sides are fitted with a turned stout wood base, the bottom of which is covered with fine baize to prevent marring the polished mahogany as the decanter was sent sliding from one guest to another —undoubtedly with decreasing precision as the evening advanced. Some of the stands are mounted on small silver wheels and occasionally two were fitted on a miniature truck of four wheels.

Though they were surely used in America, in view of the absence of any examples made here before the early 19th century, we may assume that they were among the many things imported from England; but it is possible, and to be hoped, that examples bearing the marks of American silversmiths will in due time come to light.

Dish Crosses

To an extent, the dish cross (FIG. 183) was to the English household what the brazier was to the American household—a means to keep food and drink hot. It came into use during the second half of the 18th century and is an ingenious and convenient contrivance consisting of four bars or arms; two are joined to an upper pierced ring and two to a similar ring below, in such a way as to allow them to be adjusted to the width of any dish. Each bar has a sliding socket with a bracket above and a leg below, so that the brackets may be moved along the bars to support a larger or smaller dish or a saucepan, a small spirit lamp being placed immediately under the pierced rings in the center. Dish crosses were made in America and several examples have come to light in recent years, but like their English counterparts, they are by no means numerous.

Freedom Boxes

These desirable bibelots symbolize a ceremonial recognition of individual achievement yet, in truth, perpetuate the old-time method of vote control. To be a freeman was to have the right to vote at a parliamentary election, a right formerly accorded to the privileged few, and it was not until the early part of the 19th century that any form of really democratic election was introduced in Britain—a reform which might be regarded as the first instance of England following where the United States led. For, despite the emphasis upon the rights of man in the Declaration of Independence, the right to vote in the young Republic was for some time dependent upon a property qualification and a religious test, with the result that less than one third of the people could vote.

As new States come into being and recognized manhood suffrage, regardless of property or religion, old States mended their ways and by about 1830 the franchise was extended to virtually every adult white male. And in 1835 Britain began to move toward the same goal and the old term "Freeman" lost its former significance. It was made permissible, however, for a borough to confer the distinction of honorary freeman upon any man or woman whom it deemed worthy, and the worthy one was presented with a certificate in a gold or silver box engraved with the arms of the borough and an inscription.

This custom was observed in America, and an appreciable number of the boxes including several of gold are now in different collections. New York seems to have been particularly prodigal in the use of gold for freedom boxes (FIG. 184), one of which was presented in 1702 to Lord Cornbury, Governor of New York, whom one historian describes as "the most dissolute rascal ever sent to govern an American colony, not even excepting the infamous Sothel of the Carolinas."

Most of the boxes are oval, about 3½ inches long by 2 inches wide which is approximately the size of those for tobacco or snuff and doubtless some of the Freemen later put their freedom boxes to better use than that of being a repository for a piece of vellum.

Papboats

Many of these little boat-shaped bowls have been elevated to the status of cream jug by the addition of three feet and, where necessary, a handle. Their intended use, however, was to hold soft food suitable for infants and invalids who, too weak to feed themselves, were given the food from the wide lip of the papboat. Actually, the same method is still employed, but the papboat is usually of white porcelain, though virtually the same size as those of silver.

They were made of silver in England during the 17th century, but the few that have survived date from the Georgian period; in fact, there are more American examples than there are English. Papboats, bearing the marks of American silversmiths, date from the end of 18th or beginning of the 19th centuries. They differ little one from the other, each having a quite shallow bowl and a long lip with or without a light strap handle (FIG. 185). It is not improbable that this, now obsolete, little vessel came originally from Holland, as the Dutch word *pap* is, supposedly, the sound made by infants when they are hungry. And there is an early reference to it in the saying: "To give pap with a hatchet," for doing a kind action in an unkind manner; the phrase occurs in *A Discourse of Marriage and Wiving, and of the greatest Mystery therein contained: How to chuse a good Wife from a bad,* by Alexander Niccholes, London, 1615, which warns that "he, that so old seeks for a Nurse so young, shall have Pap, with a Hatchet, for his Comfort."

Saucepans and Nutmeg Boxes

Serving hot food in a silver saucepan at table was a custom that came down from ancient Roman times, for a number of vessels similar in shape to the modern saucepan have been unearthed in Britain and other European countries. They are known in England dating from the days of Cromwell, though, at that time and for some years later, they were not the shapely vessels that appeared later, being in fact skillets rather than saucepans. Few skillets have survived, however, and it is rare indeed that one makes its appearance. This writer has met with two which were sold at Christie's in 1929 and 1930. One, hall-marked London 1656-7, is a heavy plain cylindrical bowl on three stumpy pear-shaped legs with a massive reversed S-handle; the other, hall-marked nine years later, is somewhat more refined and has three cast legs with claw feet. The latter (FIG. 186) is of particular interest because the cover resembles an American porringer.

As it appears in the illustration, it is merely a domical shape with a flat pierced handle, but, when inverted, it is in every way similar to a porringer, even to the boss in the center shown in Figure 96 and, furthermore, the cover of the skillet is the same size as the larger porringers, namely 5 inches in diameter.

Later in the 17th century, larger saucepans and stewpans were one of the many extravagances marking the reign of Charles the Gay and this method of serving hot food continued well into the 19th century. The custom was observed in America probably as early as the end of the 17th century, because large saucepans by such early silversmiths as John Coney (1655-1722) have been preserved to the present time; and that it persisted is equally evident from the large saucepans made as late as 1820-30. Doubtless many other early ones have disappeared, for as conveniences for keeping food hot in the dining room increased and table manners became more delicate, many would be sent to the local silversmith to be melted and fashioned into other domestic silver.

Various shapes were used, but the most common was the bulbous bowl tapering to the rim, the larger ones usually having covers; with few exceptions, one of which is illustrated in Figure 187, they have long turned-wood handles fitted into a silver socket. The smaller ones were used for making what is known as mulled wine which is wine heated and spiced; these are often referred to by the old name, "pipkin," which was a small earthenware cooking pot with a cover and a hollow earthenware handle set at an acute angle.

Another article related to mulling wine was a small silver box containing a steel grater for powdering the nutmeg with which the wine and other hot drinks were spiced. It is usually a cylindrical box about 3 inches high, with a tight fitting cap, the smaller grater, also cylindrical, being inside the box from which it was taken when needed. This may seem an extravagant means of protecting a steel grater, but the protection was really intended for the nutmeg inside the grater (FIG. 188).

Other varieties of nutmeg boxes were made by American silversmiths, one ingenious type, following an English pattern, being a cylindrical shallow box with two lids (FIG. 189)—that is, both the top and the bottom were hinged to open. A grater is fitted at the top near the rim and the powdered nutmeg falls through and is emptied by opening the hinged bottom. Another, which was an American invention and does not appear to have been made in England, is shaped like a small oval urn, with a domical cover, about 3 inches high. The cover is hinged and one side of the body opens on a hinge at the base disclosing a grater, the grated nutmeg being emptied from the hinged cover at the top.

Standishes and Inkstands

Any early inkstand or standish, as they were known until the 19th century, brings the realization that when adhesive envelopes and blotting paper were unknown and the fountain pen unthought of, writing a letter was a real undertaking. In fact, writing was done formerly by journeymen scriveners or clerks who traveled from place to place with their inkhorn and quills and put to paper the literary efforts of their patrons, whether it be a poem to a lady or a diatribe on the prevailing political situation. These clerks were the ancestors of modern journalists, for when writing was accepted as one of the social graces, the scriveners, lacking their customary work, began to record current events.

Only two early American silver inkstands have come within the purview of the writer and inquiry seems to indicate these are the only two known. We can therefore surmise that the romantic pewter inkstands were more commonly used. The well-known "Independence" ink-pot, as it is sometimes called, has been referred to and is shown in Figure 190. The other (FIG. 191) by John Coney (1655-1722), in the Metropolitan Museum of Art, bears some resemblance to one made by William Rainbow and hall-marked London, 1630-1 (FIG. 192).

155

This early Stuart example is the earliest known English standish. It is fitted with a double box, one section of which was for wafers and the other, presumably, for sealing wax, a cylindrical inkholder and a sandbox—sand was the blotting paper of earlier days—and on either side has a small cylinder for holding the quill pens. This interesting standish appeared at Christie's in 1909, when it brought $2,420. For thirty-five years, it was remembered but unseen; it reappeared at the same auction rooms in 1944 when part of the collection belonging to the late Sir John Noble was sold and at that time fetched $3,500.

When the two (FIGS. 191 and 192) are compared, the one by John Coney is markedly more advanced and better balanced. The wafer box has the same cylindrical shape as the inkholder and sandbox, and the stand is raised on three cast lions. The stand suggests an influence derived from Germany where the triangular shape raised on elaborate feet was used as early as the beginning of the 16th century; and lion feet are found in England during the Gothic period, a century earlier.

Tobacco Boxes and Snuffboxes

Less than a century ago, snuff taking was a widely fashionable custom, but smoking was one of the things not done—except more or less in secret. In these days many people look upon the former as an unpleasant habit, while smoking is very rarely questioned.

Mrs. C. S. Peel, writing in *Early Victorian England,* tells us that after the ladies had retired, the gentlemen put on their smoking caps and jackets or even complete suits to protect their dress clothes and hair from becoming tainted with tobacco smoke; for to smell of tobacco was a social sin and labeled the culprit a rank outsider. Men were allowed to smoke out of doors, in the stables or in the servants' hall when the servants had gone to bed, while in smaller homes smokers were limited to the kitchen.

Incidentally, Columbus discovered tobacco as well as America. Whether he was the first European smoker is not recorded, but he found it being used in Cuba in 1492. It was introduced to Spain some seventy years later, and about the same time to France by Jean Nicot who gave us the word "nicotine."

Legends have no place among facts, but we may, perhaps, be permitted to mention a quite charming fairy story we once heard when wandering in the Southwestern States. It tells of how an Indian princess, lacking in attraction to the opposite sex, prayed to her gods that the earth should swallow her and that she should rise again beau-

tiful and desired of all men. According to the story she did rise again
—as the tobacco plant.

Boxes for tobacco have loose lids, are somewhat larger and deeper
than those used to hold snuff, and are usually oval and plain except
for an engraved coat of arms or other insignia (FIG. 193). Nor was the
shape changed during the long period they were fashionable. Even in
the extravagant times of the Merry Monarch, Charles II, the tobacco
box remained plain, though a reeded or cabled ornament was added
at the end of the 17th century. One collection of about thirty which
came up at Christie's two years ago gave some indication of the value
placed upon these rarities and, taken as a whole, it showed that the
value is dependent upon the age: thus one dated 1683 brought $705,
whereas one of the late 18th century sold for less than $100.

Snuffing or sneeshing, as it is called in Scotland, did not become
popular until after smoking had become fairly general. For this, too,
the great Columbus must be given credit. The habit was first noticed
among the Indians by Ramon Pane who went to America with Columbus on his second voyage (1493-96). It was adopted in France, in
about 1560-65, as a supposed cure for a nasal trouble prevalent at that
time. The "cure" became so popular that the "patients" developed a
weakness for it and the virtues of *reniflement* spread rapidly.

As George Evans says in *An Old Snuff House,* whether snuff taking
was a nice habit or not greatly depended upon the taker, and he adds,
"Snuff, however, was without doubt surrounded by a great amount of
elegance." This elegance was observed even before the boxes were
introduced from France, when tightly rolled tobacco leaves, known as
a "carotte," were powdered by rubbing them on an iron rasp or rape.
These rasps were similar to a nutmeg grater mounted on carved ivory
or wood often inlaid with mother-of-pearl.

Snuffboxes did not come into general use in England until the time
of Queen Anne when a cargo of snuff was captured by the English off
the coast of Spain; the sale and distribution of this large quantity of
powdered tobacco popularized snuff throughout England and, within
a short while, small boxes of wood, horn, metal, silver and even gold
became as common as cigarette cases are in our time.

Some of the English snuffboxes emulate the extravagant magnificence fashionable in France, but, as a general rule, the decoration is
restricted to engraved work; and the popularity of snuff taking, resulting from the captured cargo, soon crossed the Atlantic, for boxes were
made in New England early in the 18th century.

One example (FIG. 194) by John Coney (1655-1722) has a romantic

157

history. For some time it had lain unrecognized with other knick-knacks in the window of a small London shop, until one day T. H. W. Lumley happened to see it and bought it for the proverbial song. Soon afterward, it returned to its native land and is now under the care of Dr. John Marshall Phillips, Curator of the Mabel Brady Garvan Collection at Yale University.

It is the usual oval, about 3 inches long, the lid engraved with the arms of Wentworth and the motto, *"En Dieu Est Tout,"* which, as the box was made by John Coney, allows the presumption it formerly belonged to Benning Wentworth (1696-1722), Governor of New Hampshire, who was succeeded by his nephew Sir John Wentworth (1737-1820).

Another similar snuffbox of gold is also associated with the early history of New England. It was made by Jacob Hurd (1702-58) and is engraved with the arms of Dummer of Southampton, England, granted in 1711. The box is illustrated by the late Francis Hill Bigelow *(Historic Silver of the Colonies)* who mentions it was bequeathed by William Dummer to his nephew, William Powell, and that it is in the collection of the Misses Loring. This William Dummer was the son of Jeremiah Dummer, the well-known Boston silversmith, and was acting Governor of Massachusetts for two periods in the early 18th century.

Those soft sentiments which in these days we sometimes "say with flowers" were often expressed in earlier times on the lid of a snuff box which would be engraved with tiny blossoms and birds and a heart pierced by arrows—when a heart was all aflame with love, that heart would be shown ablaze with fire and pierced by an arrow, while other arrows pass it by unharmed. Tortoise-shell boxes mounted in silver were also made in America, but examples are rarely met with.

Patch Boxes

One early 17th-century authority on the gentle art, advises the love-lorn swain, "If it be a lover's part you are to act take a black spot or two; 'twill make your face more amorous and more gracious in your mistress's eyes," which tells us that patches were not restricted to the fair sex.

How extravagant the use of patches became during the 17th century is illustrated by contemporary descriptions and pictures. One drawing of a lady of that period will serve as an example of the excessive use of patches: A crescent shape is applied under the left eye and another at the side of the right eye; below the latter, there is a large star and a large spot on the chin. To all these "minor" decorations was added a coach-and-four complete with driver, fixed to the forehead. The last mentioned was one of the more popular "designs" of the early Stuart days.

During the reign of Queen Anne, women took an active interest in politics and it was customary for those of Tory (Conservative) leanings to wear a patch on the left side of the face, while those who supported the Whigs (Liberals) wore one on the right side—where those who remained "on the fence" wore their patches is not recorded, but we might suppose they would have one on each side.

Patches were, at first, of black taffeta, but later this was replaced by velvet; and the ubiquitous compact of today is, to an extent at least, the patch box of yesterday. Some of these tiny boxes have a mirror inside the lid. That patches were still fashionable during the later Georgian days is indicated by the small boxes, about 1 inch in diameter, made of Sheffield plate with a polished steel mirror in the lid. These Sheffield plate boxes have a lift-off lid instead of the more usual hinged type and it is worth noting that the inside is neither plated nor tinned, consequently the bare copper shows.

If more or less unimportant as examples of early American silverwork, many preserved in different collections can now be connected with romance, thanks to those who have traced their original owners. Occasionally one will tell the story of the sentiment it conveys from a lover in an inscription, as for instance, *This is Thine and Thou Art Mine* with the date 1734 on a tiny heart-shaped patch box in the collection of Mrs. Miles White, Jr.; and there is one in the Clearwater Collection at the Metropolitan Museum of Art, engraved with love knots and locks of hair. This belonged originally to Lucy Mercy Noyes, a belle of Portsmouth, New Hampshire, from whom it descended. During the first World War, it was donated to a Red Cross salvage sale, where it was bought by the late Judge Clearwater.

Punch Strainers and Ladles

Any question as to the popularity of punch in Colonial times is disposed of by the number of strainers dating from the second half of the 18th century; though the fact that most of them were made by New England silversmiths might imply that this Oriental drink was more popular in Boston than in New York or Philadelphia.

Punch strainers differ little in form. The bowls are generally about

159

4 inches in diameter pierced in various geometric designs and fitted with two shaped rests or handles of fairly heavy silver to support the strainer on the rim of the bowl; in some instances, one rest is much shorter than the other, the longer being intended as a handle.

How greatly historical association can increase values was demonstrated in the 'thirties by a strainer (FIG. 195) by Jonathan Clarke of Newport and Providence, Rhode Island (1705-c. 1770), now in the Mabel Brady Garvan Collection, Yale University. When this strainer was offered at auction it realized no less than $5,500, a figure explained by the fact that it formerly belonged to Jabez Bowen who was Chief Justice of the Superior Court, Rhode Island, 1781; Deputy Governor, 1778-86, and a member of the State Convention which adopted the Constitution in 1790. The strainer was probably especially ordered from Jonathan Clarke, as the handles are far more elaborate than those of other strainers and part of the pierced design forms the words, JABEZ BOWEN PROVIDENCE JANUARY 1765 (or 1766, the last figure might be either).

There is a scarcity of ladles made specifically for dipping the punch from the bowl to the jugs which were placed on the table and from which the glasses were filled. The earliest 18th-century ladles have a round bowl with a lip and a tubular silver handle, but later this was refined to a lighter round bowl with a long turned wood handle. Similar ladles were made with whalebone handles, but wood seems to have been more commonly used both in England and America. After the middle of the century, the double-lipped bowl rather like the shape of the early sauceboats became popular and this seems to have been generally used by American silversmiths (FIG. 196).

While there may be few with the wooden handle and double-lipped bowl, it has to be remembered that there is no dearth of other American ladles of a size suitable alike for serving soup or dipping punch; and as we moderns realize, a soup ladle is equally convenient and easier to handle.

Tea Caddies

All the various accessories to the teapot which appeared during the 18th century have been retained, with the exception of the tea caddy. It might also be said that the beautiful sugar vases no longer serve their original purpose, but at least any one of these is a graceful ornament.

As we have noted in a previous chapter, tea was formerly too expensive to allow it to be in the charge of careless and wasteful

160

servants. Hence the small silver caddy which was kept under lock and key, probably in the drawing room where the tea was brewed by the mistress of the house. Incidentally, the word "caddy" is another of those curious English corruptions; it is the Anglicized form of *catty* which comes from the Malay *kati,* a small box in which tea was at one time imported to England—the box held about 21 ounces.

Silver caddies were first made in England during the time of Queen Anne and dating from that time examples still exist of the octagonal pear shape similar to, but slightly smaller than, the body of the octagonal teapots (see FIG. 81). The most popular type during the early years of the 18th century, however, was the bottle-shaped, often called a canister. These were straight-sided with clipped or canted corners. Many were plain with a short cylindrical neck and a tightly fitting cover, but some were fitted with a sliding bottom or top to allow the caddy to be filled with less risk of spilling the precious tea.

Both the straight-sided and the more elaborate caddies that came later were frequently in sets of two or three (each for a different kind of tea) and enclosed in a locked case. And the importance of these caddies is evident from the fact that the cases were covered with tortoise-shell, mother-of-pearl or shagreen with silver mounts and instances are known where the case is entirely of silver.

Tea caddies were made by American silversmiths but few seem to have survived. We might perhaps assume that as the century advanced and tea drinking in America became increasingly popular more silver caddies would be made; but it is probable that following the custom in England many Colonial homes used a pottery or porcelain caddy.

No silver caddy by a New England silversmith has yet revealed itself to the writer, but one by Garret Schanck (*c.* 1791) and one by Thauvet Besley of New York (*c.* 1727) were exhibited at the Museum of the City of New York in 1937-8. The latter is of the bottle type with straight sides and a deep vertical flute at each corner. It is inscribed, *Bohea Tea* on the shoulder and with the initials C M P on the base; these are the initials of Catherine McPheadres who married Robert Gilbert Livingston in 1740.

Here we have one of those romantic incidents connected with early American silver. When, over two hundred years ago, Thauvet Besley received the order for the tea caddy for Bohea Tea, the order included a companion caddy for Green Tea. And Catherine McPheadres became the proud owner of the pair. In the course of time, however, the two caddies were separated and one lost sight of and forgotten.

161

In 1946, an odd lot of silver consisting of an English taper stick and a caddy by an unknown maker inscribed, *Green Tea* and engraved with the initials C M P on the base appeared at Christie's. Thinking it was Continental, probably Dutch, no attention was paid to it and the lot was bought by a dealer for the taper stick alone.

However, H. R. Jessop, having seen and examined the caddy at the sale, recalled the curious incised mark, TB, in monogram, and later looked through the list of American silver marks, to discover it was American; and within a very short time he owned the caddy. Through the good offices of Miss Helen Comstock, this long-lost treasure found its way back to its native land where, it is to be hoped, it will join its twin.

Caddies made in Philadelphia in the later 18th and early 19th centuries are slightly more numerous. One by Brown and Seal (*c.* 1810), in the Metropolitan Museum of Art, is bottle-shaped but in place of being rectangular with clipped corners it is oval-shaped with slightly sloping molded shoulders—not unlike a pocket flask.

Others which were in the exhibition at Philadelphia in 1921 follow various forms of the late 18th-century straight-sided teapots. This style of caddy was sometimes made as part of a tea service as is the case with the one shown in Figure 175. It is oval in form with the slightly convex sides shaped by a series of wide flutes; and like other caddies of that type is fitted with a lock and key which indicates the value of tea even in the early 19th century.

In view of the number of other American silver articles connected with tea drinking, tea caddies are singularly few—it is not improbable that the melting pot claimed many of them after they were no longer in general use.

Dish Rings

Anything that is singular arouses both interest and speculation, and the one American dish ring (FIG. 197) makes one wonder whether it was an experimental piece by the maker, Myer Myers of New York (1723-95), or one he made to order. It is engraved with the initials SSC and is said to have belonged originally to the Honorable Samuel Cornell, a merchant of New York and New Bern, North Carolina, and his wife, Susannah.

These rings, which are essentially Irish, appeared first about the middle of the 18th century and were popular (in Ireland) until about 1820. Nothing is known definitely regarding their origin, though it has been suggested that rings were used on the table at an earlier period. These misunderstood articles, so persistently referred to as "potato rings" were intended primarily as a stand for vessels holding hot foods and so to protect the surface of the table from the heat.

One of the rings was placed on the dinner table and remained there throughout the meal, serving as an ornamental stand, in this order, for the soup bowl, the oak potato bowl, the dessert bowl and, lastly, the punch bowl. Some Irish families still possess one or more of the large turned bog-oak potato bowls, a few of which have silver rims, and the sight of such a bowl placed on a dish ring doubtless suggested to the English mind the absurd name "potato ring."

During the three quarters of a century they were fashionable, there are three distinct styles of dish rings, but the basic form remains the same. They may be divided into periods, which we will call early, middle and late; the distinctive features being in the height and decoration. Those of the early period are quite shallow, some of them being less than 3 inches high and the ornamental design an intricate combination of rococo scrolls, flowers, foliage and sometimes birds, all of which are embossed and chased and the background cut away. Other characteristics of the earlier examples are the deeper plain band above and below the pierced design, the more pronounced incurve of the spool shape, and, while smaller, they are heavier than the later examples.

Those of the middle period express in the pierced decoration all that love of fantasy which is so much a part of the Irish character. The dish rings of this time are about 4 inches high and the larger surface offered an opportunity for various pastoral scenes and figures. For example, a fashionably gowned lady gathering fruit in an orchard with a small farmhouse in the background; that the lady's hat appears likely to fall or that the fruit is suspended in mid-air did not trouble the Irish silversmith. Nor did he find any incongruity in combining Occidental with Oriental architecture, or Chinese figures wearing pancake hats with European hunters and dogs against a background of disproportionate trees with equally disproportionate birds flying wildly to escape the long fowling-pieces carried by the hunters.

Bird and figures continued to be used until the dish rings went out of fashion, but those of the third period are strongly influenced by the classic designs of Robert Adam and, in consequence, are more formal than the typically Irish designs of the earlier rings. There is a like formality with the American dish ring which is one of the few examples of the more elaborate ornamentation found among early American silver.

163

Those who have studied any representative collections realize the dominant feature is simplicity of line. This reflects the character of the people for whom the silverwork was made, for had those people demanded more elaborate work, the same craftsmen could have produced it, as is evident in those more ambitious examples such as the Coney monteith bowl, the Winslow sugar box, the Richardson kettle and stand and other examples of which some are shown among the illustrations in this book. And if, as is probable, many fine pieces passed beyond recovery before the work of early American craftsmen was fully acknowledged, this country has a heritage in both silver and furniture which demands and has, of late years, received adequate recognition.

CHAPTER SEVEN

Marks on American Silver

ANY TOPIC OF GENERAL INTEREST IS LIKE A MAGNET—
it attracts particles of information which, when assembled and col-
lated, give us a wider knowledge of the subject. Meanwhile, the
interest continues to spread and the magnet to attract. A signal
instance of this is all that has been learned and has yet to be learned
of early American crafts after starting from zero about half a century
ago. Then, few indeed gave a thought to the possibility that there had
been craftsmen in Colonial America as skilled as those of the Old
World.

But when the pioneer collectors and students lifted the curtain of
the past, the less diligent among us became curious; and curiosity
being the mother of discovery, many important facts regarding early
Colonial life and the craftsmen of those· days were brought to light—
more particularly concerning the cabinet-makers and silversmiths.

On the foundations of the history of the early American silversmiths started by such pioneers as the late J. H. Buck and others, there
has been built a "Book of Knowledge" to which new facts are con-
tinually being added. From the realization that important schools of
silversmiths had worked in America during the later 17th century,
developed an always increasing search both for examples and information about the men themselves.

As time went on, more names were added to the first tentative lists
and more facts were garnered relating to the several groups of silversmiths. The result was that an always increasing amount of silverwork, the origin of which had remained unrecognized, could at last
be definitely attributed to an American craftsman. All this valuable
information was not assembled in any short time or without untiring
observation and research. Even as late as 1925, the then most complete
list contained less than twelve hundred names, but since then that
number has been very largely increased.

Valuable as these lists were as records, they did not materially assist the layman in identifying a mark with a particular silversmith. The first contributions to this knowledge were recorded by Robert Ensko (1915) and Hollis French (1917). Ten years later, Stephen G. C. Ensko issued his *American Silversmiths and Their Marks,* in which the actual marks are reproduced and the name of the silversmith with the date and place at which he worked shown against each mark; other editions of this important work containing additional marks and names have since been issued.

Unlike Europe and Great Britain, no official stamps or date letters were ever used by the silver craft in Colonial America, nor were any records of the silversmiths kept. Consequently, it is not possible to date definitely any example of American silver or to determine exactly the period when a particular man was active, except in some few instances where information has been found in early documents.

There is, however, something to be learned from the style of the marks themselves. Through the years these develop from the forms familiar to the founders of American silvermaking in the countries from which they came to those used by craftsmen of after years. In the Boston marks of the late 17th and early 18th centuries, there is an obvious English influence in the occasional use of emblems, such as the crown and fleur-de-lys. And the use with the earlier marks, of a punch following the outline of the initials and symbols is a further indication of European influence. Again, the cutting of the punches is noticeably crude compared with those of later dates.

Symbols are seldom found in early New York or Philadelphia marks which, as a general rule, are merely the initials in a rectangular, heart-shaped, oval, circular or other simple punch. Several of the New York men with Dutch names used three initials arranged one above two or vice versa, as for instance Jacobus Vanderspiegel $I^S V$; Benjamin Wynkoop, $W_B K$; Cornelius Vanderburgh, $C_B V$; Gerrit Onkelbag, $_G B_O$; John Brevoort, $_I B V$.

Analyzing the various types of marks to the middle of the 18th century, so far compiled, shows that a far larger proportion of Boston and other New England silversmiths used the full surname, either with or without the initial, than those of New York or Philadelphia. Many of the earlier New England men had one punch with initials only and one with the surname or initial and surname.

It is sometimes suggested that initials indicate a slightly earlier date than the full-name mark; but it would seem more likely that the one was intended for small articles and the other for larger pieces. This latter view gains support from the marks on forty pieces by different early New England silversmiths, each of whom used the two marks. Of these, thirteen (mostly small articles such as casters, spoons, tiny boxes) are punched with the initials and twenty-seven (mostly large) with the surname. But that there was no fixed rule is evident from the fact that those punched with the initials included a caudle cup and a tankard and those with the full name, a spoon and small saltcellars.

Though some New England silversmiths adopted the crown, fleur-de-lys and other symbols, their number is comparatively small. It is noticeable, too, that the quite early men, such as Jeremiah Dummer, John Coney, Timothy Dwight and others used only their initials, those of Coney often being accompanied by a crown or fleur-de-lys and Dummer's with a fleur-de-lys only; Coney also used his initials with a crown above and a cony below.

As mentioned before, the two symbols as part of a silversmith's mark were introduced from France where the maker's marks invariably included a crown or coronet and, more often than not, the fleur-de-lys with various other devices. By way of illustrating the size and elaborate character of the French makers' marks that of Jean Picard (1652) will serve: At the top of the gracefully shaped punch there is a coronet and, immediately below, a large fleur-de-lys and below that two pellets and a mullet between the maker's initials. Marks of this elaborate type are found on London silver of the late 17th century, though examples are very rare. The crown and the fleur-de-lys as part of a maker's mark made their appearance in London about 1670 and, though less prevalent after 1720, they are found until about 1739.

Incidentally, "pellet" is a later heraldic term for "gunshot" and is shown as a black roundlet; a mullet, the rowel of a spur, is the distinction indicating the third son.

Earlier New York silversmiths show a decided preference for the traditional initials of the Christian and surname, for there are few instances of the surname in full; but the Philadelphia marks suggest that while the smaller punch was general, the full name was frequently used. Even during the second half of the 18th century when the surname was more commonly used throughout the country, New York silversmiths seem to have retained an affection for the initials. By the beginning of the 19th century, however, American silver is marked almost invariably with the full surname and initial of the maker, the punch with the initials only being found very occasionally.

167

If the silver itself lacks the attraction of the earlier styles, the marks of the first half of the 19th century should offer interest to any collector.

There is nothing which would suggest any form of assay or marking of silver by a constituted authority in America at any time, except the establishment of an office at Baltimore in 1814 which is dealt with more fully later in this chapter. Some control may have been exercised in Boston by the Massachusetts Charitable Mechanic Association and by the New York Silver Smiths' Society of which Myer Myers was president in 1776; but there are no records of either of these "Guilds" having directly supervised the craft.

Perhaps we may accept the wide variety of marks which appeared after about 1790 as an indication of an effort to establish some form of control. And, assuming this, the fact that these punches are found more often on silverwork bearing New York maker's marks would suggest that the New York Silver Smiths' Society was more active than any similar group elsewhere.

Upward of seventy of the devices are reproduced by Mr. Ensko and, for convenience, they may here be classified under two headings: (a) Those essentially American in origin and (b) those obviously copied from marks on British and Irish silver.

Some few in the first group are difficult to determine, but there is no question regarding the several forms of the eagle or the eagles' heads or the five- and six-pointed stars which are evidently taken from the arms of the Young Republic; the same applies to the figure of an Indian holding a bow. Another which offers some interest is an arm and hand holding a short-handled heavy hammer which suggests the symbol of a silversmiths' guild—a similar mark was used by an English 16th-century silversmith named Colville. The eagle or the eagle's head mark is found accompanied by the name of the maker in a separate punch from the later 18th century, more frequently on New York pieces, but also on some made in New England, Philadelphia and Maryland. Occasionally, the eagle is with the arm and hammer or with a wheat sheaf.

One mark that has exercised the writer's curiosity for some time is the palm-leaf-like form used by Philip Syng, who came with his father from Cork, Ireland, to Philadelphia in 1714. There is nothing among the symbols used by an Irish silversmith in any way resembling this leaf, nor is there any mention of a palm leaf as a maker's mark in the lengthy Irish, British and French records. Finally the shape inspired the rather "wild and woolly" idea that it might be associated

168

with the botanical term "syngenese" (a plant with stamens united by the anthers).

Among the marks in the second group is one which might equally belong to the first group, namely, the male profile of which there are various forms, some of which are bewigged and some with short hair. The first explanation to suggest itself is that the punch was copied from the king's head which was used on British silver as a duty mark. But it could equally well have been intended as a portrait of George Washington, even if most of them are somewhat uncomplimentary to the features of the First President.

Regarding the others in this group there is no doubt. The various quaint lions, the leopard's head, with or without the crown and the occasional letter were suggested by similar marks on English silver, probably London as that would be more familiar; the wheat sheaf, it may be assumed, was borrowed from the three wheat sheaves of Chester; the anchor from Birmingham; and the rarely used harp from Dublin.

In 1792, the United States Mint fixed the standard of silver coinage at 892 parts fine in 1,000 and, in 1837, this was raised to 900. Later, it became compulsory in some States that silverware marked COIN should not be less than the standard of the coinage, namely 900 fine; and while the word STERLING or an abbreviation of it had been used previously, this was later restricted to silver of the same standard as that required in Britain—925 parts fine.

In connection with the more or less crude reproductions of British marks, it has been put forward that after the War of Independence British silver remained popular despite the natural lack of affection toward England; and that the American silversmiths, seeking to sell their own products, used the punches to suggest an English origin. This is contradicted, at least to an extent, by the fact that some of the pseudo-marks are accompanied by the name of the place in which the articles were made.

The pseudo-marks are found (in addition to the maker's mark) in various combinations, always in separate punches and more commonly on spoons. Even if the marks themselves were good copies of the originals, the several combinations dispose of any suggestion of deliberate forging, as the following examples show:

Spoon: Male profile, figure of lion, letter G   maker's mark B. Gardiner
   punched twice   New York
" Anchor, star, male profile, letter D "   " John Elliott.
  incised

169

"	Eagle, male profile and letter D incised	"	"	Bell
"	Anchor, male profile, lion	"	"	Howe & Guion
"	Anchor, female profile, star and an animal (? a beaver)	"	"	I.W.F. (John W. Forbes)
"	Leopard's head crowned and lion	"	"	J. Ewan
Fluted teapot and stand: Lion, letter **r,** leopard's head crowned (this may be an Indian's head with feathered headdress)		"	"	I.H. (in a serrated rectangle)
Tea caddy: Lion, leopard's head crowned and male profile		"	"	Vernon
Tea urn: Lion, letter G and male profile		"	"	(no mark)

The tea urn was found by the writer some years ago in the collection of Mrs. Cornelia Dabney Tucker of Charleston, South Carolina, whose information was that it had been made by a New York silversmith; in view of the marks being the same as those on the spoon by B. Gardiner, it may be presumed he was the maker of the urn.

Never could one of these quaint "Anglo-American" marks be mistaken for that of an English assay office which are finely cut and quite definite in outline. But there are more perfect reproductions of British marks made in America during the present century which are deliberate forgeries and which are intended to deceive and have deceived the unwary. To be unwary is to ignore the adage *"Caveat emptor"* and the protection that others, more experienced, are always willing to offer.

Mention was made earlier of an assay office at Baltimore, Maryland. When Charles I gave Lord Baltimore the "miniature kingdom of a semi-feudal type" which is now the State of Maryland, he gave him the right to make his own coinage, grant titles, start a war or any other pastime that pleased him. A mint was established there nearly three hundred years ago, but it does not appear to have operated for long. Had it continued, there is little doubt that an important group of silversmiths would have been established there long before the end of the 18th century, the time when Baltimore began first to achieve prominence as a center.

In fact, so greatly did the craft develop there, that in 1814 Maryland passed what was known as the Silver Purity Act under which an assay office was established and authorized marks were impressed on all silverwork offered for sale. It is a matter for regret that this effort to

170

regulate the craft was so short-lived, for otherwise it might have served as a model for other States to adopt.

From the fairly consistent appearance of an eagle punched with the names of several prominent Baltimore silversmiths before the assay office came into operation, it may be assumed that at least some of the craft had formed a guild and adopted the eagle as their symbol. About this time, too, the surname punch was more generally used, but after Baltimore silver was officially marked, there was a tendency to revert to the earlier initials as the maker's mark. Early in the 19th century the STERLING mark is found, either in relief or incised, sometimes accompanied by the eagle; but the word COIN does not seem to have been used at Baltimore. Other punches found occasionally are the figure of a lion, a spread eagle and the head which has the semblance of a woman and may possibly have been the forerunner of the profile of Liberty later adopted as one of the official marks.

Three official marks were used by the Baltimore Assay office; namely, the head of Liberty, an annual date letter, and the arms of Baltimore which were adopted for its great seal by the State of Maryland from the arms of the Lords Baltimore, the founders of Maryland. Thus, we may regard the head-of-Liberty punch as denoting that the silver was of the legal standard of purity and the arms as the "town" mark. These marks are analogous to those of many English towns, as for instance, Exeter, Devon, which used the familiar lion passant as a standard mark and the arms of the city (a triple towered castle) as a "town" mark.

For some reason, the official notice directed that the dating should be the "dominical letter of the year." For an explanation of "dominical letter" we had better rely on that never-failing friend, Noah Webster. After telling us that the first seven letters of the alphabet are used to denote the first seven days of the year and are repeated throughout the year, he adds:

> The letter which, in almanacs, denotes Sunday, or the Lord's Day (*Dominica dies*), chiefly used to aid in finding the date of Easter. The first seven letters of the alphabet are used to designate the first seven days of the year and are repeated throughout the year, the same letter thus standing for Sunday during the year (except in a leap year). The dominical letter for any given year is the letter preceding that for the year before, or in leap years, after February 29, the second preceding. Thus, the dominical letter for 1934 is G; 1935, F; 1936, E and D; 1937, C; 1938, B; 1939, A; 1940, G and F. After 28 years, unless a cen-

turial year which is not a leap year (as 1900) is included, the letters return in the same order.

Admittedly somewhat complicated, but it can be worked out.

After being operative for sixteen years, the Silver Purity Act ceased to be enforced and, the official assaying and marking no longer being required, the Baltimore Assay office closed in 1830; though until about 1853 it remained the headquarters of an official known as the Assayer whose duty it was to decide by assay the standard of silver, where the quality was in question.

This appointment of a public assayer is explained by the fact that while freed from the compulsory official marking of their work, the silversmiths were required to punch it with figures showing the standard or proportion of pure silver. The legal standard had been 11 ounces to 12—12 ounces troy being 1 pound troy, which is always used for weighing precious metals, etc. Hence with a Baltimore maker's mark you may find a separate punch showing 10.15, 11^2, $\frac{11}{12}$, which respectively denote: 10 ounces 15 pennyweights fine silver to each 12 ounces; 11 ounces 2 pennyweights to 12 ounces; and 11 to 12 ounces.

These marks may guarantee the silver to be of "proper fineness," to use the ancient term, but they lack the romance of hall-marks however modern the latter may be. But maybe the day will come when we shall see a revival of the old Silversmiths' Guilds and the establishment of assay offices in different centers of America.

CHAPTER EIGHT

Scarcity and Collections

WHEN THE LARGE NUMBER OF SILVERSMITHS WHO are now known to have worked in Colonial America is compared with the amount of their work which has come to light, it becomes obvious that a considerable quantity of early American silverwork has disappeared across the years. This discrepancy cannot, as yet, be accounted for definitely, though several reasons explain it, at least to some extent.

In analyzing any appreciable number of important private and public collections, the fact stands out that surviving examples of certain household articles as, for example, tankards, canns, porringers and teapots are relatively more numerous than others which would have been equally in daily use. And when the former are themselves considered, it becomes noticeable that all of them are articles which would have a more or less personal association with the owners. Thus tankards would be prized by the master of the house; canns in many instances might have sentimental value as childhood gifts; porringers were regarded as necessary to the average household and again might have sentimental associations; while teapots and tea services, being essential to the social activities of the woman of the house, would be highly valued, protected, and handed down from mother to daughter through succeeding generations.

On the other hand, articles lacking sentimental value would be sacrificed to the melting pot to supply silver for others of a more fashionable style. Today, we would look upon this "transformation" as vandalism, but the practice was as prevalent in England during the later 18th and the 19th centuries as it was in America. Nor was it confined in England to private owners, because no small amount of fine early silver belonging to the great Livery Companies was melted down and the metal used to make the massive and ugly objects which became fashionable during the early Victorian days.

If, among all the Colonial silver which has come to light, there is a dearth of such pieces as standing-cups, two-handled caudle cups, tall spool-shaped salts with the brackets, the delightful little trencher salts and early spoons and forks, we should not conclude that more were not made. Customs and manners went through a series of radical changes between the time when the first silver was produced in the Colonies and the later 18th century. As we have pointed out in preceding chapters, the tradition of the standing-cup was virtually discontinued, caudle was replaced by other drinks and, moreover, table glass came into general use. The same situation applies to the large salts which, when the ceremony of the salt declined to a forgotten custom, represented nothing more than metal of some value, and similarly with the trencher salts when fashion decreed the small circular saltcellers on three legs.

Consequently, a large number of these fine pieces having become old-fashioned and useless, were sent to the silversmith who melted them down and used the metal to make other articles of a more fashionable and useful character. That many beautiful pieces were produced by this means is admitted, but the early examples from which they were made were lost forever.

Then, too, a very considerable amount of early domestic silver was given at different times to various churches, particularly in New England. This is shown very clearly when the exhibition catalogues are studied in detail. For example, the Boston catalogue of 1911 reveals that over six hundred pieces were lent by churches and among them were eighty-nine tankards, twenty-nine mugs and canns, and thirty caudle cups. In addition to these, the same exhibition included a considerable number of tall cups with baluster stems of the type known as a standing-cup, but described as a chalice when intended for ecclesiastical purposes; and, as we have remarked before, it is safe to assume that at least some of these were at one time in use as domestic wine cups.

When we consider the imposing number of such drinking vessels as tankards, canns and caudle cups which are now part of the silver belonging to the churches, it is easy to speculate that these rich gifts were inspired by what George Washington called "that little spark of celestial fire, called conscience" during temporary waves of temperance. We can concede that much of the early silver preserved in churches might otherwise have been lost, but no collector is without regret that this entailed its going "out of circulation."

Certainly, there are evidences that these sporadic periods of self-denial caused the destruction of many early drinking vessels. Some cups were melted down and made into spoons, forks or other pieces, while others were transformed or their former purpose disguised, as was the case with tankards which were turned into jugs by the addition of a spout; a number of these exist to the present time.

Again, in bygone days there was a lack of the protection against fire and theft which we enjoy in our time; and we may safely assume that in addition to the not inconsiderable amount destroyed by fire, at least as much domestic silver was stolen and melted down. Another channel through which a large amount disappeared was via the Loyalists who left the Colonies at the time of the Revolution, for it would be natural that these people would take their silver with them, if only for the reason that it was an easily portable and valuable possession. Not that all the silver they carried away was necessarily made by Colonial silversmiths, but at least a fair proportion was and, while some of it may have been preserved, more was doubtless sold by the owners in time of need when probably it found its way to the melting pot.

Mr. Bigelow in the Introduction to his book refers to the huge quantity of silver which was taken from the King's Chapel in Boston by the rector, Dr. Henry Caner, when he left the country during the Revolution. While much of this was the work of English craftsmen which had been presented by different English monarchs, there can be little question that many of the pieces were made by New England silversmiths.

The probability that a good deal of American silver was carried away by Loyalist families links up with the relatively large amount which has been found in England in quite recent years. Many of these people went to Canada and later to England, and it is a safe inference that they carried with them any silver they may have had.

It would be natural that, as time went on, this American silver should change hands and not bearing English hall-marks be regarded as of little value and melted. But even so, a number of important examples survived, as is demonstrated by the fine collection belonging to Victor A. Watson of London, which was on loan in the Victoria and Albert Museum before the second World War, where it was seen by many American visitors.

This collection was started by the late Lionel A. Crichton who, realizing that he not infrequently came upon examples of Colonial silver in England, decided to assemble as many as possible without acquiring any in the United States. As all the groups of American

175

silversmiths are represented it seems that gifts of silver to friends in England must have been frequent, aside from the contributions of the Tories.

We cannot mention all the many examples in the Watson Collection, but a few of the rarer ones are as follows: The earliest is a flat-top tankard by John Coney of Boston (1655-1722) which bears the mark IC with a crown above and the coney below impressed on the cover, the body and the bottom; and in case some reader may be able to identify them we will mention it is engraved with the initials $_N{}^H{}_S$.

Most of the tankards, however, are by New York makers and these include one by John Brevoort (1715-75) known as the Crommelin tankard. It is the usual tapering shape with a flat cover and has a double scroll handle. The front is engraved with the seal of the Collegiate Church of New York and a particularly elaborate mantling, and on the bottom is inscribed, *The Gift of The Consistory of The Dutch Church of The City of New York to Mr. Daniel Crommelin Marc^t, at Amsterdam 1764.* According to the records of the Reformed Protestant Dutch Church of the City of New York, "The Consistory . . . resolved at the meeting of May 1st, 1764, that the three gentlemen, Messrs. Longuiville, Brinshall and Crommelin each be presented with a silver tankard with the Seal of the Church Corporation inscribed on the same." It would be interesting to discover the present whereabouts of the other two.

Another tankard by William Vilant of Philadelphia in this collection is even more interesting. This has the plain tapering body and domical cover with a beaded rat-tail down the handle and a cupid head in an ornamental shield on the tip. About two thirds of the distance round the body is engraved with three joined panels each depicting a subject from Ovid and, above these, the heads of Philip, Earl of Hardwicke, Lord High Steward at the trials at Kilmarnock, Cromartie and Lovat in 1746; Simon Fraser, Lord Lovat who was beheaded for treason in 1747, and Philip, Earl of Chesterfield. This decoration was the work of Joseph Leddel probably a son of Joseph Leddel, a pewterer of New York, the back of the handle being inscribed, $_I{}^L{}_M$ *Joseph Leddel Sculp. 1750.*

Heraldic emblems and initials which may some day be identified with the original owners occur on several other pieces: A trifid spoon decorated on the back of the bowl by Edward Winslow bears the initials $_L{}^H{}_M$ and a tobacco box by Benjamin Brenton of Newport, Rhode Island, is engraved with the arms of Parker. Two excellent globular teapots are similarly engraved with arms, one by Jacob Hurd of Boston with those of Coffin and one by Thomas Hammersley of New York with arms which have not been identified—a chevron sable between three swans, crest, a salamander. A pair of small waiters by Myer Myers of New York bear the crest of the Marquess of Exeter.

The Philadelphia pieces include a small cylindrical dredger with a simple ring handle and a porringer engraved, W.C. on the handle, and on the body, *To my Esteemed friend Dr. Rush from Thomas Paine, 1775,* both by Joseph Richardson; a straight-sided fluted teapot and stand by Joseph Shoemaker; and a saucepan by Joseph Lownes.

Among the many others which found their way to England and are now in the Watson Collection are a set of four saltcellars on three feet accompanied by four spoons by Thomas Hammersley—these are engraved with the salamander crest mentioned above; a fruit dish 10¼ inches in diameter and a bowl, both made by Daniel Christian Fueter of New York, (PLATE VI-A) and examples made in Baltimore.

As in America, Colonial silver was not known formerly in England for what it was and many an example was labeled "foreign"—usually Dutch. A classic instance of this was the octagonal teapot by Peter Van Dyck which appeared in London and was long regarded as of Dutch origin. Then a dealer with more experience and knowledge recognized it as an American piece and it is now one of the many rarities in the Mabel Brady Garvan Collection at Yale. In the same collection, there are a covered sugar basin by Adrian Bancker, a tankard by Cornelius Kierstede, a salver by John De Nys and a snuffbox by John Coney, all of which were found at different times in England.

Others have been referred to previously, and more could be added, together with romantic stories in connection with the discovery of some, as for instance, a magnificent two-handled bowl by Cornelius Vanderburgh bought in the South of England and now returned to its native land.

It is to be regretted that the interest in England did not show itself as early as it did in America, because it is possible that many more examples might have been found and preserved. But today English dealers are as keen to "spot" an example as their opposite numbers and private collectors are in America.

Looking back, however, it is clear that even the present enthusiastic interest in America did not develop until relatively recent years. The reason for this was probably lack of adequate literature on the subject and the absence of any authentic records of the silversmiths and their marks. It must be remembered, too, that until the several exhibitions had been held, virtually nothing was known of American silver except

177

to those men whom we have already mentioned as having zealously started the quest.

These men might be called the missionaries by whom the less enlightened were stimulated to learn. It would not be wide of the mark, however, to suggest that the really active interest derived largely from those first few professionals who, like Robert Ensko, gave time and study to American silver and who were willing always to advise and help the younger collector. But here again the younger collector was timid of entering what to him was a new and unknown field and this was undoubtedly a hindrance to the general expansion of collector interest in Colonial silver.

Though today there are many reliable dealers to whom the beginner may apply for guidance, such men were few and far between for some years after the rediscovery of American silver. To discuss an article and at the same time be able to examine it and ask questions of someone who knows the correct answers is not only a pleasure to a collector but a means of adding to his knowledge and so adding to his zest. And as the lack of these sources of information tended formerly to retard the general interest, so in more recent years they have become one of its important stimuli.

When did the less experienced begin to be active collectors? It is possible that the later and present keenness had its beginnings when American silver began to appear in the auction rooms; for courage begets courage and many who had hesitated, on seeing others bid, themselves became bidders. And such timid beginnings have proved the nucleus of more than one splendid collection.

LINE ILLUSTRATIONS

Illustrations on facing page:

1. Tapering cylindrical cup with baluster stem and domical spreading foot. New England, late 17th century. *H: 8 in.*

2. Cup with spirally fluted calyx, baluster stem and gadrooned band around foot. New England, late 17th century. *H: 8 in.*

3. Beaker with band of frosted or matted decoration. New England, late 17th century. *H: 3⅞ in.*

4. Beaker with molded base, showing Dutch influence in the style of the engraved decoration. New England, late 17th century. *H: 6½ in.*

5. Plain beaker with flaring lip and molded base. New England, early 18th century. *H: 5½ in.*

6. Beaker engraved in the Dutch style with intersecting bands, flowers and panels. New York, late 17th century. *H: 7 in.*

Illustrations on facing page:

7. Tumbler cup. New York, early 18th century. *H: 1¾ in.*

8. Cylindrical dram cup or wine taster with cabled wire scroll handles. New England, late 17th century. *H: 1½ in.*

9. Hemispherical dram cup. New England, late 17th century. *H: 1 in.*

10. Two-handled bowl embossed with floral designs in panels after the Dutch style. By Cornelius Kierstede, New York and New Haven (1675-1757). *H: 4¼ in.*

182

7

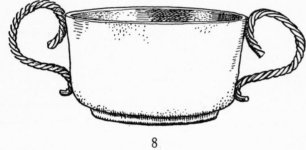

8

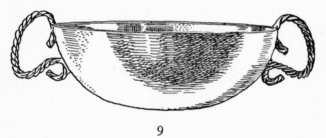

9

10

Illustrations on facing page:

11. Bowl embossed with flowers in panels. By Cornelius Kierstede. *H: 3½ in.*

12. Plain bowl with cabled wire handles. By Benjamin Wynkoop, New York (1675-1751). *H: 3 in.*

13. Tankard with 'ram's horn' thumb-piece and cherub-head handle tip. New England, late 17th or early 18th century. *H: 5¾ in.*

14. Tankard with dolphin and mask thumb-piece, V-shaped tongue below handle joint, small tube on handle, shield-shaped tip. New England, early 18th century. *H: 6½ in.*

· Domino · THOMÆ DARLING · Tutor Dic Winn Liv Co

11

12

13

14

Illustrations on facing page:

15. Large tankard with eagle thumb-piece and cherub-head handle tip. By John Coney, Boston (1655-1722). *H: 8½ in.*

16. Tankard with cut-card work design on lid and at lower handle joint. By Jeremiah Dummer, Boston (1645-1718). *H: 5½ in.*

17. Tankard with beaded rat-tail grip, cherub-head tip, foliated band and zigzag wire at base and rim. By Peter Van Dyck, New York (1684-1750). *H: 7½ in.*

18. Tankard with engraved medallion on lid and rat-tail spine at back of handle. New York, early 18th century. *H: 7½ in.*

19. Tankard with ornamentation on handle and above base molding and double-spiral or corkscrew thumb-piece. New York, early 18th century. *H: 7½ in.*

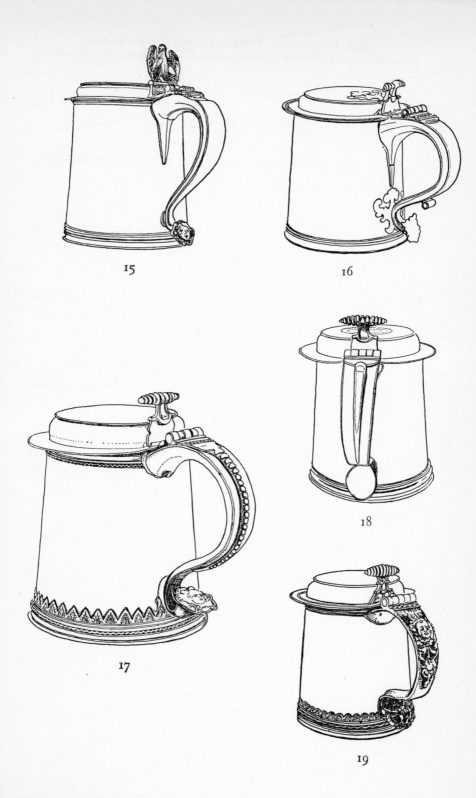

15

16

17

18

19

Illustrations on facing page:

20. Mug with bulbous body, cylindrical neck, and fluted decoration. By John Coney, Boston (1655-1722). *H: 3½ in.*

21. Mug with fluted base and band below rim. New England, late 17th century. *H: 3¼ in.*

22. Beaker-shaped mug with molded strap handle. New England, early 18th century. *H: 3½ in.*

23. Tapering cylindrical mug. New England, late 17th century. *H: 4 in.*

24. Tapering cylindrical mug with molded rib and beaded ornament on handle. New England, late 17th century. *H: 4 in.*

25. Mug with cherub head on handle tip. New England, late 17th century. *H: 4½ in.*

20

21

22

23

24

25

Illustrations on facing page:

26. Mug with molded rib and strap handle. New York, late 17th century. *H: 3½ in.*

27. Mug with tubular handle and ornamental band above base molding. New York, late 17th century. *H: 3½ in.*

28. Plain caudle cup, bulbous or ogee shape. By Jeremiah Dummer, Boston (1645-1718). *H: 3 in.*

29. Caudle cup with embossed and chased figure of cupid, flowers and foliage, scroll caryatid handles. By John Coney, Boston (1655-1722). *H: 5½ in.*

30. Caudle cup with fluted base and beaded scroll handles. New England, early 18th century. *H: 5 in.*

31. Caudle cup and cover-fitted spool-shaped foot-handle. By John Coney, Boston (1655-1722). *H: 7 in.*

32. Two-handled cup and cover embossed acanthus and palm leaves. Ascribed to Jacob Boelen, New York (1654-1729). *H: 5⁷⁄₁₆ in.*

33. Caudle cup with scroll handles by Gerrit Onkelbag, New York (1670-1732). *H: 5¼ in.*

190

26

27

28

29

30

31

32

33

Illustrations on facing page:

34. Spout cup with tankard-shaped body, handle and thumb-piece. Made at Plymouth, England, circa 1690. *H: 5 in.*

35. Two-handled spout cup. By Jeremiah Dummer, Boston (1645-1718). *H: 4½ in.*

36. Spout cup decorated with cut-card work on cover; wood handle. New England, late 17th century. *H: 5½ in.*

37. Spout cup with domical cover and molded strap handle. New England, early 18th century. *H: 4½ in.*

38. Spout cup, pear-shaped body, domical cover and tankard handle. New England, early 18th century. *H: 5 in.*

39. Spout cup of simpler type without cover. New England, late 17th century. *H: 3½ in.*

34

35

36

37

38

39

Illustration on facing page:

40. Elizabethan silver-gilt standing-salt. London 1588-89. *H: 12 in.*

40

Illustrations on facing page:

41. Octagonal standing-salt with four scroll brackets on the rim. New England, late 17th century. *H: 5½ in.*

42. Circular trencher salt. New England, late 17th or early 18th century. *H: 2½ in.*

43. Sugar box embossed and chased with lobes etc. on cast scroll feet. By John Coney, Boston (1655-1722). *Length: 8½ in.*

44. Sugar box embossed and chased with swirling flutes. By Edward Winslow, Boston (1669-1753). *L: 7⅛ in.*

41

42

43

44

Illustrations on facing page:

45. One of a pair of columnar candlesticks made by Jeremiah Dummer of Boston, probably in 1686. *H: 10¾ in.*

46. Two types of baluster candlesticks. By John Coney, Boston (1655-1722). *Heights: 6⅛ in. and 6¼ in.*

47. Baluster candlestick by a London maker, 1690-91, showing outline of a drinking cup in the larger knop. *H: 6½ in.*

48. Snuffer stand by Cornelius Kierstede, New York and New Haven (1675-1757). *H: 8 in.*

45

46 A

46 B

47

48

Illustrations on facing page:

49. Dish or salver engraved carnations, tulips and cherubs' heads. By John Coney, Boston (1655-1722). *Diameter: 11¼ in.*

50. Cylindrical caster with bayonet fastener. New England, late 17th century. *H: 5½ in.*

51. Cylindrical caster, fluted top and foot, ornamental band at base. By Gerrit Onkelbag, New York (1670-1732). *H: 5¼ in.*

52. Tankard with dolphin and mask thumb-piece, showing the transitional form of lid and use of small finial. New England, early 18th century. *H: 7½ in.*

49

50   51

52

Illustrations on facing page:

53. Tankard of the more pronounced tapered shape with domical lid retaining the flat top. New England, early 18th century. *H: 6¾ in.*

54. Tankard with ornamental band above base molding copied from the New York tankards. By Samuel Vernon, Newport, R.I. (1683-1735). *H: 7¼ in.*

55. Tankard showing New York influence in the foliated band at base. By John de Nys, Philadelphia, early 18th century. *H: 7 in.*

56. Tankard with beaded rat-tail on handle and cherub-head tip. By William Vilant, Philadelphia, circa 1725. *H: 7½ in.*

53

54

55

56

Illustrations on facing page:

57. Cann or mug with scroll handle. New England, circa 1735. *H: 4½ in.*

58. Cann or mug with double scroll handle. New England, circa 1750. *H: 5½ in.*

59. Cann or mug showing transition from straight-sided to bulbous shape. *H: 5 in.*

60. Two-handled cup with fluted cover and base, melon-shaped finial, and scroll handles with terminal heads. By John Coney, Boston, (1655-1722). *H: 10 in.*

61. Two-handled cup with fluted body and cover, melon-shaped finial, and plain handles. By Edward Winslow, Boston (1669-1753). *H: 11 in.*

62. Two-handled cup and cover decorated with cut-card work, and harp-shaped handles. By Charles Le Roux, New York (1689-1745). *H: 10¼ in.*

57

58

59

60

61

62

Illustrations on facing page:

63. Punch bowl of the monteith type in the rococo style. By John Coney, Boston (1655-1722). *D: 11 in., H: 8½ in.*

64. Plain monteith with molded scalloped rim. By John Coney, Boston. *D: 11½ in., H: 9 in.*

65. Plain punch bowl. By John Hutton, New York, early 18th century. *D: 10 in., H: 6 in.*

66. Octagonal trencher salt. New England, early 18th century. *H: 1½ in.*

67. Circular trencher salt. New York, early 18th century. *H: 1½ in.*

63

64

65

66

67

Illustrations on facing page:

68. Salver on foot. New England late 17th or early 18th century. *D: 9½ in.*

69. Cylindrical dredger. New England, early 18th century. *H: 3¼ in.*

70. Octagonal dredger. New England, early 18th century. *H: 3¾ in.*

71. One of a pair of pear-shaped casters with bayonet fastener. By John Coney, Boston (1655-1722). *H: 5 in.*

72. Cylindrical dredger on feet. New York, early 18th century. *H: 3½ in.*

73. Set of three casters with bayonet fastener. New York, circa 1730. *H: 7⅛ in. and 5¾ in.*

68

69

70

71

72

73

Illustrations on facing page:

74. Octagonal baluster candlestick with molded domed foot. By John Burt, Boston (1692-1745). *H: 7¼ in.*

75. Octagonal baluster candlestick with 'saucer' base. By Nathaniel Morse, Boston (c. 1685-1748). *H: 6 in.*

76. Octagonal baluster candlestick. By Bartholomew Schaats, New York (1670-1758). *H: 9 in.*

74

75

76

Illustrations on facing page:

77. Pear-shaped teapot with short duck-neck spout. Engraved with the arms of Mascarène. By John Coney, Boston (1655-1722). *H: 8 in.*

78. Pear-shaped teapot with cut-card work on cover. By Peter Van Dyck, New York (1684-1750). *H: 8 in.*

79. Pear-shaped teapot. By Peter Van Dyck, New York. *H: 8 in.*

80. Pear-shaped teapot with molded cover and faceted spout. By Peter Van Dyck, New York. *H: 7 in.*

81. Octagonal pear-shaped teapot. By Peter Van Dyck, New York. *H: 7⅛ in.*

82. Globular teapot. Engraved with the arms of Phillipse. By Jacob Boelen, New York (1654-1729). *H: 6½ in.*

77

78

79

80

81

82

Illustrations on facing page:

83. Cylindrical tapering chocolate-pot with stopper in cover. New England, mid 18th century. *H: 10 in.*

84. Coffee-pot with low molded cover. New England, early 18th century. *H: 9½ in.*

85. Chocolate-pot with vase-shaped body and cylinder above cover. By John Coney, Boston (1655-1722). *H: 7⅞ in.*

86. Chocolate-pot with pear-shaped body showing use of the thumb-piece and heavy hinge borrowed from the tankard. By Edward Winslow, Boston (1669-1753). *H: 9½ in.*

83

84

85

86

Illustrations on facing page:

87. Tapering cylindrical coffee-pot with thumb-piece. New York, early 18th century. *H: 10½ in.*

88. Kettle with band of zigzag wire at rim. By Cornelius Kierstede, New York and New Haven (1675-1757). *H: 10¼ in.*

89. English brazier with cylindrical bowl on claw and ball feet. Circa 1685. *H: 4 in.*

90. English brazier with hemispherical bowl. London 1700-01. *H: 2¾ in.*

91. Cylindrical brazier with claw feet. By John Coney, Boston (1655-1722). *H: 3 in.*

87

88

89

90

91

Illustrations on facing page:

92. Brazier showing rococo influence in style of the pierced work. New England, early 18th century. *H: 3½ in.*

93. Brazier with primitive supports and feet. By Peter Van Dyck, New York (1684-1750). *H: 3½ in.*

94. Brazier by John de Nys, Philadelphia, late 17th or early 18th century. *H: 2⅞ in.*

95. Brazier with plain bowl. By Philip Syng, Philadelphia (1676-1739). *H: 2⅞ in.*

92

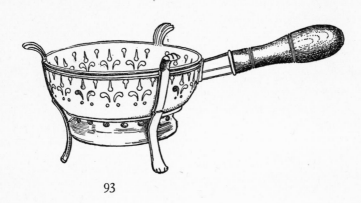

93

94

95

Illustrations on facing page:

96. Porringer showing the boss or print in center of bowl. *D: 5 in.*

97. Types of pierced designs found with porringer handles.

98. Covered porringer. Probably New England, late 17th century. *D: 6¾ in.*

99. Two-handled porringer with cover. Attributed to Jan Van Newkirke, New York, early 18th century. *D: 6½ in.*

100. Plain beaker with molded rim and base. Later New York type. *H: 5¼ in.*

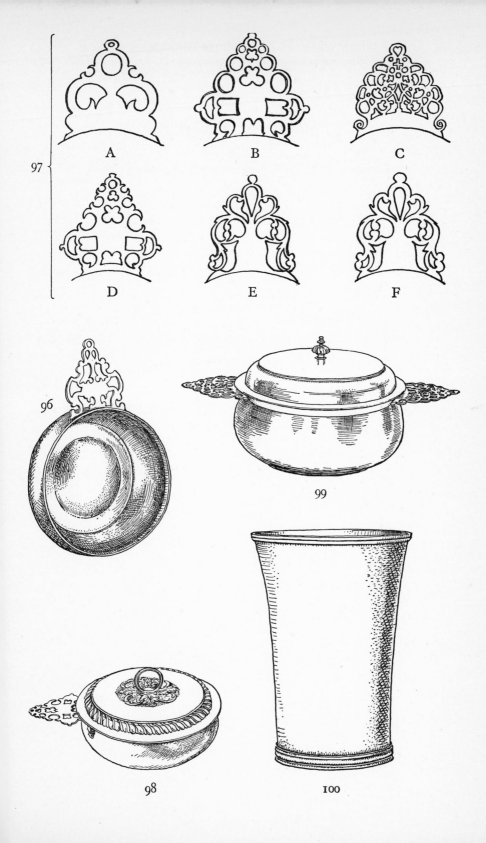

97 A B C

D E F

96

99

98 100

Illustrations on facing page:

101. Large tankard with open thumb-piece and pineapple (or cone) finial. New England, circa 1770. *H: 11½ in.*

102. Tankard with tall scrolled thumb-piece, baluster finial, drop on upper part of handle, and cherub-head tip. New England, circa 1760. *H: 8½ in.*

103. Tankard with plain domed lid (no finial knob) and volute at handle tip. New England, 1st half of 18th century. *H: 6 in.*

104. Tankard with engraved medallion on cover and disk at handle tip, baluster drop on handle, and interlaced thumb-piece. By Elias Pelletreau, New York (1726-1810). *H: 7 in.*

105. Tankard with scroll thumb-piece and long baluster drop on handle. By Nicholas Roosevelt, New York (1715-69). *H: 7¼ in.*

106. Bulbous or pear-shaped tankard with domical lid. New York, circa 1750. *H: 5½ in.*

101

102

103

104

105

106

Illustrations on facing page:

107. Tankard showing transition to the bulbous type. By Philip Syng, Philadelphia (1703-89). *H: 9 in.*

108. Bulbous-shaped tankard with plain domical lid. By Peter David, Philadelphia (1707-55). *H: 9½ in.*

109. Two-handled cup and cover. By Jacob Hurd, Boston (1702-58). *H: 12 in.*

110. Plain punch bowl. By William Homes, Boston (1717-83). *D: 9⅞ in.*

111. Punch bowl of the monteith type with removable rim. By Daniel Henchman, Boston (1730-75). *D: 10¾ in.*

107

108

109

110

111

Illustrations on facing page:

112. Plain circular saltcellar on three legs. New England, circa 1760. *H: 1½ in.*

113. Circular saltcellar with shaped gadrooned rim. New England, circa 1760. *H: 1½ in.*

114. Saltcellar decorated in the rococo style on dolphin feet. By Charles Le Roux, New York (1689-1745). *H: 1¾ in.*

115. Sauceboat on shell-shaped feet. New England, circa 1770. *H: 3 in.*

116. Sauceboat on shell feet with shell ornament at joint of the leg. Philadelphia, circa 1760. *H: 3 in.*

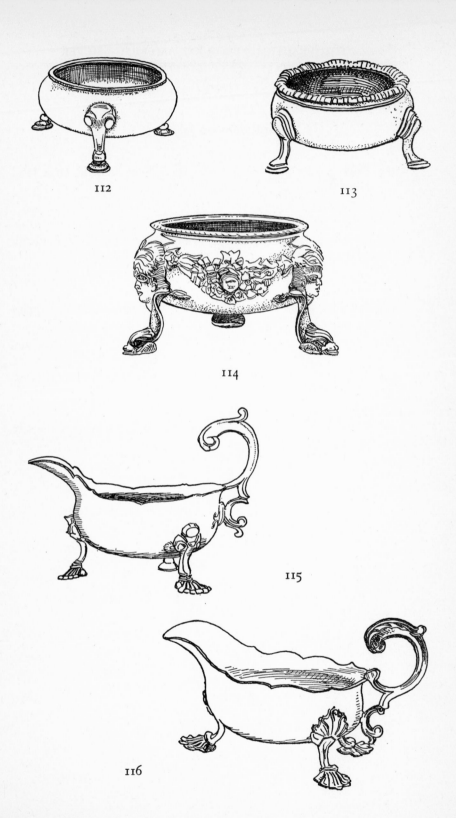

112

113

114

115

116

Illustrations on facing page:

117. Octagonal caster. New England, 1st half of 18th century. *H: 6½ in.*

118. Plain caster with pierced paneled top. New England, circa 1760. *H: 5 in.*

119. Pyriform caster with pierced paneled top outlined in trellis pattern. New England, circa 1760. *H: 5 in.*

120. Dredger with double scroll handle. New York, circa 1740. *H: 4 in.*

121. Cast fluted candlestick showing restrained rococo influence. By Jacob Hurd, Boston (1702-58). *H: 7 in.*

122. Candlestick in the florid rococo style. By William Thomson, New York, circa 1810. *H: 9 in.*

123. Candlestick showing use of rococo ornament. By Myer Myers, New York (1723-95). *H: 8 in.*

117   118   119

120

121   122   123

Illustrations on facing page:

124. English globular teapot with faceted spout. London 1722-23. *H: 5 in.*

125. Globular teapot with faceted spout. By Jacob Hurd, Boston (1702-58). *H: 5½ in.*

126. Globular teapot with pronounced downward taper and low domical lid. By Nathaniel Hurd, Boston (1730-77). *H: 5¾ in.*

127. Globular teapot with conical-shaped lid and tall wood finial. By Jacob Hurd, Boston (1702-58). *H: 5 in.*

128. Globular teapot with flat lid. By Jacob Hurd, Boston. *H: 5 in.*

129. Inverted pear-shaped teapot with chased decoration. By Benjamin Burt, Boston (1729-1805). *H: 6 in.*

130. Inverted pear-shaped teapot on three feet. New England, mid 18th century. *H: 7 in.*

124   125

126

127   128

129   130

Illustrations on facing page:

131. Globular teapot with inset lid. By Stephen Bourdett, New York, circa 1730. *H: 4 in.*

132. Teapot with marked downward taper. By Thomas Hammersley, New York (1727-81). *H: 5 in.*

133. Inverted pear-shaped teapot embossed and chased with flowers. New York, circa 1750. *H: 8 in.*

134. Inverted pear-shaped teapot decorated with immature embossed and chased work. New York, circa 1770. *H: 7½ in.*

135. Tea service of three pieces decorated in the rococo style. By Peter de Riemer, New York (1738-1814). *Height of teapot: 6¾ in.*

131

132

133

134

135

Illustrations on facing page:

136. Coffee-pot with tapering body rounded at base. By Daniel Hench-man, Boston (1730-75). *H: 10 in.*

137. Plain pear-shaped coffee-pot with cast spout and pineapple (or cone) finial. By Benjamin Burt, Boston (1729-1805). *H: 11½ in.*

138. Coffee-pot with inverted pear-shaped body and silver handle. By Benjamin Burt, Boston (1729-1805). *H: 13 in.*

139. Coffee-pot inverted pear-shape. By Ephraim Brasher, New York (w. 1786-1805). *H: 14 in.*

136   137

138   139

Illustrations on facing page:

140. Inverted pear-shaped coffee-pot. By Joseph and Nathaniel Richardson, Philadelphia, circa 1785. *H: 13 in.*

141. Kettle, globular shape with stand and spirit lamp. Engraved with the arms of Lowell quartering Leversedge. By Jacob Hurd, Boston (1702-58). *Height to top of handle: 14½ in.*

142. Inverted pear-shaped kettle in the rococo style. By Joseph Richardson, Philadelphia (1711-84). *Height to top of handle: 15 in.*

140

141

142

Illustrations on facing page:

143. Pear-shaped cream jug. New England, mid 18th century. *H: 3½ in.*

144. Cream jug on three feet. New England, mid 18th century. *H: 4¾ in.*

145. Cream jug, chased in the rococo style, on claw and ball feet. New England, mid 18th century. *H: 5 in.*

146. Inverted pear-shaped cream jug with punched beads round rim. New England, circa 1775. *H: 4¾ in.*

147. Pear-shaped cream jug on three feet. By Jacob Ten Eyck, Albany, N. Y. (1704-93). *H: 4 in.*

148. Cream jug on shell feet. By Nicholas Roosevelt, New York (1715-69). *H: 4¼ in.*

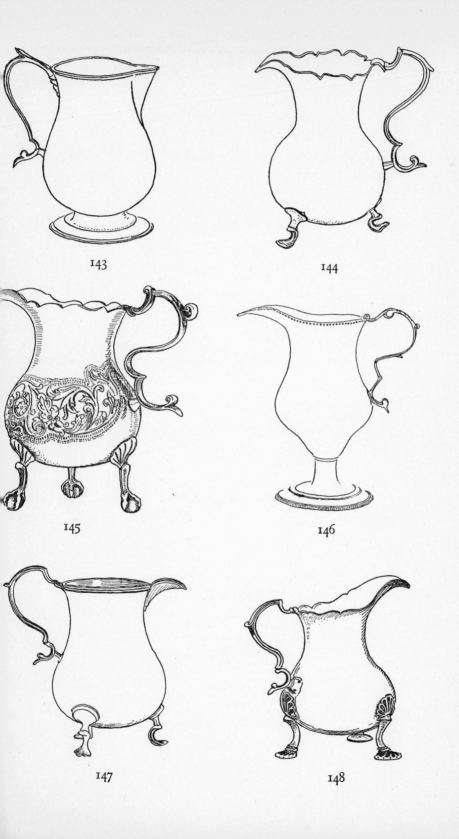

143

144

145

146

147

148

Illustrations on facing page:

149. Cream jug with long vertical lip. By Elias Pelletreau, New York (1726-1810). *H: 5 in.*

150. Plain cream jug. Philadelphia, circa 1770. *H: 5 in.*

151. Cream jug chased with flowers. By Abraham Dubois, Philadelphia, circa 1777. *H: 5⅛ in.*

152. Sugar bowl and cover-fitted 'foot-handle.' By John Burt, Boston (1691-1745). *H: 4 in.*

153. Sugar bowl, inverted pear shape, decorated in the rococo style. By Paul Revere, Boston (1735-1818). *H: 6 in.*

154. Sugar bowl on feet, cover with foot-handle. By Thomas Dane, Boston (c. 1724-c. 1760). *H: 4¾ in.*

155. Sugar bowl embossed and chased. By Jacob Boelen II, New York, circa 1755. *H: 5 in.*

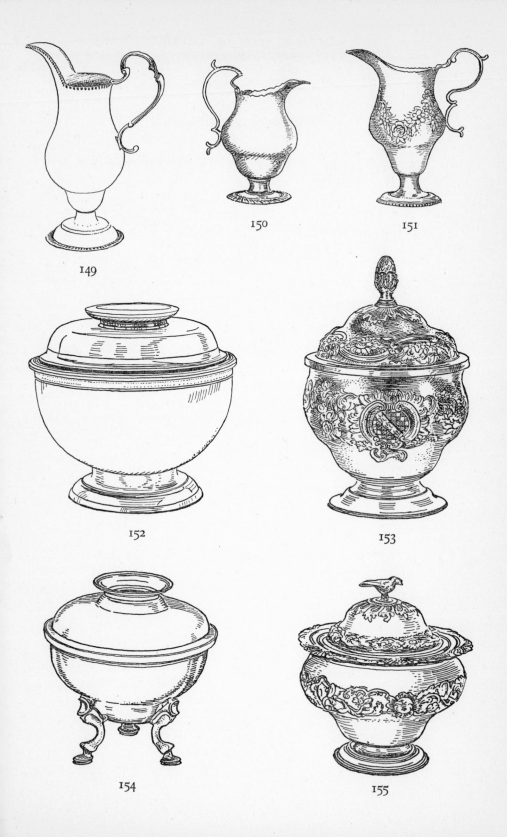

149

150

151

152

153

154

155

Illustrations on facing page:

156. Sugar bowl with pierced gallery and plinth. By John Letelier, Philadelphia, circa 1770. *H: 7¼ in.*

157. Shaped salver. By Jacob Hurd, Boston (1702-58). *D: 6¼ in.*

158. Salver with scroll and shell border. By Paul Revere, Boston (1735-1818). *D: 13 in.*

159. Oval tray with handles. By Paul Revere, Boston. *L: 17 in.*

160. Salver with gadroon border. By John Le Roux, New York (c. 1725). *D: 9 in.*

161. Salver with gadroon border on claw and ball feet. By Joseph and Nathaniel Richardson, Philadelphia, circa 1785. *D: 10 in.*

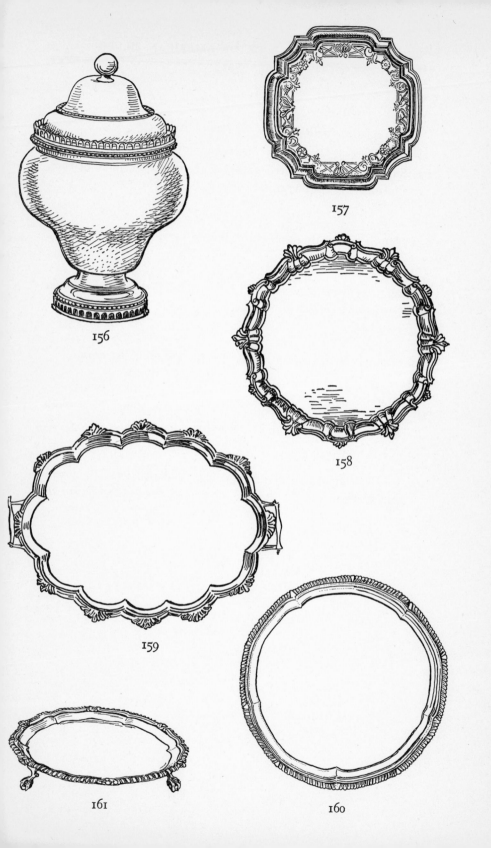

156

157

158

159

160

161

Illustrations on facing page:

162. Bowl decorated with band of bright-cut engraving. By Ephraim Brasher, New York (w. 1786-1805). *D: 9¾ in.*

163. Shaped pitcher. By Robert Evans, Boston (c. 1768-1812). *H: 7½ in.*

164. Boat-shaped saltcellar. New England, late 18th century. *H: 2½ in.*

165. Sauceboat with gadroon mounts. By Richard Humphreys, Philadelphia, circa 1775. *H: 6¼ in.*

166. Caster with conical body and simple pierced top. New York, late 18th century. *H: 4½ in.*

162

163

164

165   166

Illustrations on facing page:

167. Columnar candlestick. By Isaac Hutton, Albany, N. Y. (1767-1855). *H: 8¼ in.*

168. Candlestick. By Joel Sayre, New York (1778-1818). *H: 8¾ in.*

169. Cylindrical teapot with inset lid. By Joseph and Nathaniel Richardson, Philadelphia, circa 1785. *H: 6 in.*

170. Vase-shaped urn ornamented with bright-cut engraving. By Paul Revere, Boston (1735-1818). *H: 19 in.*

171. Oval teapot with spool-shaped lid and pineapple finial. By Daniel Van Voorhis, Philadelphia and New York, late 18th century. *H: 7¼ in.*

167

168

169

170

171

Illustration on facing page:

172. Tea service in the Empire style. By John Targee, New York, early 19th century. *Height of teapot: 9 in.*

172

Illustrations on facing page:

173. Octagonal teapot with engraved decoration. Philadelphia, late 18th century. *H: 5½ in.*

174. Vase-shaped teapot with pierced gallery and square plinth. Philadelphia, late 18th century. *H: 11 in.*

175. Teapot, tea-caddy with lock and sugar bowl. By Joseph Lownes, Philadelphia, circa 1790. *Height of teapot: 5½ in.*

176. Vase-shaped coffee-pot with pierced gallery. By Joseph Lynch, Baltimore, Md. (1761-1848). *H: 13 in.*

177. Helmet-shaped cream jug, fluted and engraved. By Christian Wiltberger, Philadelphia (1770-1851). *H: 7 in.*

173

174

175

176   177

Illustrations on facing page:

178. 17th-century spoons:
   A. Puritan type. By John Hull, Boston.
   B. Puritan type. By Jeremiah Dummer, Boston.
   C. Irish spoon showing transition from plain to trifid end.
   D. Trifid end. By Edward Winslow, Boston.
   E. Decorated end. By Jeremiah Dummer, Boston.
   F. Decorated wavy-end. By John Coney. (This Coney spoon is the companion to the wavy-end fork in FIG. 181-*C*.)

179. 18th-century spoons:
   A. Old English pattern. By Francis Richardson, Philadelphia.
   B. Showing disappearance of the ridge. By Philip Syng, Philadelphia.
   C. Bright-cut engraved decoration. By Joseph Anthony, Jr., Philadelphia.
   D. Feather edge. By Samuel Drowne, Portsmouth, N. H.
   E. Pointed end, bright-cut. By John David, Philadelphia.
   F. Clipped end, known as coffin-spoon. Late 18th and early 19th century.
   G. Marrow-scoop. 2nd half of 18th century.

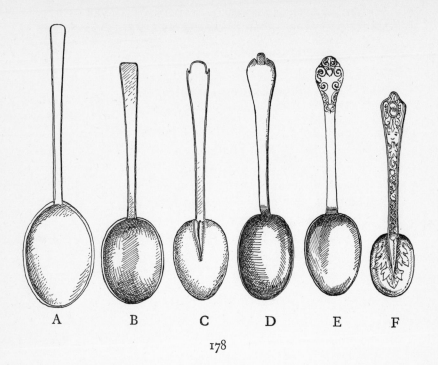

A   B   C   D   E   F

178

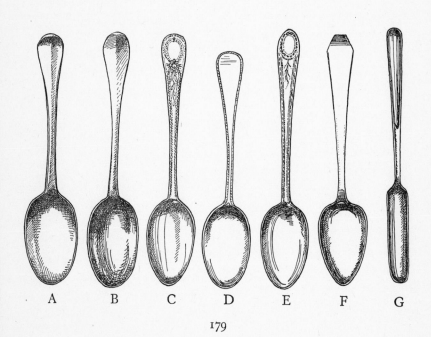

A   B   C   D   E   F   G

179

Illustrations on facing page:

180. Scissor-type sugar tongs. New York, early 18th century. *L:* 4½
in.

181. *A.* Sucket fork. By John de Nys, Philadelphia.
B. Wavy-end fork. By John Noyes, Boston.
C. Wavy-end. By John Coney, Boston (companion spoon shown
in FIG. 178-*F*).
D. Old English pattern. By unknown American maker.

182. Argyle or gravy holder. By Seril Dodge, Providence, R. I. (1765-
1803). *H:* 7½ *in.*

183. Dish cross with spirit lamp. New York early 19th century.
L: 12 in.

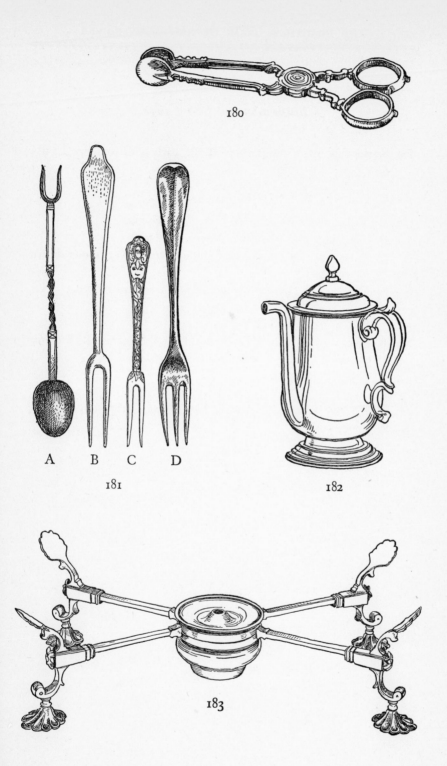

180

A   B   C   D

181

182

183

Illustrations on facing page:

184. Freedom box. New York, late 18th century. *L: 3½ in.*

185. Papboat. New York, early 19th century. *L: 5 in.*

186. Posset pot or skillet. With cover similar to an American porringer. London, 1665-66. *H: 4½ in.*

187. Saucepan with silver strap handle. By Nathaniel Coleman, Bur-
lington, N. J., circa 1775. *H: 5 in.*

184

185

186

187

Illustrations on facing page:

188. Cylindrical nutmeg grater and silver case. New England, late 17th or early 18th century. *H: 2½ in.*

189. Oval nutmeg grater in silver box with a hinged lid top and bottom. London, 1784-5. *L: 2⅛ in.*

190. Inkstand made in 1752 by Philip Syng, Philadelphia. *L: 10¼ in.*

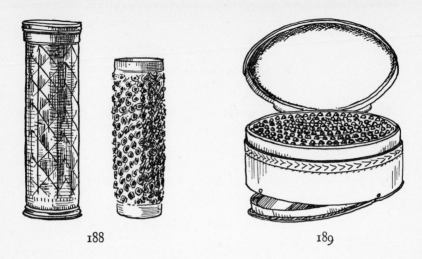

188

189

190

Illustrations on facing page:

191. Inkstand. By John Coney, Boston (1655-1722). *H: 4¼ in.*

192. Inkstand. Hall-marked London 1630-31.

193. Tobacco box. Engraved with the arms of Barnardiston. Early 18th century, probably New England. *L: 4⅝ in.*

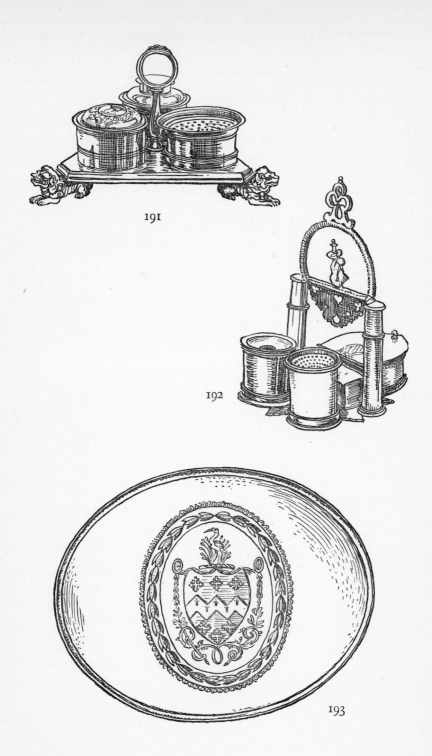

191

192

193

Illustrations on facing page:

194. Oval snuffbox. Engraved with the arms of Wentworth. By John Coney, Boston (1655-1722). *L: 2¾ in.*

195. The Jabez Bowen punch strainer. By Jonathan Clarke, Newport and Providence, R. I. (1705 to c. 1770). *L: 11⅞ in.*

196. Punch ladle with wooden handle. New England, early 18th century. *L: 11 in.*

197. Dish-ring. By Myer Myers, New York (1723-95). *H: 4⅜ in.*

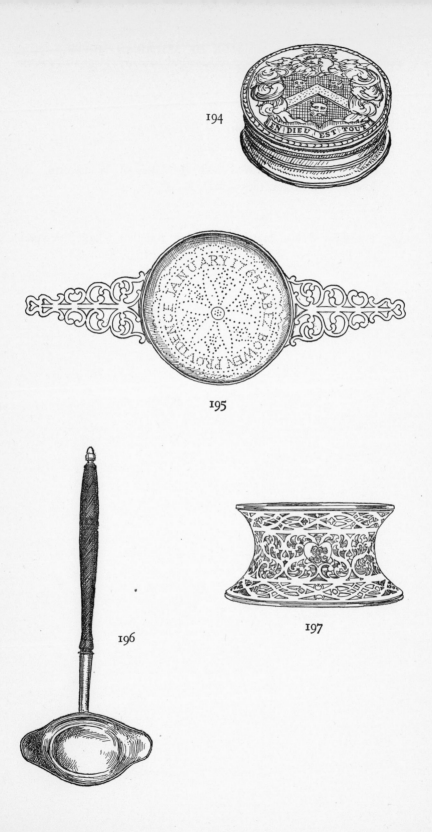

194

195

196

197

BOOKS OF REFERENCE

AVERY, C. LOUISE: *Early American Silver,* 1930

BIGELOW, FRANCIS HILL: *Historic Silver of the Colonies and Its Makers,* 1917

BRIX, MAURICE: *List of Philadelphia Silversmiths and Allied Artificers from 1682 to 1850,* 1920

BUCK, J. H.: *Old Plate, Its Makers and Marks,* 1903

BURTON, E. MILBY: *South Carolina Silversmiths, 1690-1860,* 1942

CLARKE, HERMANN FREDERICK: *John Coney, Silversmith, 1665-1722,* Introduction by Hollis French, 1932

CLARKE, HERMANN FREDERICK and FOOTE, HENRY WILDER: *Jeremiah Dummer, Colonial Craftsman and Merchant, 1645-1718,* Foreword by E. Alfred Jones, 1935

CURTIS, GEORGE MUNSON: *Early Silver of Connecticut and its Makers,* 1913

CUTTEN, GEORGE B. and CUTTEN, MINNIE WARREN: *Utica Silversmiths,* 1936

ENSKO, ROBERT: *Makers of Early American Silver and Their Marks,* 1915

ENSKO, STEPHEN G. C.: *American Silversmiths and Their Marks,* 1927

——, *American Silversmiths and Their Marks,* No. III, 1948

FRENCH, HOLLIS: *A List of Early Silversmiths and their Marks,* Walpole Society, 1917

——, *Jacob Hurd and His Sons, Nathaniel and Benjamin, Silversmiths,* 1939

HARRINGTON, JESSIE: *Silversmiths of Delaware,* 1939

JONES, E. ALFRED: *Old Silver of American Churches.* Privately printed, National Society of Colonial Dames of America, 1913

——, *Old Silver of Europe and America,* 1928

PHILLIPS, JOHN MARSHALL: *American Silver,* 1949

PLEASANTS, J. HALL and SILL, HOWARD: *Maryland Silversmiths, 1715-1830* with illustrations of their silver and their marks and with a facsimile of the design book of William Faris, 1930

PRIME, ALFRED COXE: *Arts and Crafts in Philadelphia, Maryland and South Carolina, 1721-1785,* Gleanings from newspapers. Walpole Society, 1929

——, *Arts and Crafts in Philadelphia, Maryland and South Carolina, Second Series 1786-1800.* Walpole Society, 1933

Catalogues and Bulletins

Boston, Museum of Fine Arts: *American Silver, the Work of Seventeenth and Eighteenth Century Silversmiths.* Exhibition, 1906. Technical description by J. H. Buck, Introduction by R. T. H. Halsey
   American Church Silver. Exhibited 1911. Introduction on Early Connecticut Silversmiths by George Munson Curtis
   The Philip Leffingwell Spalding Collection of Early American Silver, by Edwin J. Hipkiss, 1943
Cleveland, Museum of Art: Bulletin, November 1940. *A Collection of Early American Silver. Gift of Hollis French,* by Helen S. Foote
Hartford, Connecticut: Wadsworth Atheneum and Morgan Memorial. *Early Plate in Connecticut Churches Prior to 1850.* Exhibited 1919. Catalogued by Florence Paull Berger
New York, Metropolitan Museum of Art: *The Hudson-Fulton Celebration.* Catalogue of an exhibition held 1909. American silver, Vol. II, part 3
   Catalogue of an Exhibition of Silver Used in New York, New Jersey and the South. With a note on Early New York Silversmiths by R. T. H. Halsey, 1911
   American Silver of the XVII and XVIII Centuries: A study based on the Clearwater Collection, by C. Louise Avery, 1920
   An Exhibition of Early New York Silver, by C. Louise Avery, 1932
Museum of the City of New York: *Silver by New York Makers, Late 17th Century to 1900.* Exhibited 1937-8. Preface by Luke Vincent Lockwood. Introduction by V. Isabelle Miller
Philadelphia, Museum of Art: *Exhibition of Old American and English Silver,* 1917

Bulletin, June 1921. *Catalogue of Loan Exhibition of Silver, American and English*. Introduction by Samuel Woodhouse

Rhode Island School of Design: *Exhibition of Silver*. Introduction by William Davis Miller, 1936

Washington, D. C., National Gallery of Art: *Exhibition of Early Paintings, Miniatures and Silver*, 1925

Worcester, Massachusetts, Art Museum: *Old Silver Owned in Worcester County*, 1913

Yale University, Gallery of Fine Arts: *Connecticut Tercentenary, 1635-1935. Early Connecticut Silver, 1700-1830*. Introduction by John Marshall Phillips, 1935

Masterpieces of New England Silver 1650-1800. Foreword by Everett Victor Meeks. Introduction by John Marshall Phillips. 1939

INDEX

Adam, J., 130
  James, 99
  Robert, 99, 128, 131, 163
Adam style, 99
Albany, N. Y., First Reformed Church, 12
Alexander, Edward P., v
Allen, John, 53
Alloy, 41
All Souls' College, Oxford, 31
American Antiquarian Society, 20
American Church Silver, ix
American Collector, 124
American Silver in England, 176
American Silver of the XVII and XVIII Centuries, viii
American Silversmiths and their Marks, xi, 166
Anderson, William, 85
Andrews, William Loring, viii
An Old Snuff House, 157
Anthony, Joseph, 105
Argyles, 28, 148
Arms, 9, 25, 38, 53, 61, 76, 77, 90, 158, 176, 177
Ashmole, Elias, 5
Ashmolean Museum, 5
Auction sale prices, xi, xii, xiii, 31-33, 50
Austin, Josiah, 82
Avery, C. Louise, vi, viii, 52

Baldwin, Elizabeth M., Mrs., 143
Bancker, Adrian, xii, xiii, 177
Bates, Elizabeth M., 61
Bayonet fastener, 39, 55
Beakers: New England, 10, 11, 71, 72, 101; New York, 10-12, 72, 101; origin of shape, 10; Pennsylvania, 72, 101, 102; South, 102
Belcher, Jonathan, Gov., 35
Bellarmine, Cardinal, 20
Besley, Thauvet, xii, 61, 161
Biddle, George, Mrs., 104
Bigelow, Francis Hill, viii-xi, 32, 105
Bleeding Bowls, 66
Boelen: Henricus, xii, 44, 139; Jacob, 25, 26, 61, 68, 86, 139

Boke of Keruynge, 29
Books of Reference, 265-267
"Borde," 30
Bortman, Mark, v
Boss or Print, 66
Boston Churches: First Church, 7, 9, 10; Brattle Square, 9; King's Chapel, 53, 175; Old South, 109; West Boston, 125
Boston Museum of Fine Arts, *see* Museum of Fine Arts, Boston
Bourdett, Stephen, 86
Bowen, Jabez, 160
Bowls: bleeding, 66; punch, 29, 49, 50, 77, 78, 79, 107, 108; sugar, 93, 94, 131-134; wine, 13, 14
Boxes: freedom, 152, 153; nutmeg, 155; patch, 158, 159; snuff, 156-158; sugar or sweetmeat, 33-35; tobacco, 156-158
Bradbury, Frederick, 115, 150
Bradford, Gamaliel, Capt., 117
Brandewijnkom, 14
Brashier, Ephraim, 108, 141
Braziers or Chafing Dishes: New England, 64, 65; New York, 65; Pennsylvania, 65
Brenauer, Joseph, 68, 119
Brenton, Benjamin, 176
Brevoort, John, 61, 68, 166, 176
Bridges, Margaret, Mrs., 22
Bright-cut engraving, 101, 107, 108, 117, 118, 130, 141
Bristol (Eng.) pottery, 27
British Museum, 146
Brooklyn Museum, v
Brown and Seal, 162
Buck, J. H., viii, ix, 36, 165
Buckles, x, 148-151
Buhler, Yves Henry, Mrs., v
"Bunch of Grapes" tavern, 78
Burnett, Charles, 102
Burr, Ezekiel, 140
Burroughs: Thomas, 67; Mary, 67
Burt: Benjamin, xi, xiii, 140; John, xi, 51, 56, 57, 81

269

Burton, E. Milby, v
Butter Tasters, 147
Byrd, William, 124

Cabot, Samuel, Mrs., 132
Cabriole, derivation of, 80
Caddy, derivation of, 161
Cadwalder, John, 90
Candle Sconces, 57
Candle Snuffers, 36, 57
Candlesticks: New England, 35, 36, 56-58,
    84, 114; New York, 36, 37, 58, 84,
    85, 114, 115; Pennsylvania, 115; The
    South, 115
Candlesticks, method of casting, 56
Caner, Henry, Dr., 175
Cann, derivation of, 74
Canns, see Mugs and Canns
Casters: New England, 39, 54, 55, 83,
    113; New York, 39, 55, 56, 83, 84,
    113, 114; Pennsylvania, 84, 114; The
    South, 114
Caudle and Two-handled Cups: New Eng-
    land, 21-24, 47, 48, 75-77; New
    York, 24-26, 48, 77
Chafing Dishes, see Braziers
Chalices, 9
Charger, 37
Charleston, S. C., Museum, v
Chesterfield, Philip, Earl of, 176
Chinese influence, see Oriental influence
Chocolate, introduction of, 42, 62
Chocolate-pots: New England, 62, 63, 88,
    125, 126; New York, 63, 64, 89, 126;
    Pennsylvania, 89, 90, 127; The South,
    127, 128
Christie's, vi, vii, 8, 15, 19, 32, 34, 64, 79,
    154, 156, 157, 162
Churchill, Jesse, 125
Clarke: Hermann F., 53, 57; Jonathan,
    160
Classic period, 99-136
Clearwater, A. T., viii, x, xi, 150, 159
Clement: Augustin, 22; Elizabeth, 22
Cleveland Museum of Art, v, vi, xi, 86
Close plating, 151
Clubs, London, 62
Coasters, 151, 152
Coen, Daniel, 119
Coffee-houses, 62
Coffee, introduction of, 42, 62
Coffee-pots: New England, 62, 63, 88, 89,
    125, 126; New York, 63, 64, 89, 126;
    Pennsylvania, 89, 90, 127; The South,
    127, 128

COIN, mark, 169, 171
Colonial Dames, ix
Colonial Williamsburg, v
Columbus, 62, 156, 157
Commonwealth of Massachusetts, 78
Comstock, Helen, 162
Concord, First Parish, 22
Coney, John, x, xiii, 17, 22, 24, 34-36, 38,
    39, 47, 49-51, 54, 56, 59, 63, 65, 67,
    145, 154-158, 167, 176, 177
Conner, Edward, 135
Constitution, The, 108
Cornbury, Lord, 153
Cornell: Samuel, 162; Sussanah, 162
Courtauld, Samuel, 75
Cowell, William, 47
Cream Jugs: New England, 91, 92, 128;
    New York, 92, 129; Pennsylvania,
    92, 93, 129, 130; The South, 130,
    131
Crichton: Bros., 34; Lionel A., 175
Crommelin, Daniel, 176
Cunningham, Stanley, Mrs., v, 90
Cups: caudle, 21, 22, 47; dram, 13; rac-
    ing trophy, 43, 75; spout, 27; stand-
    ing, 7-10; two-handled, 47, 48,
    75-77; tumbler, 13, 103
Curiosities of London, 4
Custis, Nellie, 102

Dally, Phillip, 126
Dalton, Henry R., 82
Dartmouth College, 78
David, Peter, 68
Davis, Edward M., III, v, 124
Dawes: Ambrose, 77; Thomas, 77
Decanter Stands, 151
Decatur, Stephen, Commodore, 135
Deerfield, Mass., First Congregational
    Church, 105
De Lamerie, Paul, 64, 81, 84, 98, 117
Dennis, Faith, vi
De Nys, John, 45, 65, 177
De Peyster, Frederic, 48, 52
Derby, Elias Hasket, 95
De Riemer, Peter, 87
Detroit Institute of Arts, 35
De Worde, Wynkyn, 29, 30
Dining-room introduced, 31
Discourse of Marriage and Wiving, 153
Dish Crosses, 152
Dishes and Salvers: New England, 37, 38;
    New York, 38; see also Salvers
Dish Rings, 98, 162-164; use of, 163
Dixwell, John, xi

Dodge, Seril, 148
Domestic Silver of Great Britain and Ireland, 34
Dominical letter, 171
Dooley, W. Germain, vi
Dorchester: First Church, 22; Second Church, 22
Dram Cups, 13
Dredgers, *see* Casters
Drinking customs, 4-6
Dubois, Abraham, 93
Dummer: Jeremiah, xii, 18, 22, 27, 28, 35, 56, 158, 167; William, 158
Dunn Gardner sale, vii
Du Pont, H. F., v
Dutch influence, 3, 10, 12, 14, 18, 23, 25, 26, 39, 45, 64, 66, 122
Dutch West India Company, 8
Dwight, Timothy, 38, 167

Eagle thumb-piece, 17
Early American Silver, 52
Early Victorian England, 156
Edwards: John, 9, 53; Samuel, 95; Thomas, 67
Elers: David, 59; John, 59
Elliott, John, 169
Empire style, 100, 110, 120, 121; source of, 100
Ensko: Robert, x, 166, 178; Robert, Inc., vi, 137; Stephen G. C., v, xi, 11, 35, 79, 105, 146, 166, 168
Essex Congregational Church, 10
Essex Institute, v, vi, xii, 76, 137
Evans, Robert, xiii
Ewan, J., 170
Exhibitions, ix, xii, 9

Farnam, Rufus and Henry, 126
Farr, Willoughby, 34
Feurt, Peter, 76
Fielding, George, xiii
Finials, 43, 47, 59, 72, 83, 89, 98, 103, 118-120, 123, 126, 127
Flagons, 125
Fogg Museum, 56
Foote, Helen S., v, vi
Foot-handle, 93
Forbes, John W., 170
Ford, Edsel, 38, 51
Forks, 144-146
Fraser, Simon, Lord Lovat, 176
Freedom Boxes, 152, 153
French, Hollis, viii, x, xi, 95, 166
French influence, 3, 18, 24, 26, 29, 42, 48, 55, 58, 60, 66, 71, 76, 77, 82-84, 87, 100, 138, 140, 145, 167
Fueter: Daniel Christian, 79, 177; Lewis, 134
Fused Plate, 150, 151

Gardiner, B., 169, 170
Garrison, Lloyd K., Mrs., v, 61
Garvan: Francis P., x, xi, 78; Mabel Brady Collection, xi, 24, 35, 53, 76, 95, 97, 108, 109, 158, 160, 177
Gazette, New York, 79
German influence, 3, 10, 15, 19, 20, 26, 28, 45, 54, 66, 72, 156
Gidds, Samuel, 141
Gilbert, William, 118, 129, 132
Glover, Jose, Reverend, 32
Goldthwaite, Joseph, 146
Good, Joanna, 141
Gordon, Alexander S., 133
Gould, Marshall Hopkins, 67
Graham, John M., 2d., v
Grand Turk, The, 95
Green, Nathaniel, Gen., 102
Grundy, William, 91

Hale, Mathew, Sir, 4
"Hall-feasts," 4
Halsey, R. T. H., viii, ix, x
Hammersley, Thomas, 86, 177
Hanap, 7
Hanaper, 7
Hanners, George, 48, 79
Hardwicke, Philip, Earl of, 176
Harris, Isaac, 109
Hartt, Edmund, 117
Harvard University, 32, 56, 109
Harvey, Alexander Duer, Mrs., v, 60
Hearst Collection, 98
Health, John, 96
Henchman, Daniel, xiii, 77
Hendricks, Ahasuerus, 12
Hengist, 4
Heraldic insignia, *see* Arms
Herculaneum, 99
High Standard Period, 4, 36, 38, 40-69
Hipkiss, Edwin J., vi, xii
Historical Society of Pennsylvania, 97, 98
Historic Silver of the Colonies, xi, 158
History of Old Sheffield Plate, 150
Hoare, Richard, Sir, 60
Homes, William, 77
Hooper: Mary, 67; Robert, 67
Hope, Henry, 76
Howe & Guion, 170

Hudson-Fulton Celebration, ix
Huguenots, 3, 42, 43, 56, 70, 71, 74, 75, 77, 91, 95
Hull: Isaac, Commodore, 108; John, 9, 137, 138
Hull and Sanderson, 9, 11, 22, 137, 138
Humphries, Charles P., 105
Hunt, Leigh, 70
Hurd: John, xi, xiii, 76, 90, 95, 158, 176; Nathaniel, 86
Hutton: Isaac, 114; John, 50

Ihing potteries, 59, 122
Illustrated History of English Plate, 28
Inkhorn, 155
Inkstands and Standishes, 155, 156
Irving, William, 110

Jackson, C. J., Sir, 28, 34, 36, 98
Jay, Pierre, v, 61
Jayne, H. F., vi
Jeffords, Walter M., 79
Jeffries: B. Joy, Dr., 35; David, 35; John, Dr., 35
Jessop, H. R., 162
Jones, E. Alfred, 105
Jug, derivation of, 107
Jugs, *see* Cream Jugs, Pitchers

Kettles, *see* Tea-kettles
"Keyhole" pattern, 69
Kierstede, Cornelius, 14, 36, 37, 56, 64, 90, 177
Kirk, Samuel, 112
Knives, 146
Koke, Richard J., v

Ladles, 159, 160
Lamerie, *see* De Lamerie
Lansing, Jacob Gerittse, 61, 104
Lawton, Herbert, 102, 109
Leddel, Joseph, 176
Le Roux: Bartholomew, 11, 48, 52, 53; John, 96; Charles, 48, 61, 77, 81
Letelier, John, 79, 123
Leverett, Knight, 58
"Liberty" spoon, 141
Livery Companies, 5, 49, 52, 145, 173
Livingstone, Robert Gilbert, 161
Lord: Abigail, 17; Richard, 17
Loring, Joseph, xi
Loring, The Misses, 158
Lowell, James Russell, 90
Lownes: Edward, 89; Joseph, 105, 107, 123, 127, 177

Loyalists, 175
Lumley, T. H. W., 158
Lustres, 58

McCall, George, Mrs., 103
McCoy, W. Logan, Mrs., 123
McMullin, John, 135
McPheadres, Catherine, 161
MacSwiggan, A. E., Mrs., v
Manners and customs, *see* Table manners
Marks on silver: Baltimore Assay Office, 170-172; pseudo-English and Irish, 168-170; symbols, 166-168
Marrow Scoops, 147
Marston, John, 78
Massachusetts Charitable Mechanic Association, 168
Massachusetts Historical Society, 117
Mazers, 66
Meissonier, Juste-Aurèle, 70
Mercers' Company, 32
Metropolitan Museum of Art, vi, viii, ix, x, 14, 24, 37, 45, 51, 53, 59, 60, 62, 63, 67, 68, 75, 78, 96, 104, 108, 112, 118, 119, 126, 129-131, 133, 135, 139, 143, 147, 150, 155, 159, 162
Middlecott, Sarah, 51
Milk Jugs, *see* Cream Jugs
Mills: Edward, 76; Mary, 123
Milne, Edmund, 101, 102
Minneapolis Institute of Arts, 38
Monteiths, *see* Punch Bowls and Monteiths
Morgan, Pierpont, 15, 49, 78
Morton, Marcus, Jr., 53
Moulton, William, 109
Muffineers, *see* Casters
Mug Houses, 20
Mugs and Canns: New England, 20, 21, 46, 74, 106; New York, 21, 46, 74, 75, 106; Pennsylvania, 75, 106, 107; The South, 107
Mug, derivation of, 20
Mullet, 167
Museum of Fine Arts, Boston, v, vi, ix, xii, 9, 22, 27, 34, 35, 38, 48, 51, 53, 55, 68, 77-79, 82, 95, 96, 109, 117, 125, 145, 146
Museum of the City of New York, 24, 33, 38, 48, 55, 68, 77, 82, 85, 96, 108, 109, 119, 126, 132, 133, 139, 141, 161
Myers, Myer, 96, 162, 168, 177

Nashe, Tom, 6

Nelme, Anthony, 64
Neponset, Mass., Church of the Unity, 48
New York: Collegiate Church of, 176;
    Corporation of Trinity Church, 53;
    Dutch Reformed Church, 87, 176;
    Historical Society, v, 14, 134; Silver
    Smiths' Society, 168
New York *Gazette*, 79; *Sun*, 35, 78, 79,
    138, 146; *Times*, 78
Niccholes, Alexander, 153
Nicot, Jean, 156
Noble, John, Sir, 156
Norfolk, Va., Museum of Arts and Sci-
    ences, v
Notes and Queries, 5
Noyes: John, xiii, 146; Lucy Mary, 159
Nutmeg Boxes, 155
Nys, Johannis, *see* De Nys

Ogee shape, 22, 74
Old English pattern, 140
Old Plate, viii, 36
Old Silver in American Churches, 105
Old Standard of silver, 70
Oliver: Daniel, 35; Elizabeth, 35; Peter,
    35; Sarah, 35
Onkelbag, Gerrit, 25, 26, 39, 166
Onslow pattern, 143
Oppenord, Gilles, 70
Oriental influence, 24, 28, 49, 59-61, 63,
    70, 74, 80, 85, 93, 107-109
Orekovsken, 14
Ornamental forms and decoration, acan-
    thus, 17, 23, 25, 26, 99, 110; anthe-
    mion, 99, 110; beaded, 89, 110, 116,
    118, 122, 127, 129, 130, 132, 133,
    141; bright-cut, 101-103, 107, 108,
    117, 118, 130, 135, 141, 142, 144;
    chased, 22, 23, 34, 71, 81, 87, 89,
    91-93; cherub heads, 17, 44-46, 49,
    79; classic, 99; cornucopia, 120, 121;
    cut-card, 18, 28, 41, 48, 54, 60, 61;
    embossed, 14, 22, 23, 25, 26, 34,
    71, 87, 93; Empire, 99, 110, 120,
    121; faceted, 61, 63, 90; feather-edge,
    141; fluted, 24, 38, 41, 47, 63, 79,
    86, 88, 110, 116, 129-133; gadroon,
    36, 41, 52, 80, 89, 96, 97, 109, 113;
    matted or frosted, 10, 67; palm
    leaves, 17, 23, 25; pierced, 94, 122,
    123, 131, 133, 163; rococo, 71; shell,
    80-82, 85, 92, 95-98, 140; scrolls, 71,
    82, 85, 95-98; terminal heads and
    busts, 14, 24, 47; wire, 18, 19, 43,
    44, 64

Paine: Thomas, 177; William, 35
Palmer, George, 35
Papboats, 153
Parke-Bernet Galleries, Inc., vi, 142, 143
Parke, Hiram H., Maj., vi
Parker, Daniel, 82
Parkman, William, 35
Parsons, Ella, 123
Patch Boxes, 158, 159
Patches, 158, 159
Patera, 66
Paul Revere and His Engraving, viii
Pellet, 167
Pelletreau, Elias, xii, 77
Pennington, Edward, 97
Pennsylvania, Historical Society of, 97, 98
Pepys, Samuel, 31
Perry: Marion Lincoln, 78; Marsden, 78
Petersen, Peter, 10
Philadelphia: Marine and City Hospitals,
    135; Museum of Art, vi, xii, 27, 52,
    54, 65, 90, 93, 103, 104, 121, 123,
    129
Phillips, John Marshall, Dr., v, xi, 102,
    158
Phillipse, Eve, 25, 33
Picard, Jean, 167
Pickman: Benjamin, 76; collection, 38
Pierced gallery and plinth, possible sources
    of, 94
Pipkin, 154
Pitchers: New England, 108, 109; New
    York, 109, 110; Pennsylvania, 110;
    The South, 110, 111; pottery with
    silver mounts, 110
Pompeii, 66, 99
Porringers: Evolution, 66; New England,
    66, 67; New York, 68; Pennsylvania,
    68; The South, 68, 69
Posset Pots, 27
Posset, The, 28
"Potato rings," 98, 163
Powell, William, 158
Prices, *see* Auction sale prices
Print or boss, 66
Punch Bowls and Monteiths: New Eng-
    land, 49, 50, 77-79, 107, 108; New
    York, 50, 79, 108; Pennsylvania, 79
Punch, derivation of name, 48
Punch Ladles, 159, 160; Strainers, 159,
    160

Quaich, 66
Queen's College, Oxford, 5

Quincy, Mass., First Congregational Church, 10

Racing Cups, 43, 75
Rainbow, William, 155
Raising, 22, 116
Rasp or rape, 157
Reeves, Enos, 69
Reid, Sam C., Capt., 109
Revere: Paul, Sr., x; Paul, Jr., ix-xiii, 67, 78, 88, 93, 95, 107, 108, 117, 124, 126, 128, 131, 134; Pauline, 67
Richardson: Joseph, Sr., 68, 90, 91, 96-98, 177; Joseph, Jr., 98; Joseph and Nathaniel, 97, 143
Richmond, Va., Virginia Museum of Fine Arts, 124
Ridout, George, xiii, 82
Rivoire, Apollos, x
Robert, Christopher, xiii
Rococo, 70-98
Rogers, Daniel, 141
Roosevelt: Harriet Howard, 68; James, 68
Rowe, Charles, 76
Rowena, 4

Sale, Edith Tunis, 124
Salem, Mass.: Essex Institute, v, vi, xii, 76, 137; First Baptist Church, 126
Salisbury Court Glasshouse, 27
Saltcellar, derivation of, 50
Saltcellars: New England, 31-33, 51, 80, 111; New York, 33, 51, 52, 80, 81, 111; Pennsylvania, 52, 81, 111; The South, 112; standing, 29-32
Salver, derivation of, 94
Salvers and Trays: New England, 52, 53, 95, 134; New York, 53, 96, 134, 135; Pennsylvania, 96, 97, 135; The South, 135, 136
Sandbox, 156
Sanderson, Robert, 9
Sauceboats: New England, 81, 82, 112; New York, 82, 112; Pennsylvania, 82, 83, 113; The South, 113
Saucepans, 154
Sauce Tureens, 112
Sayre, Joel, 114
Scandinavian influence, 3, 10, 15, 17, 18, 19, 45, 72
Schaats, Bartholomew, xiii, 58
Schanck: Garret, 161; John, 118
Sconces, 57
Setauket, L. I., Presbyterian Church, 24
Sever, Emily, 51

Sheffield Plate, 110, 115, 150, 151, 159
Shapard, William, Gen., 108
Shepherd, Thomas M., Mrs., 51
Shoemaker: Joseph, 177; Sara, 97, 98
Sillabub, 27
Silver Purity Act, 171, 172
Skewers, 147
Skillets, 154
Skittowe, Timothy, 10
Smith, Henry Barney, 109
Smoking, 156
Snuff, 156, 157
Snuffboxes, 157, 158
Sons of Liberty, 78
Sotheby & Co., vi, 27
Soumaine, Simeon, 45, 96, 142
Sowers, Thomas, 135
Spalding Collection, xii, 55, 79, 82
Spalding, Philip L., x, xii
Spoons: New England, 137-141; New York, 139, 141, 142; Pennsylvania, 142, 143
Spout Cups, 27, 28
Standards of silver, 40, 41, 169
Standing-cups, New England, 8-10
Standing-salts, 29-32; significance of, 29, 30
Standishes and Inkstands, 155, 156
Steeple Cups, 7, 8
STERLING mark, 169, 171
Stillman, Webster, 17
Stow: Charles Messer, v, 34, 35, 78; Millicent D., Mrs., 79, 138, 146
Strainers, 159, 160
Sucket Forks, 146
Suckets, 146
"Sucking-spout," 28
Sugar boxes, see Boxes
Sugar bowls: New England, 93, 131, 132; New York, 93, 94, 132, 133; Pennsylvania, 94, 133, 134
Sugar loaves, 143
Sugar Tongs, 143, 144
Sun, New York, 35, 78, 79, 138, 146
Swan, William, 76
Sylvester, Brinley, 67
Syng: Philip, M.D., 135; Philip, Sr., 52, 65, 68; Philip, Jr., 97, 168

Table customs and manners, 29, 30, 37, 144, 145, 154
Tankard Bearer, 15
Tankard, origin of, 14, 15
Tankards: horn, 15; New England, 16-18, 43, 44, 72, 73, 103, 104; New York,

18, 19, 44, 45, 73, 104; peg, 15; Pennsylvania, 45, 46, 73, 74, 104, 105; The South, 105
Targee, John and Peter, 109
Taylor, Samuel, 98
Tazze, 38, 52
Tea: introduction of 42, 58, 59; prices, 59
Tea Caddies, 160-162
Tea-kettles: New England, 90; New York, 64; Pennsylvania, 90
Teapots: New England, 59, 60, 85, 86, 116, 117; New York, 60-62, 86, 87, 118-121; Pennsylvania, 87, 88, 121-124; The South, 124, 125
Tea Services: New England, 117; New York, 119-121; Pennsylvania, 123, 124; The South, 125
"Tea table," 134
Ten Eyck, Jacob, xii
Thayer, Nathaniel, Mrs., 126
The Salt, 30
Thomson: John, 110; William, 84, 109
Thumb-pieces, 15, 16, 17, 19, 44, 45, 46, 60, 63, 64, 72-74, 103-105, 107
Tiffany & Co., 35
Times, New York, 78
Tingley, Samuel, 96
Tobacco Boxes, 156, 157
Townsend, William S., 95
Tray, origin of, 94
Trays, see Salvers and Trays
Trencher, 31, 37, 145
Trencher Salts, 31-33, 51, 52
Trenton, N. J., First Presbyterian Church, 105
Tucker, Cornelia Dabney, Mrs., 170
Tumblers, 13, 103
"Tutor Flynt" cup, xiii
Tyler: Andrew, xiii; David, 132
Tyng, Edward, Capt., 76

Underhill, Andrew, 96
United States Naval Museum, 102
Urns, 117, 118, 124
Usher, Elizabeth, 35

Van Cortlandt: Jacobus, 25, 33; Oloff Stevenszen, 139
Vanderburgh, Cornelius, 33, 139, 166, 177

Vanderspiegel, Jacobus, 33, 38, 53, 166
Van Deursen, Henricus, 139
Van Dyck, Peter, xii, xiii, 24, 44, 48, 60, 61, 65, 68, 82, 177
Van Inburgh, Peter, 44
Van Newkirke, Jan, 68
Van Renselaer, Maria, 139
Van Voorhis, Daniel, 119
Vernon: John, xiii; Samuel, 44
Verstegan, Richard, 4
Victoria & Albert Museum, 27, 57, 66, 91, 122, 175
Vilant, William, 176
Vinton, David, 132
Voider, 37
Vortigern, 4

Wall Brackets, 57
Walpole Society, xi
Ward, John, 79
Warner: Andrew E., 112, 135; Daniel, 57; Sarah (Hill), 57
Washington Centennial, 36
Washington, George, 101, 102, 169, 174
Watson, Victor A., vi, 79, 86, 96, 175
Wentworth: Benning, 158; John, Sir, 77, 158
Westover, 124
Wheelock, Eleazor, Revd., 78
White, Miles, Jr., Mrs., 130, 159
Whitenack, Charles, vi
Wilkes, John, 141
Williamson, Samuel, 105
Wiltberger, Christian, 124
Winslow, Edward, xi, 34, 47, 51, 53, 63, 176
Winthrop, John, 7
Wishart, Hugh, 68, 104, 110, 119
Woburn, Mass., First Congregational Church of Christ, 48
Woolsley, Theodore S., Dr., viii-x
Worcester, Mass.: Art Museum, vi, xii, 28, 44, 126; American Antiquarian Society, 20
Wynkoop, Benjamin, 14, 68, 166

Yale University Art Gallery, v, xi, 17, 24, 35, 53, 57, 76, 90, 95, 97, 108, 158, 160